Glimpses Of Utopia

Real Ideas For A Fairer World

Jess Scully

16pt

Read How You Want
LARGE PRINT BOOKS, BRAILLE & DAISY

Copyright Page from the Original Book

PANTERA
PRESS

First published in 2020 by Pantera Press Pty Limited
www. PanteraPress.com

Cover design: Luke Bird
Cover illustrations: Lala Aliyeva/Alamy
Publisher: Lex Hirst
Editor: Anne Reilly
Proofreader: Pauline O'Carolan
Indexer: Catherine Page
Author photo: Walter Maurice
Text design and typesetting: Kirby Jones
Printed and bound in Australia by McPherson's Printing Group

TABLE OF CONTENTS

For Elinor, and the future her generation
deserves

INTRODUCTION

Rays through the storm clouds

What if the future we need is vastly different to the future we've been told to want?

What if real progress doesn't look like driverless cars or hoverboards? Instead, let's imagine a world in which we value our most human instinct: the drive to care for each other and our planet.

What if we stopped swallowing lines from politicians about what is a burden and what is an investment, and recognised that we have the power to decide how we gather and spend money as a society? We have more than enough money to pay for the generous, principled society that we all deserve, and we can direct our leaders to deliver it.

What if our cities were designed for people, not property portfolios? Let's imagine our cities as centres of human flourishing: productive, diverse and just; tools of environmental regeneration and social empowerment. The places we live can be designed to unlock our potential to contribute and be part of the solutions we need.

What if we stopped shouting at each other? Imagine a public sphere where we could talk about values and the kind of future we want to build together, a media and civic realm where big decisions could be made deliberatively and collectively.

All of this is necessary if we are to address the planetary-scale challenges that confront us. Despite the enormity of what lies ahead, this book is a manifesto for hope in the face of cataclysmic change. The heroes of our time aren't working to *save* the world as it is: instead, in the ashes of the old, they're building a new world that's designed from the outset to be fair and sustainable, caring and creative. With imagination and a shared intention, we can be a part of that change and claim that fairer future.

I know it can be really hard to stay optimistic when we're in the midst of a pandemic, on the verge of an economic depression, and we can see the effects of climate change moving from theory to reality. While I was finishing the first draft of this book, most of the east of Australia burned: every week brought another day of catastrophic fire danger. When the air in the Blue Mountains, where my parents live, became so thick with smoke and ash that they were getting migraines, Mum and Dad temporarily moved into our place in Sydney. Thousands of Australians lost their homes, and millions of animals perished in the most horrible way.

While our continent burned, to our north Jakarta flooded, and close to 70 people died in floods and landslides: authorities there went so far as geo-engineering – seeding clouds with sodium chloride – to try to break up the rain clouds.

This is only the beginning. This is the future climate scientists have been predicting, the volatile, violent natural world we can expect if we persist with business-as-usual behaviour.

As if that wasn't hard enough, it's not *just* climate change we have to contend with. Skyrocketing inequality is its twin: devastating and divisive, cutting lives short and stealing potential, turning people against each other and making it harder for us to pull together against the torrent ahead. Like climate change, it has been slowly, steadily building over the course of decades. It is also a wholly *un* -natural disaster, also human in origin, the utterly predictable result of bad policy being written by the powerful to cement their privilege.

From the Stone Age until now, parents could have a reasonable expectation that their kids would be better off than they were, that they'd live a longer, easier life. It's natural to assume that because things have steadily been getting better for the past 100 or 200 years – life expectancy extending, literacy expanding, child mortality falling, ascent out of poverty accelerating – that the upward trends will continue, and that life will get better and easier for everyone. We can't take that for granted anymore.

In a time of astronomical innovation and unparalleled plenty, we're beginning to see the trends reverse: after stalling since 2011, in 2017 life expectancy in the UK actually *declined.*[1] In the United States, 2017 was the second consecutive year of declines in life expectancy, the first time a backward trend has been recorded since the 1960s. If this trend continues, it means that kids born today would live shorter lives than their parents. On current trends, the next generation will also be worse off financially: Harvard economist Raj Chetty has called it the 'fading American dream' and demonstrated how income mobility has spluttered to a halt as inequality grows.[2] In early 2018, the World Economic Forum released a report revealing that both rich and poor countries are failing to deliver intergenerational equality: instead, what they're passing on to future generations is massive debt and climate damage.[3]

***

Why are we on such a downward spiral?

We're living in the richest, most privileged time in human history, yet we're increasingly seeing life get shorter and more unfair for many people. Even as we're hurtling forward with technology, with better communications and connections across the planet, we're seemingly taking big steps backwards on the metrics you'd think would matter most. Why?

This is not yet because of war or natural disaster: it's the result of the business-as-usual mindset. I think our problems arise because we're running a 21st-century world with a set of 19th-century institutions and rules. We've been rolling along without updating the software our system operates on, and so many foundational assumptions and policies are now completely outdated and out of sync with the way the world works today.

There are alternatives to the status quo already in motion, but in the noise of our information-overloaded lives, we're missing out on hearing about and learning from the people who are proving that another future is possible.

Here's the good news: because humans created these problems, we can also fix them. The even better news is a lot of this work has begun.

There are movements, organisations and individuals in every corner of the world who are modelling alternatives to the extractive and exploitative mindset that got us here, and for the first time in history, they can connect with each other to support and amplify their efforts. In *Glimpses of Utopia,* you'll meet some of them and hear their stories, and how their efforts and ideas are shaping a better future for us all. The innovators you'll meet in this book are many and various: they're teachers and designers, technologists and researchers, artists and activists, policy-makers and politicians.

You'll learn about the approaches that unite these diverse catalysts for change, and most importantly, find out how you can be a part of the solutions too. It's true that we're living through dark times, but that's not the whole story. I want you to feel as hopeful as I do that a better world is within reach. But it's going to take some work from all of us, as both citizens and advocates, to bring it into being.

The challenge that climate change presents is the undercurrent of *Glimpses of Utopia* – alongside a focus on the inequality that's tearing us apart – and we need all the scientific and environmental genius in the world focused on preserving our planet. But, as you've probably noticed, science and technology won't do the job on their own. We've got plenty of smart tech out in the world, but without the policy changes to fund or enable them, these things stay in the realm of the prototype or the luxury accessory. There is also some exciting big-picture thinking on the economic models we could shift to, from degrowth,[4] an alternative to endless economic growth, to the 'doughnut economics'[5] model setting planetary and social boundaries for the economy. Brilliant models and cutting-edge science are important, but they'll stay on the margins until we transform our social institutions: the way we make decisions, set priorities and debate what we value as a society.

It's not just about having better models or even compelling examples of alternatives: we also have to have space to talk to each other about them. Our societal conversation – the discourse, or public sphere – is so important because it's the space within which we can contest ideas like these, put forward competing visions and weigh up what matters. It's the place – whether metaphorical or literal – where we make sense of the world and talk about the future we want. That space is becoming more splintered and polarised as many people no longer trust the news media or experts, making it harder for a fact-based and thoughtful debate to take place.

You've probably noticed a growing number of conspiracy theories bubbling up as people try to articulate what's wrong with a system that's not working for many in society. Rather than mock individual theories, let's try to connect with that underlying, well-founded disillusionment with the status quo.

The challenge right now is to pull back and describe the bigger picture that leads to this feeling of exclusion and distrust. To me it seems essential that more of us make the connections between what can seem like abstract or distant policy decisions and their impacts on our lives. Imagine what could be achieved if most of us could see that there are real alternatives and better stories out there, and that there's a future that includes us all.

The most exciting innovation right now would be to upgrade our policies, processes and public sphere to serve a 21st-century operating system. More of us have more to gain – or lose – than ever before.

1

Rethink utopia

'But miss, why think about the future for?' Sara asked.

The 13-year-old held my gaze and, for a few seconds, I couldn't answer her. No one had ever asked me this before.

I spend most of my time thinking about the future: what our cities are going to look like in five or 50 years, what art will explore, how information will be distributed, what laws we'll need, how people will spend their days, how we'll work, how our economy will shift and change. I've always assumed that thinking about the future was a natural thing to do, something that everyone did all the time, driven by motivations that were so obvious that I ... well ... so obvious, that I couldn't really think of any of them, right now.

Casting about for an answer, I looked out the classroom window, at the building next door. As fate would have it, I found myself looking at the hospital I was born in. All that separated me from this girl and her classmates was a couple of decades. Most of them were the first in their families to be born in Australia, like me. Many of their parents had come here seeking opportunity – like my dad, Bryan, originally from India – or fleeing political conflict and seeking asylum – like my mum, Trish, who'd come here from Chile. Kids navigating different cultures and languages; kids who'd seen enough of life to know progress is bumpy and, as they say, the future is unevenly distributed and fair can be hard to find.

Finally, I landed on a response.

'Because you'll live in the future,' I said, feebly. 'In 25 years from now, you'll be my age. And you'll want clean water to drink and air to breathe. You'll need to earn money, you might want to have kids, and you'll be interested in what kind of world you all live in...' I trailed off.

Sara gave me the kind of gently condescending look that 13-year-olds everywhere are the masters of. That look that says, *I'm not a kid anymore.*

I don't believe in fairytales. I'm not buying what you're selling, lady, but nice try.

'Sure, miss, okay. But who cares what I think about the future? I mean, it's just going to happen anyway, no matter what I think.'

She had me floored, again. I couldn't imagine what it was like to feel like your voice doesn't matter. For better or for worse, people have cared about my opinion for years now, or at least, they've been polite enough to nod along as I've shouted my ideas from the soapboxes I've been given: festivals and events, radio shows and media interviews, and all the opportunities that come with electoral politics. The girls in this class had been through more in their short lives than I could imagine: many of them had come from war zones, places where their lives and the lives of everyone they knew had been disrupted forever. Was Sara right: was I naive to think that the ideas of one or two people could make a difference? Was I selling false hope by suggesting that the future was something she could direct?

In less than an hour, this class of 13-year-old girls in Sydney's south-west had punctured the blissful bubble I lived in, a privileged realm of 'changemakers', where everyone felt informed about issues, empowered to make their mark and ready to make change. Suddenly, I was outside the bubble, looking in, and it was much harder to explain how one person could shape the course of their own life, let alone their city, their country, the world.

***

I've done a lot of things that have scared me, but standing up in front of that class of young teenagers, trying to get them excited about the future, was one of the toughest.

Knowing my work and focus on the future, my friend Matt Roden had asked me to be a guest speaker at a couple of sessions with year 7 and 10 students at Liverpool Girls High. As an educator with the Story Factory, Matt visits a lot of schools. He works with kids who rarely get asked to shape the future, coaching them to turn their experiences and ideas into stories. These classes could be hard going, he'd warned me.

That turned out to be true, but I was shaken when I arrived at the school and suddenly realised the extent of my personal connection to this place. My own life started right here, and it felt fated, somehow, to be standing here thinking about my past while talking about the future.

I was born in Liverpool Hospital, immediately next door to this school. Back then, my family lived nearby in Fairfield in Sydney's south-west. My mum's family had arrived on transit visas in 1975 and overstayed, fleeing Chile under Pinochet, while my dad's big Anglo-Indian family were adjusting to some serious culture shock, having swapped Bangalore for Canley Vale in 1973. Then, as now, Fairfield, Liverpool and this part of south-western Sydney represented a port of arrival for migrants: you can chart the flows of Australia's migration intake though the changing shopfronts. When we lived there, the stores were Vietnamese bakeries, Turkish cafes and Latino *pasteleros:* today, these remain, but with Nigerian churches and Persian restaurants alongside.

It's a place that offers a welcome, and safety compared to what many have left behind, but not a place that immediately offers access to the halls of power. It's hard to have your voice heard from this part of town. Fairfield is ranked as the most disadvantaged suburb in Sydney, with unemployment at almost double the state average and a constantly renewing community of new arrivals. I can understand how, as a kid living in this part of the city and sensing that the social, cultural and economic tools of empowerment are located elsewhere, you wouldn't feel like the world was keen for your input: you'd be lucky to find a university place or a job waiting for you.

In my own life, I'd gone from being one of these first-generation Aussie kids in Liverpool and Fairfield to being a Deputy Lord Mayor of Sydney. I feel extraordinarily lucky that I had the opportunity to study at an incredible selective public high school, to receive the kind of thoughtful, focused education I might have received at a private school – something my family could never have afforded to pay for. I feel so fortunate to have had teachers who had the time to see my enthusiasm for learning and carve out an accelerated program for me, to give me pathways to thrive and dive deeper into language and history and art, all of which were formative for me. I know not every kid gets to have this kind of attention from a public education system that's being systematically starved and worn down. I feel lucky that I could study at university before fees started creeping higher and higher, and that I could afford to live relatively cheaply in the heart of my city in my 20s, as I threw myself into poorly paid but impactful projects that helped me build a career. I feel like I was one of the last to benefit from the golden days of Australia's social welfare state, and that the red carpet has since been rolled up, and a velvet rope set up to keep the likes of me out. But the luck of my birth at the right place and right time gave me advantages and opportunities that I'm so grateful for today.

These days, my office is in the front corner of Sydney Town Hall, a majestic sandstone landmark in the heart of one of the wealthiest cities in the world. I feel privileged to be able to have a say, and have my voice heard, on the issues that matter most to me: on how we make this city a fairer place, on how we build it to be more resilient socially and regenerative environmentally, on how we get more life and creativity on our streets, on how we open up the halls of power to make sure everyone else has their voices heard too.

Would it help Sara to know that this journey was possible, if she wanted it? Was it naive to think it still was? In my lifetime, I've seen Australia's pride in its egalitarianism shrink and the gap between rich and poor grow. Worse still, governments have been actively widening that gap, making political choices that entrench disadvantage and pool wealth and access at the top, putting up walls where once there were pathways. Today more than ever, your postcode can predetermine your life outcomes. Opportunity is being distributed unevenly across our cities and countries, dictating how long you spend on waiting lists to see specialists in public hospitals, for example, or even your lifespan.[1] While I'm talking about Sydney, as I know it best, this kind of geographically distributed opportunity is so common around the world it even has a name: spatial injustice.

In 2018, University of Sydney student magazine *Honi Soit* published a playful interactive map which charted the distribution of fast food restaurants and boutique grocers around the city under the headline, 'Food fault lines: mapping class through food chains'.[2] The 'Red Rooster Line' had already been quoted in research, but this project added other brands, depicting the concentration in 'The Affluent North' of upmarket chain Chargill Charlies and contrasting this with the 'El Jannah Line', in what they dubbed 'The Ethnic West'. It was a potentially silly but highly descriptive way of depicting where social and ethnic groups find themselves in Australia's largest city. If you're west of the Red Rooster Line, you're likely to earn less, travel longer distances in traffic to get to work, cop more heat in heatwaves and even see your life expectancy reduce. Fairfield is squarely on the 'have-nots' side of the 'Quinoa Curtain', which is the term my colleague on council Jess Miller likes to use, rather than the more ubiquitous 'Latte Line'. The *Honi Soit* map makes it starkly clear that there isn't just one Sydney. Instead, your experience of the city depends very much on where you live, and the type of food you have access to serves as a metaphor for the range of opportunities you might have access to as well.

CityPulse, a 2018 research project by multinational professional services firm PwC ranked every suburb in the city based on access to work, green space, transport and education, with points deducted for crime and a lack of housing affordability. Once again, a version of the Quinoa Curtain emerged from the data, with the 25 most advantaged suburbs being those that ring Sydney's glittering harbour.

Before our eyes, a country that once saw itself as free of class divides and open to social advancement (justifiably or not) is becoming dramatically less equal. Australian Bureau of Statistics (ABS) data shows that the richest 20 per cent of Australian households have average wealth of around $2.5 million, or more than 70 times higher than the average net worth held by households in the bottom 20 per cent of the wealth distribution. Not double. Not ten times richer. Seventy times richer.

Imagine how different your experience of the world would be if, for the rest of your life, you were 70 times wealthier than you are. What would you stop worrying about? What would you have time to do that you don't have time for now? Such a situation is hard even to picture. It wouldn't mean you'd have no problems, but your everyday problems would be so very different from the ones you currently have that – even if you were the most empathetic person in the world – you'd soon struggle to understand what struggling really feels like.

You might have trouble grasping what your neighbours a few suburbs away were going through. You might struggle to understand how some people might be too stressed out or time poor to be interested in politics or big issues, even if they really affected them, and might readily accept the simplest explanation coming from the loudest voice. You might not be able to appreciate how being short on cash from day to day and week to week stops you from being able to do things that might save you money in the long term. Having no money can be really expensive: you can get charged fees for late payment and those fees then stack up and if you have to take repayment options, you'll pay more than those who can pay in full. You might have to use payday lenders or get caught in other vicious cycles of debt; you might miss a repayment and get a bad credit rating, then find yourself having fewer and fewer options about where you live, how you get around or what you can afford to do with your time.

As the dividing line between rich and poor grows wider and wider, it becomes a moat around the castle walls of decision-making. Inside the castle, you have the people who have time to take an interest in the rules of the game we're all playing, the time to get involved and, often, the language and tools to have their say. They're typically the people who have their voices heard, they know how to lodge a complaint or demand that the system meets their requirements, and their experiences of the world can often be so astronomically different to those of their poorer neighbours, who're living day to day, that the divisions are reinforced. Over time, the moat gets steadily deeper.

When a society divides into haves and have-nots, how does that impact who has a say and who has a sense of agency over their future? What does a community lose when a huge percentage of its greatest wealth – the imagination, ideas, experiences and creative energy of its next generation – is trapped on the wrong side of an invisible divide? That Latte Line, as it arises in this city and in the forms it takes in many other places, has the potential to lock out a powerful source of new solutions to the big challenges that face us all.

***

Even without these stats and images, signs of exclusion, I shouldn't be surprised that Sara and her classmates had a gloomy view of the future: the stories we've been telling her generation about it have truly sucked. From *The Hunger Games* to *The Handmaid's Tale,* from *Westworld* to *The Walking Dead,* the future visions we're offering a 13-year-old in 2020 are absolutely grim. At some point in our recent past, we stopped imagining that we'd live in a future of convenience, connection and plenty, and instead became convinced that it would be brutal and divided, with a privileged few born into wealth and comfort, and the rest battling to survive. We stopped imagining that technology could be a tool to enhance our lives and make the world easier for everyone, and instead we fell into telling stories about how that tech controls, surveils and entraps us. The stories we tell ourselves have power, and one of the first things we need to do is change them so we can visualise a future worth fighting for.

The Story Factory works with kids to help them conceptualise, write and publish their own stories. Later, reading what the students I visited had written, I was floored by the pessimism that pervaded the visions of the future articulated by Sara and her schoolmates. They were full of surveillance culture, addiction to screens, automation and suppression, overwork and disconnection.

It wasn't always like this.

There have been outpourings of utopian future-thinking throughout history, starting with Thomas More's 1516 book of the same name: projecting forward to a better tomorrow as a form of social dreaming, either to critique the present day or to suggest alternative ways of living together.

The last decades of the 19th century had some major parallels with our times, and were rich in the work of utopian thinkers who inspired people to believe in a fairer future and to take action towards building it. People in the Victorian era were living through a time of unprecedented technological change and scientific discovery, feeling the effects of the industrial revolution and how it transformed work and family life, the seismic cultural impact of Darwin's theory of evolution, and being amazed by the disruptive innovation of the tech gurus of the day: Thomas Edison, Nikola Tesla, Guglielmo Marconi. This was the dawn of the electric age and of radio communications, lighting up the night and connecting the world through communications in ways that had never been imagined. As a result, the fundamentals of society and faith were being questioned, challenged, reset. It sounds a lot like this moment of rapid innovation and disruption that we're living through right now. Some people gathered around the idea of 'the march of intellect', a movement to expand access to knowledge and education beyond the strict class confines of earlier eras, and there was a flurry of tech-fuelled imaginative storytelling, some of which we still read today, like Jules Verne's *20,000 Leagues Under the Sea* or HG Wells' *The Time Machine,* for example.

There are a couple of lesser known stories that I love, and that I think are useful for this story I want to share with you – mostly because they're such vivid illustrations of the paths we tend to go down when we drift into utopian future thinking.

Among the most detailed and influential books of that era, but one that isn't widely discussed today, is called *Looking Backward 2000–1887,* by Edward Bellamy, published in 1888. In *Looking Backward,* the protagonist Julian West has himself hypnotised to deal with his chronic insomnia, but it's a hell of a cure: he slips into suspended animation for over a century then wakes up in the year 2000. The premise requires a bit of suspension of disbelief (the 'I went to sleep and woke up in the future' trope was probably a shade fresher in the late 19th century than it is now) but bear with me.

In Bellamy's vision, Boston in the year 2000 is a spectacle of urban grandeur, offering a 'universal reign of comfort': high quality of life and equality for all. The bounty of the world is at your fingertips, thanks to technology and a new form of social organisation, allowing everyone to eat well, live comfortably and retire at 45. Accruing wealth has become unnecessary and is socially shunned. This new way of sharing the benefits of modern life communally was achieved by countries dispensing with their armies and navies, taxation, capitalism and competition, and by nationalising every industry. The production and distribution of everything needed in society was now powered by an 'industrial army' of workers – all of them equal in pay and respect.

Of course, you might recognise some classic elements of the dream of communism in here, along with ideas that are once again fashionable today, such as Universal Basic Income (more on that later), and a few ideas that seem like predictions that came true, such as globally connected communications and trade, debit cards, or music and performance being streamed direct to every home.

Meticulously detailed, it's more a love letter to economics and political fantasy than a work of literature. It's not exactly easy beachside reading: there's a lot more time spent describing distribution logistics than the flimsy romantic element or any kind of human drama, which is why it's staggering to learn that *Looking Backward* stayed in print for a century and was the third-highest selling book of its time. Why?

People were attracted to a vision of the kind of future they wanted to live in, and it spread faster than a 21st-century meme: fans set up 'Bellamy Clubs' as far away as New Zealand to discuss the book's ideas and how to turn this vision into reality. The Garden City movement, an influential philosophy of urban design initiated by Ebenezer Howard in the late 1800s, was inspired by Bellamy's vision of perfectly sustainable neighbourhoods that combined the green spaces of the country with the convenience of city life. Bellamy might not be a household name today, but his influence endures in the form of the garden city. There are dozens upon dozens of them around the world, from the original Letchworth in the UK to suburbs in Sao Paolo and other Brazilian cities, from Tel Aviv to Canberra and Mount Royal in Canada. I now think of Bellamy when I'm waiting at a roundabout. If you come across a city with a radial design, with grand avenues of concentric circles, featuring cul-de-sacs and green belts – there lies an echo of Bellamy.

Bellamy didn't confine his utopian thinking to urban planning: the classless, caring society he portrayed was dramatically different from the Boston that Bellamy would have known. For a while, Bellamy made socialism very hip for the middle class. People ran for political office as 'Bellamyites' and a magazine, *The Nationalist,* launched to promote ideas from the book, starting with nationalising the railways and telegraph. It inspired dozens of imitations and detractors, and continued to influence politics and society for decades.

Reading it today, there's a lot that's appealing: a vision for a global society that managed to transition peacefully to sharing resources, honouring all work equally, and treating crime as a symptom of social inequality rather than human evil or weakness. Admittedly, worrying elements are present: there's no room for dissent and very little discussion of cultural difference or gender roles – though Bellamy's sequel, *Equality* focused on a more equal role for women in work and the world.

Bellamy's wasn't the only positive, alternative vision of the future sparking the popular imagination at the time. In 1890, a different but equally optimistic vision of the future was articulated in a book called *News from Nowhere.* Its author, William Morris, best known as a designer – for his beautiful wallpaper and textile prints and for spearheading the British Arts and Crafts movement, was also a prolific writer and committed socialist, and this book combines all these loves in one.

While *News from Nowhere* and *Looking Backward* had a similarly communitarian mindset, Morris had loathed Bellamy's ultra-technocratic image of the future and wrote some pretty spicy reviews of it and its shortcomings. He didn't understand the appeal of a future in which everyone aspired to be a consumer and a middle-class city-dweller. In his counter-vision, people dedicate themselves to work and craft as a passion, and live closer to nature.

Like Bellamy's book, Morris's *News from Nowhere* opens with a Victorian-era man, William Guest, going to sleep troubled by the inequality, misery and pollution of his time. He wakes up in the same bed in London, but sometime in the 2000s, in a place transformed beyond recognition: from a commercial hub of the industrial age into a blissful semirural paradise. The narrow streets, iron bridges and Georgian and Victorian architecture of London had been torn down in the 'great clearing of 1955': Trafalgar Square was now an orchard of apricot trees, while down the road, the UK Houses of Parliament had been repurposed into a dung market.

The inhabitants of this new world are healthy and hearty, and Morris lingers over his descriptions of the 'firm, comely' women and bronzed, handsome men who spend most of the book laughing at Guest's bizarre 19th-century ideas about paying people for their services or products, dressing according to their job or social station and so on. This new, perfect world had emerged following an all-out class war in the

1950s which pitted the workmen versus the gentlemen. Now money and private property are a thing of the past, along with the 'World-Market', the engine that drives mass production.

Freed from having to work for survival and from the 'cheapening of production', people turn their talents to making beautiful things for their friends and neighbours, leading to a world in which everyone is an artist or scientist, farmer or builder, sometimes all at the same time. Schools are ancient history. Instead, children learn by living in the woods that have reclaimed London, teaching themselves the skills they need and following their interests and instincts.

Cleared of factories and the ravages of industrialisation, the scarred landscape regenerates, and the people of this time are driven by a deep 'love of the very skin and surface of the earth on which man dwells', putting conscious consumption and environmentalism at the core of this utopia.

On the face of it, these visions of the future are very different from each other: Bellamy imagined a tightly controlled industrial army, in a rigid social structure, living in a highly urbanised world. In Morris's vision, the 2000s are a semi-pastoral idyll, where people dedicate themselves to artistry, craft and fieldwork as they desire, switching from job to job based on their moods and the seasons. Transferred to today, you could almost say Morris offers the tree-changed creative worker ideal versus Bellamy's version of the 'smart city'.

What they do have in common, though, is an optimism that people can organise society to share wealth and opportunity, and use technology to make life easier and more fulfilling for everyone. They both tapped into a growing enthusiasm for genuine equality and they fuelled it with these vivid depictions of a world that could be, if only we could come together to work for the common good.

So far, so uplifting: these utopian imaginings served to energise the people of their time. But today's challenges are going to need a different tactic to inspire sustained optimism and action towards change. While I love the ambition and positivity of Bellamy and Morris's visions, I think there's something we need to avoid here too.

With Morris's literal 'great clearing' and Bellamy's regimented citiscape, both these stories took the blank slate approach to imagining the future: as though tomorrow will land like a spaceship, settling over everywhere we live and everything we do. In each of these stories the future is a settled case, all-encompassing and absolute.

This tabula rasa thinking actually holds us back. What we need right now is an ability to recognise future visions with transformative potential but that are still in seed form. The future we need could be sprouting all around us, unseen: we need to be able to spot the future we want in unassuming little slivers, experiments, prototypes of what could be.

They might be a little more imperfect and pragmatic, aspirational but incomplete. Maybe then we'd be able to recognise them and make them real in the here and now.

***

There is one utopian thinker who can help us out of this conceptual cul de sac: Ernst Bloch. Bloch lived through some of the darkest moments of the 20th century and yet is the philosopher who focused his attention most completely on the concepts of hope and utopia.

For Bloch, there was a big difference between an 'abstract utopia' – basically, wishful thinking, even if that wishful thinking looks expansive, impressive and complete – and a 'concrete utopia'. A concrete utopia is one that goes beyond expressing a desire for a particular kind of future, and instead, works towards *enacting* that hope for a new way of living. But that's not to say only the detailed, comprehensive plans are the 'concrete' ones. You don't need to have the whole solution laid out before you to have an inspiring, concrete utopian vision: all you need is to give a glimpse of the possible, and to have some latent potential in your idea that can blossom into something significant in the future, to be a maker of a utopia.

This is what I want us to find in our world today – glimpses of utopia –

ideas and projects laden with the possibility of transformative, systemic change.

Another idea of Bloch's that sticks with me is this concept of the 'Not-Yet'. Bloch says it's easy to be overwhelmed by 'What Has Been', to imagine the future in the shape of the past, so much so that we can actually fail to notice those slivers of possibility, forward glimpses of tomorrow that are around us today. Bloch calls them the 'Not-Yet-Conscious, Not-Yet-Become': the tendencies and latencies for a better world that exist in our reality, waiting to be nurtured and developed. He says there is a 'huge occurrence of utopia', seeds of it, in this imperfect today which is in the process of becoming our tomorrow.

I remember sitting on a train as I first read Bloch's words and feeling a shiver actually run up my arm, like an electric charge being transmitted from the page to my brain. Finally, here was someone who spoke to the reason I feel a stubborn optimism about the future, despite all the challenges mounting against us. You don't wake up and find a utopia fully realised and perfectly formed. They happen a little bit at a time, unevenly, erratically, and if we know how to look, we can see glimpses of them everywhere.

My own privileged access to positive, proactive visionaries from every corner of the world, through my work as a curator in the creative community and as a citymaker, gives me daily moments of wonder at the inventiveness of people and movements. For the past 20 years I've worked as an advocate and instigator of projects shepherding in the new: supporting designers, city-makers, artists and other visionaries who propose innovative ways of doing things. The best thing I can do right now is share the most compelling visions I've encountered, and weave them together, because more people need to hear that there are alternatives to the status quo and that a better world awaits us.

Sure, there's no one big, catch-all solution, no one ideology or utopian vision that we could all get behind to address the environmental, social and economic challenges that surround us. But there's more than one way to remake the world, more than one future we should be working towards.

The glimpses of utopia I want to share with you aren't one-size-fits-all solutions. They're each responding to the challenges of their own corner of the globe and piecing together solutions from the tools very different communities have to hand. They may be new currencies that make money a tool for exchange, not hoarding, or banks that serve people over shareholders. Perhaps they're fresh mindsets for valuing the most human things we do – care for each other – and reimagined tax systems that can actually pay for it. Elsewhere, people are reshaping the tools of social decision-making (otherwise known as politics) so more voices are heard and broader priorities considered. Whether in finance or work, politics or media, or in the way we build the places we live, that's a recurring theme in all these utopian sparks: opening up and offering more seats at the table. The same old thinking, by the same old minds, won't get us where we need to go. Time after time in these stories, we'll see the wisdom and generosity of everyday people being elevated, and the knowledge and capacity of the marginalised being centred.

These are the kinds of utopias we need to uncover and the heroes we need to champion. Incomplete, imperfect 'Not-Yet' utopias are being created by people all over the world every day. Right now we need Bloch parties more than Bellamy clubs.

I set out on this journey positive I could improve the stories we tell each other about the future we could have. I would find those seeds of potential, the glimpses of utopia being put into action: in how we redesign work to work for more of us, how we redistribute power, plan the places we live, find new ways to organise, debate and relate as a global community to address our planetary challenges.

I owed it to every young girl I spoke to in that class who didn't feel like there was a future worth caring about. Already, I could think of dozens of people, organisations and movements turning optimism into action and building concrete utopias in wildly divergent, unexpected ways, all over the world. If we could see some of these new utopias gathered in one place, would we start to have a brighter view of what the future holds, and start to claim our own place in it?

2

Recentre the citizen

Australia in early 2020 was covered in a smoky haze: we were consumed with watching the raging bushfires scorching whole swathes of the country, too focused on our own tragedy to pay a whole lot of attention to the rest of the world. I read stories about the city of Wuhan in China being shut down with an unknown new virus spreading out of control and watched drone shots of empty streets. But for some reason I, like most Australians, somehow didn't think it could happen here. In my work as a local representative I was much more focused on looking out for local Asian communities who were being unfairly targeted by racist media coverage and providing support to businesses as people abandoned Chinatown, right at the usually busy time of Lunar New Year. I thought we had enough to deal with, and that was as bad as it would get, so I posted pictures on social media eating yum cha, encouraging people to keep calm and carry on (eating dumplings).

Then it started to spread: first Japan and South Korea began to confront it, then Singapore, Italy and Spain. The government flirted with closing our borders, and the social media drip started turning into a torrent. And then, one weekend, Hollywood actor Tom Hanks was diagnosed with the virus on a film set on the Gold Coast.

I don't know why, but I'm ashamed to say that was the moment it became real for me. Tom Hanks? Gold Coast? You mean, rich people in holiday destinations get this too? My husband Pat and I lay awake that night and whispered about it in the dark. Was this thing really about to happen here too?

Within a week, everything had changed. A global pandemic was declared and I'd never known time to move so fast. Friends whose arrival we had been counting down to on our wall calendar cancelled their trips as their countries locked down. Other friends in Germany, the USA and the UK began posting about their positive test results. I watched in horror as the American health system began to buckle, cities closing down, states scrambling for medical equipment, unemployment skyrocketing. We stopped leaving the house.

Like many privileged people, I was confronted with a reality we can often avoid: the world is small and interconnected. The global pandemic made it clear we're all in this together, but it also revealed tears in the social fabric, widening the gap of inequality. Some said we're all in same storm but not in the same boat. As the lockdown took an economic toll, in Australia it fell hardest on women and young people – more often working in sectors that shut down – and low-income workers were twice as likely to be out of work as high-income earners.[1]

There were two other big lessons for me in all of this. One is that despite its prominence in the language of our leaders, none of us can live in an economy alone. Most of the measures of success, the goals that we set as a nation, are focused solely on economic indicators: for the most part, that takes the form of GDP, a measure that was never designed to be a full picture of what a good society looks like. There are better ways of working out if our system is working for people, and we need to elevate them so we all start having more useful conversations about what our governments are doing on our behalf and whether these efforts are giving us the world we want.

The second lesson, one that gave me hope among the panic and uncertainty of the COVID-19 pandemic, was just how quickly major policy pivots can be enacted in the face of an immediate threat. Many sacred cows of conventional politics were revealed to be less than holy, and suddenly even the most conservative leaders found themselves turning to the tools of redistribution and social democracy. There's a political concept called the Overton Window.[2] It's a way of describing what is considered socially acceptable within the spectrum of political possibility. This historical moment has busted that window right open: ideas that might once have been considered too radical even to be on the agenda have been catapulted into the mainstream. For example, during the crisis, Spain declared that they would introduce a Universal Basic Income (UBI) – a payment without strings attached, that all citizens are entitled to, in order to help them meet their basic costs of living – not just to deal with the COVID-19 shutdown, but as a permanent policy. The idea of a UBI has been growing in momentum around the world over the last few years, and there are some examples of a 'social dividend' paid in some parts of the world, but it has never been introduced at the level of an entire country. I'm not convinced that UBI is the best approach for creating a fair society (I prefer the Universal Basic Services model that Anna Coote and others have advocated for – more on that shortly) but what's really significant is that we're beginning to see a discussion growing about what it means to live in a society.

The conversation could now shift to cover not just what we're obligated to do, such as following the law and paying our tax, but what we're entitled to expect in return from our governments. As people around the world have self-isolated and made sacrifices, part of that has been an act of self-preservation in avoiding the virus, but it has also been an act of care for our neighbours. Can we take that further in the era that follows the pandemic? Does preserving public health and safety extend to ensuring people have everything they need to live a healthy, secure life beyond the crisis, such as a viable planet or sufficient services and income? If so, how are our nations tracking on that front?

We have to be vigilant for the snap back to business-as-usual and also to make sure the economic recovery doesn't become an excuse for cuts to the care sectors we came to prize more than ever through the crisis. But for a brief moment that Overton Window is wide open, and we have to be ready to leap through it. We might be able to redefine our relationships to the state and to each other. To demand that we be considered as citizens, not just consumers, and that our fullest selves – not just our capacity to make and buy – are explicitly included in the social contract.

People are finding better ways of setting priorities and measuring what matters. This is a moment when we can ask: what do we owe each other? What does it mean to live in a society? And most importantly of all: what kind of world do we want, and are our actions and policies taking us there?

Enable flourishing

There's a beautiful term in philosophy called *eudaimonia,* which means human flourishing, or achieving the best possible conditions for a human being. Aristotle said it was that which made life worth living. It's not just prosperity, though it does include having the capacity to thrive and live a good life. It's not just happiness, though that's important, but it means living well: leading a life with meaning and purpose, a virtuous life that is in line with your values, achieving your potential, in whatever way you define that.

It's a word that fills me with wonder and pushes me to question my actions and choices every time I think about it. It's a very high standard to aspire to as an individual: so just imagine making 'enabling eudaimonia' the goal for society. What if unlocking potential and ensuring human flourishing was the key performance indicator we assessed politicians against, when they stood for re-election every few years? What if, instead of only talking about the state of the economy, we actually counted the stuff that matters to people and communities: the health of our environments and the quality of life our children experience, for example.

Since the 1930s, the primary way we've measured whether a country is flourishing is by measuring how much stuff gets made, or services bought and sold, tallied up as Gross Domestic Product (GDP). Even Simon Kuznets, the creator of the concept, specifically warned against the way we see it being used (famously saying, 'The welfare of a nation can scarcely be inferred from a measurement of national income'[3]) as the default measure of the prosperity or success of a country. We use it because it's easy to measure output, but harder to measure impact or benefit, and for the last few decades many policymakers have pushed the line that what's good for the economy must be good for everyone. GDP doesn't measure fairness, or whether people are healthy and happy in our community. GDP doesn't differentiate between harmful or socially beneficial activity – cutting down a forest could be great for GDP this year, but terrible for the planet, society or economy in the long run. GDP doesn't measure the work we do for free, like care for each other, or volunteer: for example, the value of unpaid work in Australia has been calculated to amount to an extra, invisible one-third of the country's GDP, but it isn't counted.[4]

GDP is a flawed indicator, but it's so pervasive I've found myself referring to it in this story, even though I'm conscious of its limitations. Thankfully, there are thinkers pushing the conversation beyond GDP as well as cities and countries finding better ways of counting what matters and using more human-centred KPIs to determine the best use of public money.

At a local level, at the City of Sydney we judge our performance using Community Wellbeing Indicators,[5] which we determine by measuring over 100 different factors that are very different to simply counting how much money changes hands. We ask people in our community how much trust they have in each other, for example, and then we implement programs and support projects that seek to improve people's feelings of trust. When we started measuring trust in our neighbours in 2007, it was at 45 per cent, and by 2019 that had increased to 72 per cent (though there was a dip along the way). We don't measure only crime statistics, but also whether people feel safer. 95 per cent of our residents say they're willing to offer social support to neighbours. People say they have really meaningful relationships, something that most stats don't measure.

It's not all rosy, though – people in our community are worried about issues like being able to afford housing to live in, about more people becoming homeless, or the growing gap between rich and poor, and how we care for each other as we age. Around half of our residents feel that they don't have the time or opportunity to actively participate in life outside of work – in the arts, culture and sporting activities – things which you could certainly connect back to that sense of eudaimonia. Most of these are issues the City does not necessarily control, but we can try to advocate and push upwards to other levels of government to invest in and recognise these needs.

This is all the so-called 'soft' stuff, the human, the emotional, the sensory – for too long, we've swallowed the lie that this can't be measured, doesn't make money, and so doesn't matter. Or that it's personal, not political. But if the work of politics is helping society achieve its shared goals, and maybe even that higher goal of making a society that enables eudaimonia, doing this work is critical. At the City of Sydney, we generate the Indicators by surveying our residents every four years, and we compile that feedback with data from the ABS, NSW Health and Department of Education. We then use this information as a key input into the goals and targets outlined in our community strategic plan, the document that guides our budgets and long-term plans.

At a national scale, the Australian National Development Index[6] is a project in the works to develop a better set of metrics to measure progress based on what people actually value in their lives, which aims to engage with 500,000 Australians and a host of experts, researchers and community organisations. They're interested in measuring not just performance to date, but also the aspirations of the community, with the goal of creating a policy tool that describes 'the Australia we want'.[7]

Across the Tasman, New Zealand are one step ahead: in 2019, Prime Minister Jacinda Ardern introduced the Wellbeing Budget, a way to put a human flourishing lens on the work of government. New Zealand's wellbeing approach is a way of setting new KPIs the government will be measured on, ones that are more about the quality of life of their citizens, and in particular, their most vulnerable ones: child poverty figures are going to be presented as part of the budget every year, as are child hospitalisation rates related to deprivation, rates of homelessness, youth suicide and mental illness diagnoses. For the first time, political leaders will be explicitly, deliberately held to account for a country's performance on metrics like soil erosion and waste, pollution in waterways, social indicators like overcrowding in housing, or innovation as measured by investment in research and development.

The New Zealand Wellbeing Budget requires that any new government spending that ministers want to propose has to work across traditional portfolios and be a collaborative response that relates to one of five government priorities, such as improving mental health, addressing the inequalities faced by Indigenous Māori and Pasifika people and transitioning to a sustainable economy. This shift has already resulted in increased spending for mental health services, child poverty and measures to tackle family violence, including NZ$200 million for victims of domestic and sexual violence. Crucially, through this approach New Zealand will treat public spending as an investment that saves money in the long term rather than a cost to be minimised, which provides for a stronger focus on prevention, something which the business-as-usual model isn't designed to do.

This is an incredibly courageous path for a government to walk: many of these challenges are intractable, multifaceted 'wicked problems', and under PM Ardern, New Zealand politicians are inviting scrutiny of the kind of stats that usually get swept under the carpet. It's dramatically different to the usual focus on economic growth (or as Australian politicians like to say, jobs and growth) as the only indicator of success. We have to watch and wait to see if changing what's measured by governments shifts the dial in people's lives and enables more human flourishing.

Remove unfreedoms

When we talk about human rights, social justice and the role of government, does that mean protecting people from really terrible outcomes – like being victims of a global pandemic, for example – or does that extend to more than just the bare right to life?

Philosopher Martha Nussbaum and economist Amartya Sen set the bar higher and give us a picture of what human rights look like in action. They've developed their own framework, the Capabilities Approach, which consists of the things we need to be able to build a dignified life. In the Capabilities Approach the key question is, 'What is this person *actually able* to do and be?'

Martha Nussbaum lists ten 'Central Capabilities'. At a minimum, we all have a right to life that isn't cut short, to physical health and to having autonomy over our own bodies. We all have a right to experience a range of emotions, and to use our senses, imagination and reason, to spend time with and form relationships with other people, to play and enjoy leisure, and to participate in politics or other forms of social organisation.

Amartya Sen refocuses that 'development' we hear so much about: the goal of aid and social welfare and public spending should be 'the removal of various types of unfreedoms that leave people with little choice and little opportunity of exercising their reasoned agency'.[8] Sen and Nussbaum have given us a more human-centred approach to understanding what justice looks like in our everyday lives. And by their standards, some very wealthy countries are failing some or all of their residents.

One way to tip the scales towards fairness is through an unconditional payment for everyone: Universal Basic Income (UBI). Some UBI advocates, like Australian sociologist Eva Cox, say it could give each of us choice over how we use our time. For instance, we could turn more of our energies towards the social care that underpins society, the environmental efforts we need to make in the face of climate change, and the creative and life-affirming work that brings humanity together. 'The unpaid work that makes societies function and contributes to making our lives pleasurable is substantial, realistically valued against GDP. So, let's recognise these contributions to our common-wealth via a universal social dividend that covers basic living costs. This would give all the capacity to budget their time preferences between their paid and unpaid contributions,' Eva says.

It's a concept that has been trialled since the 1970s: giving people income support with agency and autonomy – in a way that interventions like cashless welfare cards don't – and with transformative impacts. While UBI sounds impossibly expensive, there are existing payments and rebates it could replace, and not everyone would need it. Plus it's taxed, so much of it would return to national revenue. Its sheer simplicity offers advantage over the means-tested welfare system, which can be punitive and stigmatising. Eva says, 'If you give income support that deals with people with dignity, you don't have to spend as much on social services repairing the damage.'

Interestingly, variations of basic income have developed, with advocates and opponents of different versions on all sides of politics. The UBI has now been thrust into the spotlight by the COVID-19 crisis. As mentioned earlier, to aid economic recovery, Spain's socialist government announced the national roll-out of the largest minimum income scheme proposed anywhere in the world. They're starting with one million of the poorest families in the country in May 2020 and there are plans for it to become permanent.[9]

In recent years, the UBI has become popular in the US tech sector, promoted by the likes of Tesla CEO Elon Musk and, Facebook's Mark Zuckerberg. Entrepreneur Andrew Yang, one of the many contenders for Democratic Presidential nominee, proposed that every citizen over 18 should receive a 'Freedom Dividend' of US$1000 a month as a way to balance out the job losses that result from disruptive technology and automation.

The mindset of such champions gives me pause about the UBI. Right now, tech gurus have a broad political influence. Do we want a more libertarian version of basic income taking hold? Do we want to risk governments using minimum income as a way to cut back the hard-won social safety net? Eva reassures me that the UBI discourse isn't related to the privatisation of public services, but I worry we might need more supports in place to protect those rights in action that Martha Nussbaum talked about.

'These individual bodily needs are invariable, not subjective choices,' Anna Coote says. The head of social policy for the UK's New Economics Foundation, she focuses on encouraging investment in meeting a set of shared essential needs – Universal Basic Services (UBS) – that work best when we provide for them together.[10]

UBS is an investment into the social protections we need to have a fair society – policies and programs to reduce the impacts of disadvantage and support us at our most vulnerable: the stuff people call welfare – as well as an investment in the social commons, that shared infrastructure that we as humans require to survive. That includes healthcare, education, shelter, food, transport, information, legal services and participation in democracy: some of them are already provided for free, to an extent, in countries like Australia and the UK, but they've been underfunded and overloaded over the past few decades. UBS reinvests to properly fund core public services to give us all a more generous social safety net, with the goal of every citizen having guaranteed access to material safety, opportunity and participation.

You might have heard of Maslow's hierarchy of needs – a pyramid that stacks up the essential needs that motivate us as humans, starting with the basics and becoming more sophisticated and abstract as it rises – I see UBS as the concrete that sets the foundations of that pyramid. Once our physiological and safety needs are met, those 'unfreedoms' Amartya Sen writes about are removed, and only then are we really capable of delivering on our potential and making a contribution to our society. Removing unfreedoms unlocks our potential to achieve more for ourselves and give back more to help each other.

'The care economy is part of the social commons,' Anna tells me. 'This is part of a process of claiming and controlling the resources we need to look after one another.'

Right, I can hear the cynic in you asking, *and just how would we pay for that?* UBS is not cheap, but it's not as expensive as you might think. The Institute for Global Prosperity at University College London (UCL) and Anna's co-author Andrew Percy have done the modelling on UBS in a UK context: they've estimated that it would require an increase of expenditure of about 2.3 per cent of GDP, which is nothing to sneeze at. But let's think about what side of the ledger this spending falls on: these are investments more than expenses. UCL have suggested this outlay could include building 1.5 million new homes to double the stock of social housing in the UK, creating an asset that will keep delivering for future generations; more funding for public transport, which would have a further positive impact on the human and environmental costs of pollution and congestion; and the provision of phone and internet services for all citizens, which would boost productivity and access to work, as well as the ability to participate in the kind of digital democracy platforms I explore later in this story.[11]

I'm not disputing that there are substantial sums at play here, but the UCL research also finds there are opportunities for 'economies of scale achieved through generalised provision, thus circumventing the premium of satisfying individual requirements purchased individually' Basically, we get better value for our public spending when we all pitch in and pay for these public goods together, rather than sending us all out into the marketplace with our individual UBIs and asking us to negotiate our own deals.

UBS doesn't have to result in monolithic or centralised outcomes either: this doesn't have to be a grey, one-size-fits-all future. The services we could invest in as a society would work best and provide even more efficient outcomes by being closer to the people they serve. They can take a lot of forms. Anna Coote tells me about time banks and care co-operatives that she sees as good models, people who are providing local alternatives to top-down provision. The research backs it up, finding cost savings of up to 14 per cent 'when services are locally designed and delivered with intimate knowledge and understanding of specific local circumstances efficiency can be further increased'.[12]

There's a precedent for this kind of big-picture thinking and investment in our shared human needs: in the UK following the Second World War there was a strong sense of solidarity and a shift in national priorities. For a country with deeply ingrained class divisions, the conflict had heightened awareness of social connection and responsibility, and part of the response was the creation of the National Health Service. It endures, somewhat degraded, but still the most beloved and prized UK institution (over 90 per cent of Britons support its core principles) and one that proved priceless during the COVID-19 pandemic.[13]

In Australia, the post-Second World War recovery was the moment that kick-started national-scale investments in public housing through the Commonwealth State Housing Agreement: an ambitious plan to provide 700,000 homes within ten years that were safe, dignified and affordable. The goal was that a family living on minimum income wouldn't spend more than 20 per cent of their income on rent. While disputes between the states and commonwealth, and a change of government, saw the potential of this project cut short, this postwar housing focus still resulted in almost 100,000 publicly owned homes, one in six homes built in the period. This shows us that in times of great crisis, governments can be compelled to build social infrastructure with an eye to fairness and to the future. We're in a moment of crisis recovery right now: could the next leap forward in caring for each other, the next institution that fills us with pride, be born out of a people-first response to this challenge?

Some say you don't have to pit one solution against another, and the concepts of UBI and UBS aren't mutually exclusive. There is, however, a limit to how much money can reasonably be spent, and there's growing evidence that this sort of direct-payment redistribution is less effective than us pooling the same investment and working collectively. In her book, Anna quotes an International Labour Office (ILO) study which estimated the costs of a UBI that is sufficient, not just token, in 130 countries, and found that it would cost between 20 to 30 per cent of GDP. That's enormous compared to the 2.3 per cent estimate for enlarging investment in public services.

If you look at where the money for something like Yang's Freedom Dividend would come from, he proposed introducing a Value Added Tax (a tax on things and services you buy like our own GST) and from 'consolidating' existing social services, among other things. What we see time and again is that consumption taxes have a disproportionately heavy impact on those who have the lowest income, as they're more likely to spend more of that income on essential needs. Cuts to other forms of welfare also take from those who need the most support. When the budget 'savings' from the cuts are redistributed to everyone, those who are already doing okay benefit.

My conversation with Anna Coote early in writing this story blew wide open my view of what kind of policy tools we need to be fighting for and the places we should look to find innovation. My focus for so much of my career has been the creative economy – the stories we tell to connect with each other; the art we make to express ourselves; people designing solutions to problems large and small, aesthetic and social. But there is a world of creativity to be celebrated in the care economy, in how we structure businesses and public service to be more bottom-up and responsive and in how we approach policy and government.

'We need municipal support programs and constitutional change that embeds this structural role for government in doing three things: providing equality of access, distributing funds and guaranteeing standards,' Anna says. 'And this ought to be decided by a democratic dialogue over who owns what and what government does.' That's one reason why democracy and our politics needs a 21st-century upgrade.

3

Refocus politics

All the chips are stacked against change. Those who are doing well out of business-as-usual generally have access to the algorithms of influence and levers of power, so they're well placed to keep things working in their favour. They hold the microphones and can broadcast the message that if it ain't broke, don't fix it. If you're on the outside looking in and you're feeling broken by the system, it's likely that you lack the time, money or platform to be heard: you might even struggle to put your finger on just what the problem is.

The political process is supposed to be the great leveller between the powerful and the many. We elect people to represent our best interests and to reflect what we value when they decide how to direct our shared resources – our common wealth, if you will – towards those goals. It feels impossibly naïve to tell you engaging with politics is at the foundation of the solutions we need: but the people and movements I want to introduce you to are rehabilitating the political process and carving paths for more representative and direct decision-making.

We need the solutions they present because we're experiencing a widespread erosion of trust in politics as a tool for justice in society. The democratic process now feels skewed to favour a fortunate few at the expense of everyone and everything else, even the viability of life itself on our one and only planet.

People have been losing confidence in public institutions, and politics is at the top (or should that be bottom?) of the list. The University of Cambridge's Centre for the Future of Democracy have been measuring people's attitudes towards democracy since 1995, surveying four million people in 154 countries. Their 2019 results show that the majority of people – 58 per cent – are dissatisfied with the condition of democracy in their country.[1] In 2018, *The Guardian Australia* published a survey that found that 63 per cent of

Australian Millennials believed politicians have a negative impact on society, while only 23 per cent said they had a positive impact.[2] Maybe that's because people are exasperated at seeing the issues that matter to them neglected, with little action despite years of talk. In that *Guardian* study, the top five issues of personal concern were: terrorism (31%), climate change and the environment (30%), income inequality (24%), unemployment (23%) and war (22%).

One of the most profound political ideas that guide my work comes from Edmund Burke, an Irish politician and political philosopher in the 1700s, who made it clear that the social contract isn't just to be negotiated between the competing groups in our community today but instead, is a partnership between the generations. He said: 'Society is indeed a contract ... The state ... is ... a partnership not only between those who are living, but between those who are living, those who are dead, and those who are to be born.'[3]

What Burke is telling us is that the social contract – the concept that, by an unspoken agreement, individuals surrender some of their personal liberties to the state and in return receive certain state-organised protections – is intergenerational. This contract between generations isn't being kept in business-as-usual politics. No one is donating on behalf of tomorrow and toddlers or school kids aren't a marginal seat, so no one is taking their 'special interest' in an inhabitable planet or fair society properly into account. It's one of the reasons we've seen such dismissive comments from politicians talking about the brilliant Fridays For Future movement kicked off by Greta Thunberg and the school strikers. These politicans don't see their jobs today as having a responsibility to the voters of tomorrow.

When you look at how our politics is dealing – or not dealing – with big intergenerational issues, like climate change or inequality, we can see a lot of problems being put off, pushed onto the next generation who are set to inherit a warming planet and spiralling unfairness. No wonder people are disillusioned.

In my experience, the political parties we see tussling for power today are so caught up in internal feuds between conservatives and moderates, city and country, that they've lost sight of what matters to people outside of their party rooms, much less what they owe to the next generation. It doesn't help that these so-called representatives are richer, older and whiter than the rest of us.

In Australia today, 50 per cent of us were either born overseas or have at least one parent born overseas: but if you look at our federal parliament, that's not what you see. Of the 226 Australians in federal parliament, only 20 come from a non-English-speaking background. That means our community is more than ten times more culturally diverse than our elected representatives are.

According to the 2016 census, the 'typical' Australian is a 38-year-old woman, but according to a BuzzFeed analysis of our federal parliament, the typical politician is a 51-year-old man.

They called him 'Andrew' (because there were eight Andrews in federal parliament at the time): he was born in Australia – as were his parents – and his family has English ancestry. He's got two degrees, including a law degree. Andrew's married with two children and owns two homes. All of which means that Andrew is richer, older and much more culturally homogenous than the Australians he's supposed to represent.[4]

In the United States, the typical member of Congress is 12 times richer than the average American family: the median net worth of a member of the House of Representatives is US$900,000 and for a senator US$3.2 million. Meanwhile, the typical US household has a median net worth of US$97,300. In the UK, things aren't better: 2 per cent of the UK population are millionaires, but about two thirds of Cabinet are. The UK also fails on the representation of women and minorities plus is weighted heavily towards the legal profession.

When our representatives are wealthier and more comfortable than most of the population, they live a dramatically different life. Even with the best of intentions, they're unlikely to understand what life is like for people who are struggling to get by. If the system is working for you, you'd have to be an exceptional individual to be motivated to deeply rethink it.

Another cause for concern is how our political process is funded. Even at a local government level, the cost of running an election campaign can run into hundreds of thousands of dollars: at a federal level, Australian political parties are estimated to spend about $15 million each per election campaign, while one minor party spent up to $60 million influencing the 2019 election.[5] That's staggering, but it's small change compared to the US electoral circus. In the USA, presidential election campaigns run into the billions. The 2008 US presidential campaign is estimated to have cost US$2.4 billion, while the 2016 race cost a staggering US$6.5 billion. In funding those campaigns, the return on investment of a grass-roots supporter drive is low compared to investing time and energy into courting the patronage of the mega-rich. Politicians find themselves running expensive fundraisers that give only big business or the privileged access to their prospective representatives, appealing to wealthy donors. No doubt, once elected, the successful candidates end up taking those donors' calls.

The activists, visionaries, technologists, community organisers – and, yes, politicians – we'll meet in this chapter face these challenges and this well-founded cynicism head-on. They're not trying to win the political game the traditional way: they have no intention of replicating the power structures that got us here. They're bringing politics into everyday life beyond elections; they're making real change in people's lives using the tools of local government; they're broadening the pool of decision-makers and they're engaging young people and those who are usually left out of the political conversation. None of it is going to be easy, but democracy can be saved, and here are the people who are showing us how.

Devolve decision-making

Budgets are an expression of priorities – we'll spend on this project instead of another – and one of the hardest jobs at any level of government. Who gets to decide where the money goes?

Where political leadership is unrepresentative and the priorities of the community are ignored or misunderstood, one way to bypass that is by handing over decision-making directly to the people. Known as 'participatory budgeting', it gives a broader segment of the community more power over where public money is spent. It was first introduced by the Brazilian Workers Party in the city of Porto Alegre in the late 1980s, and has been spreading around the world since then.

The way participatory budgeting works varies from place to place, but across the board, it's clear that it takes a lot of time, patience and the political will to make processes more transparent. In the Porto Alegre model, the budgeting process covers expenditure on water supply and sewage, street paving, parks and schools. To kick off the nine-month long process, the local government presents the accounts for the previous year's budget plus the investment plan for the 12 months ahead in public assemblies in each part of the city's 16 districts. The citizens rank the proposals for works within their districts and debate competing needs across the whole city. There are also thematic streams, in which experts play a role alongside the public-facing budgeting, and this approach has allowed a diversity of social groups to be represented.

There's an old saying that is attributed to Oscar Wilde: 'The trouble with socialism is that it takes too many evenings.' That's what comes to mind when I think not just about participatory budgeting, but all deliberative, community-driven processes. This stuff gobbles up a lot of time: you can understand why most of us have decided to outsource all this debate and deliberation to our elected officials. I'm one of them, so I can vouch for how much reading and work goes into making these choices – and know that not everyone has the time or interest to do this. But if we want a different set of priorities from our governments, want to have new voices at the table, or to have more transparency in how our money is spent, participatory budgeting is one compelling way to try something new.

In Porto Alegre, 50,000 citizens participate, in a community of 1.5 million, in allocating 650 million reals (approximately AU$230 million) of the city's budget. Their investment of time has paid off: the number of schools has quadrupled since participatory budgeting was introduced, and in the first ten years of the scheme the proportion of the city's budget spent on health and education increased from 13 per cent (in 1985) to almost 40 per cent (in 1996). Driven by the priorities of people not usually included in the decision-making process, Porto Alegre has also seen an increase in spending on public housing, enclosing open sewers and connecting people to town water.

Further north in Brazil, the city of Belo Horizonte adopted participatory budgeting in 1993, and now half of the city's local investment resources are allocated through the process. The projects are primarily UMEI (municipal infant education units) preschools, alley- and road-widening projects to improve access to settlements, and covering over the open sewers that flood regularly and cause health problems for residents of the *vilas* (also known as *favelas*), the neighbourhoods of settlements. There's a fascinating documentary by João Ramos de Almeida, *Op Belô*, which puts the viewer on the buses touring the competing projects over the course of one year, and in the middle of the horse-trading and frantic bargaining between communities when it comes to the votes.

It's tough watching projects that are equally worthy having to compete with each other for the votes of their neighbours. Still, it's a true expression of the push and pull of budgeting. It's always hard to choose, but it is uplifting to see so many people actively involved in making these tough choices, weighing up competing interests. It's not all rosy: residents raise doubts about the cost estimates for each project set by the city council's experts, and after the vote, those who lose out express frustration that some projects seem to get special treatment. Despite the criticisms, the residents seem to remain supportive of the process, some explaining it takes years of presenting their projects to be successful.

It's not a perfect solution, but participatory budgeting does expand the pool of decision-makers and raise priorities that might have been overlooked in the past. It could be one way we can rebuild trust in the role government can play in improving people's lives. Technology is now allowing other cities – and even countries – to implement the principles of participatory budgeting in a less time-intensive manner that actually fits with the way we live today.

Escalate feedback

'For the first 1100 years, things went pretty well,' Robert Bjarnason observes of Icelandic democracy. 'There was relatively high trust in the parliament. Yes, there's been people on different sides, you know – more left-wing or more right-wing, whatever. But the trust in the whole institution has always been very high, like 70 or 80 per cent. It was something that was respected: both the institution but also the parliamentarians themselves.

'But then just in a matter of a couple of weeks, all that was gone. The trust plummeted into the single digits.'

Throughout my conversations with people for this book, one theme that has emerged again and again is how the toxic half-life of the 2008 global financial crisis has played out in unexpected ways, and in unlikely places. I knew it would be an important factor when I set out to write this story but I never realised its extent: how catalytic a moment it had been for transformation in the political and economic trajectory we'd been (and mostly still are) travelling on. One of the most important lessons we can take from that time is that the so-called recovery efforts, resulting in public sector cuts labelled austerity, ended up having as devastating an effect as the initial crash. In the aftermath of the COVID-19 pandemic, we'd do well to remember that we'll be paying off the response for a long time; let's ensure that we're putting public money into policies today that will deliver a more equal and sustainable world tomorrow. While many countries and communities found the GFC and austerity accelerated divisions, I take hope from the fact that in some instances people took advantage of a moment of disruption to demand a new system, and amazingly, in a few places we'll discover that they actually got one.

Iceland was ravaged by the GFC economically and socially. The backstory is that in the early 2000s, banks were deregulated and Icelandic bankers began to play with high-profit, high-risk financial inventions (we'll be diving into those a little later on in our story). Within half a decade, this isolated island of about 350,000 people was suddenly a global financial player. Iceland started producing billionaires and financiers – labelled the corporate vikings – who were buying up high-street chains in the UK and Scandinavia to borrow against, weigh down with debt and strip of assets, playing the currency exchanges abroad and at home, and generally riding the wave of financialisation.

For an idea of the scale of the change this wrought in seven or eight short years, try to picture Tasmania positioning itself almost overnight as a banking mecca and Tasmanian banks advising residents to take out cross-currency loans when they refinanced their mortgages. Unsurprisingly, when the party ended, the hangover was catastrophic. The crash hit hard, wiping out the island's three banks, sinking the Icelandic currency and leaving mortgagees repaying their ballooning home loans at enormous losses in yen and pounds.

But Iceland didn't react like the rest of the world to the crash. They refused to bail out their banks, held the risk-taking corporate vikings accountable, turfed out their parliament, rewrote their constitution and took advantage of that moment of chaos to reform their financial sector and politics in a meaningful way. Their recovery hasn't been perfect – confidence in parliament may only have climbed back up to about 17 per cent, well short of the long highs Robert spoke about – but it is exemplary.

Public participation in politics beyond and between elections was central to this transformation, and Robert Bjarnason's work as co-founder of the Citizens' Foundation had a lot to do with it. But more on that in a minute. After the crash came the Pots and Pans Revolution (there are some well-named revolutions in this chapter, but I think this one takes the cake) when ordinary Icelanders hit the streets, banging their pots and pans outside the Icelandic parliament, demanding accountability for the policy decisions that let the financial sector destabilise society.

The clanging pots and pans worked. In a matter of weeks, the parliament had resigned, were replaced by a left-leaning coalition government, and soon the process whereby ordinary citizens could help rewrite the Icelandic constitution had begun. Twenty-five

Icelanders were chosen at random for the task and given the astonishingly short time of eight weeks to decide on their country's new constitution. Imagine getting tapped on the shoulder for that one: it makes jury duty sound like a holiday. The constitutional committee did what any of us would do these days: they put out the call for suggestions on Facebook and YouTube, crowdsourcing ideas from the comments. This gave Icelanders the first taste of an active role in online democracy, and I think is one of the reasons why they've been so successful in using participatory platforms to make decisions, set priorities and allocate budgets in the decade since.

Robert recalls that volatile time:

Me and some other entrepreneurs, we started to think can we use the internet to connect citizens to politicians? In the beginning we were thinking more like direct democracy – let's just get rid of the politicians! – but that was in the heat of the moment. We quite quickly realised that even with all its faults, representative democracy has a lot of positive elements to it, but the problem is that it's not been upgraded for one hundred or two hundred years.

One hundred years ago, people used to go on horseback or walking for a couple of days to go to the voting poll, and then they would meet their congressman or the representative in Reykjavik. There were like 20,000 people in the country. People were much closer to their representatives: voting for somebody for four years totally made sense then. But the thing is that now, just having the interaction at the moment of the time of those votes, every four years, that's not working as well with this modern world changing so fast.

Robert, his co-founder Gunnar Grímsson and their fellow geeks built a platform to upgrade politics to a 21st-century operating system. They called it Better Reykjavik and launched it in 2010.

We're creating something more agile by giving different groups of citizens access to policy-making on more of an ongoing level. So, the political campaigns are not only about, 'So, well, for the next four years I will do this; you just tick all the boxes in four years; let's meet then.' It's rather: 'I want to work with you on solving those issues with actual input from the crowd.' It also has this practical element in that it actually leads to better policy.

The crowdsourcing platform is also a co-creation platform: it's not really the city versus the citizen, but it's the city versus a large group of citizens that have come together with an idea to debate the pros and cons, to sort of flesh it out, and then maybe a thousand people have liked it, maybe another 500 have not liked it. So, actually this also helps increase the quality of ideas: if it's an idea that many people get around, it's more likely that it has quality in it and it's more likely that it has impact.

Then a happy accident helped, one which was born of the disenchantment of Icelanders at this unique moment in their nation's long political history. One of the leading figures of the Pots and Pans Revolution, comedian Jon Gnarr, deciding that he couldn't do a worse job than Iceland's politicians had, created 'The Best Party' and stood for election as mayor of Reykjavik in 2010. Robert explains:

The Best Party had a good theme song [a parody of the Tina Turner song 'Simply the Best'] but they did not have any policies, aside from psychedelic policies like putting a polar bear into the children's petting zoo, things like that. They promised, 'We will break all our promises', and still they were polling like 38 per cent in the polls. They jumped on Better Reykjavik and told their supporters: 'You go in and edit it; help us make the policy for the next four years.'

We got over 40,000 people who participated – there's only 100,000 people on the voting registry in Reykjavik – it was like a mass participation event.

Amazingly, Jon and The Best Party won, and ended up in a coalition with the social democrats. Crucially, they continued to use crowdsourcing through Better Reykjavik to engage directly with residents. Despite this push from the political side of things, Robert remained focused on making sure the platform wasn't exclusively the tool of one political party, but that it gained acceptance by bureaucracy and government.

'So, it created this irresistible force to get it accepted within the bureaucracy, but it still took us 15 months to sign the agreement with the city administration, because we wanted to make sure this was not a political project: it had to be a part of the administration,' he says.

That was a smart move. The Best Party disbanded after four years, but by then Better Reykjavik had become a part of the architecture of the state, expected by residents and accepted by bureaucrats. This is a vital lesson for anyone who wants to follow in their footsteps: embed the tools of systemic change beyond the modus operandi of one party or social movement, and do the work of building your tools of change into the machinery of government. Today, Robert tells me, every municipality around Reykjavik has adopted the platform (now rebranded as Better Neighbourhoods), and citizen participation in decision-making is growing.

Robert's prior life as a game designer has given the Citizens' Foundation an edge: the man knows how to keep an audience engaged. The trick is, participation has to be easy and fun or people simply won't do it. They also have to have a clear sense that someone is listening to their contributions – even if they can't all be delivered on – and this is achieved through feedback mechanisms. There's a lot the world of game design can teach anyone interested in making politics more participatory and engaging.

'Well, the first element maybe is to figure out what's "not fun": complexity is not fun. A lot of reading is not fun. That's like when you make a video game: don't make it overly complex with, like, a thousand buttons, and don't make people read 20 pages before they can go to the next stage of the game. Basic rules. And totally applies to this,' Robert says.

Make it simple. Encourage people to use images. In the past few months, we've also added video, and people can add audio comments. Have everything sort of light. For the Our Budget eVoting tool, that is more of a gamified experience where, basically, you are asked to come up with the budget for your neighbourhood. You select the neighbourhood that you live in. Then – let's say you have $20,000 to spend – you can select how many ideas you want. Do you want to do two big projects and two small projects? Do you want to do ten small projects or just want one project? So, you are the mayor of the neighbourhood and you're in total control.

I think that the key is the simplicity and also feedback ... like, when you are pressing something, it changes colour. And [there's] meaningful feedback from the game or the app ... when somebody's ideas get into the process; for example, the agenda-setting tool. So, let's say there's an idea about some cycling-related things. It goes into process into the planning department, and then it goes into a meeting and it's decided to send it forward to some experts. And then the city employee puts a short status update into the system, which then sends an email to everybody who supported or opposed the idea. So, that feels like a feedback mechanism.

You can't have a fun experience if it's just an empty hole and you keep on writing into it but nothing comes back from it. Feedback: that's also how you let people know that you're listening.

Most people are quite sensible, they know that there's not a high chance that their idea will just be accepted by the city and will just be built immediately. Very few people have that sort of expectation.

I mean, people obviously are happiest if they get a 'Yes, thank you. Your idea has been melted now into this policy and will be a part of this going forward.' But if you get a 'no' that explains it in human language not in Bureaucracia, people understand why it's not possible.

The 'no' is actually a lot more important than a 'yes' because it's an opportunity to teach people about the city and how it works. If there's a thousand people who supported that idea or two hundred who opposed it, you then send out a mass email about that specific issue that people are interested in. So, it's a highly targeted feedback mechanism, just to people who were interested in that idea, in that neighbourhood.

From my perspective as an elected official, I think one of the most important things this kind of participatory dialogue can provide is context for citizens about what their neighbours and peers think: is their proposal actually 'common sense', as they often tell us; are their opinions popularly held or shared by their neighbours? Sometimes the most vocal members of a community may not represent the majority: we're all in our own echo chambers until a process like this expands our world view.

Adds Robert, 'I've also seen situations where quite controversial, long-running problems within the city – taking positions about something that had very entrenched interests and views inside the city – were moved along by this process, by seeing large groups of citizens helping to tackle this issue. And so, it helps the politicians directly, to an extent, in that you know it creates more fluidity if you like, or more liquidity in the whole situation.'

Citizens Foundation has grown beyond Iceland. In 2012 and 2013, they helped Estonia in crowd-sourcing changes to Estonia's electoral laws, to help rebuild trust in democracy after a series of political scandals. The Citizens Foundation-powered People's Assembly (Rahvakogu) website helped thousands of Estonians propose and debate changes to laws. Of 15 ideas presented to the parliament, seven were adopted as Estonian laws. One of those formalised the status of citizens' petitions: now, if a Rahvakogu petition gains more than 1000 signatures, it must be considered by parliament.

'Now that we've done projects in over 20 countries, and wherever those citizen-participation projects are put in front of people – where they know about them, that's always a challenge – there's always demand. People want to participate. I think that the past ten years of social networks has been a fantastic training grounds for citizen participation. You know, people know how to make comments; they know how to like things, build communities, things like that. They take this idea and spread it.

'It's just like social media in a way, you know, but it just has a bit more meaning.'

Fork the government

Like Iceland's story, this tale from Taiwan begins with an evocatively named revolution, and ends in an entirely new approach to government and participation in politics.

Taiwan is an ancient culture with a young democracy: their first presidential election took place 30 years ago, and a military dictatorship is still in living memory for many Taiwanese. To my surprise, Taiwan's Digital Minister, Audrey Tang, tells me that's what's given her country a head start when it comes to reshaping politics. 'For people who don't have a legacy system, there's less inertia because there's not five hundred years, two hundred years of republican tradition to honour,' she says.

'We're literally the first generation that can actually do democracy because it was illegal in our parents' age. Because of that, there's a lot more room to innovate. There's a lot less inertia to fight. The public service generally sees the internet and digital technology as something that can potentially take away the risks, improve their efficiency and share the credit.'

Political turmoil engulfed Taiwan in early 2014 when the Sunflower Movement, made up of students and citizen groups, occupied parliament determined to block the signing of a trade agreement that they saw as tipping the balance too far in favour of their big neighbour, China, at the expense of locals and small businesses. Unlike passionate protests in many other countries, in Taiwan people didn't just occupy, they debated. They took to the streets, but they took their phones with them, and they continued their conversations online. The Sunflower Movement – the protestors carried the flowers as a symbol of hope – used the tools of the digital age to overcome the single-focus nature of protest, to craft a broader social project that could include as many people as possible and incorporate nuanced, structural demands.

'From my perspective,' says Audrey, 'the Sunflower Movement is the first time that people have seen with their own eyes, with half a million people on the street and many more online, that it is possible for the 20 or so NGOs to converge over time. They occupy the environment, rather than diverge, as many other "Occupy" [movements] did. A focused conversation is possible. That is an existential proof that collectively raised imagination of "democracy merges" as a citizen assembly ... we can actually converge into something actionable with professional facilitating and civic technology.'

The occupation – there were up to 500,000 people, mostly students, participating (extraordinary numbers in a country of under 24 million) – and conversation generated by it undermined the authority of the ruling Kuomintang (KMT) party, culminating in a retreat on their pro-China policies. While the Sunflower Movement didn't topple the KMT from power immediately, they generated enough momentum that the long-time opposition party, the Democratic Progressive Party, won government at the next national elections, in 2016, and more open-democracy advocates were elected in other roles. What was most lasting, though, was the mindset shift initiated: those citizen deliberations of the period of occupation brought people together to work through their differences and find common ground between disparate social movements and causes.

Taiwanese people started to think, 'What if it could always be like this?'

'I think that's the main thing,' Audrey says. 'The main legacy is of course that, in Taiwan, many people now expect to participate in democratic affairs between elections. People's imagination has been opened. Other mayors – like some who are following the Sunflower Movement who did not have an open government plan – lose their platforms. People who do have an open government plan or who participate in the Occupy find themselves mayors sometimes without expecting it.'

This is what government by digital natives looks like. Audrey's generation in Taiwan are creating a political process that reflects the transparent, open-source and collaborative digital world that they've grown up in. Open government takes many forms, and in Taiwan Audrey Tang is at the heart of it. She grew up in online culture and was a successful tech founder before turning her attention to public life. Audrey and her peers are bringing the language, mindsets, tools and techniques of programming to politics: the foundations are radical transparency and meticulous record-keeping, cross-disciplinary collaboration, participant feedback loops, flat non-hierarchical systems and 'forking the government' – which isn't quite as combative as it sounds.

In programming, forking means creating alternative approaches to a subset of a program (that is, writing some new code) and testing those in parallel with the status quo. Once the alternative code is working well, it's merged into the system permanently. In spaces like the Social Innovation Lab (more on that soon), through process like vTaiwan and working with the g0v (Gov Zero) community, forking is now part of politics in Taiwan. Audrey explains:

> It used to be the case, when I first participated in the free software community, that forking was taken very seriously, because it's very difficult to merge things back. If you fork something, it's forked for good. But now with Git [a version-control system from

open-source culture] and all the different equivalents of Git – in, for example, co-creation of documents, co-creation of spreadsheets, all those collaborative editors and so on – suddenly it becomes very easy to fork anything, and still with the pretty good hope of merging it back. I think that is a really great metaphor of governance. This is what we intentionally incorporate, as I said, as the sandbox regulations.

That means suspending the usual rules for a short time (a concept called 'sandboxes' in the start-up world) to give start-ups, NGOs and other innovators room to experiment and develop alternatives to the status quo which can then be brought back into the mainstream if they work. It's one way public policy thinkers in Taiwan can test out new paths with less risk or without having to leap blindly into deregulation in the name of market innovation, and it's something we could borrow from them.

***

The appointment of Audrey Tang to Taiwan's Cabinet in August 2016 was always going to shake things up. Taiwan's youngest ever cabinet minister – then 35 – and first transgender minister was also a programming expert who'd been a tech entrepreneur in her teens. As you might expect after what you've read so far, she has an unconventional approach to running a portfolio.

'My office is literally horizontal, like one person poached from each [other] ministry, and so I don't give them orders, I don't take orders from them, I just ask people to work out loud. That's the only ask that I have. Because of that, any project that arose out of my office is by definition a reconstellation of many different values across ministries,' she explains. 'We don't have one dominant ministry and neither one dominant value. It is a cross-cutting, cross-silo organisation.'

By having representatives of each department in the room, the views from each arm of the state are represented, which results in short-cuts and knowledge-sharing.

It leads me to wonder how Audrey gets public sector buy-in to citizen participation in democratic affairs. How does she manage that? And how have frontline bureaucrats adapted to having walk-ins come by to have their say on government, for instance? The secret, she assures me, is respecting what bureaucrats value and valuing their contributions and expertise. This is great to hear because, in my experience, the public service is all too often unfairly criticised and accused of being the opposition to innovation.

Audrey talks me through the three main priorities of bureaucrats as she sees them: management and reduction of risk; efficiency (effective allocation of resources) and certainty of service; and due credit. 'If a public servant innovates, then they want to be recognised, not having the ministry taking all the credit and only absorbing the blame when things go wrong.'

***

A key tool opening up Taiwanese decision-making is vTaiwan, which combines digital democracy and real-world deliberation.

The four-stage vTaiwan process begins with proposals that come from the community or in weekly in-person hackathons hosted at the Social Innovation Lab, a space designed to facilitate and incubate collaboration. Government departments review the proposals. If they like a proposal enough to take responsibility for it, that proposal can move to the next stage. By putting in place accountability and a way forward for every project, ideas at stage two don't languish as post-it notes on workshop walls, the place where most brainstorm ideas go to die. Stakeholders and communities impacted by the proposal are invited to contribute and to bring more people into the conversation, which mostly takes place using online tools like Discourse and Pol.is. Core to Taiwan's open-government mindset is that they always use pre-existing open-source platforms rather than spending money on proprietary systems. There's a feedback loop and accountability at this stage too: if you make a comment or ask a question, the relevant government authorities have to reply to you within seven days.

The next stage is reflection, which brings representatives from the impacted community, academics, public sector workers, experts and industry together into a room. This all happens as a live stream, as a facilitator works through the contributions gathered over the first few months of the process, all while receiving questions over the stream from around the country. Conversation and contributions are documented in real time, and so more input is gathered.

The final stage, legislation, is about getting an outcome. This could be either a change to government policy or else the proposal is framed into a new bill to be presented in parliament for debate. At the time of writing, 26 national issues have been explored through this process, and more than 80 per cent of those have resulted in government action.

The best example of the effectiveness of this process is how Taiwan dealt with Uber and other ride-sharing services. As in countries the world over, these had swept in and disrupted the taxi industry. In the vTaiwan conversation, four broad opinion groups surfaced: taxi drivers, UberX drivers, UberX passengers and non-UberX passengers. You'd expect the trenches to be dug between the antis and the pros, but that isn't what happened. Within a short time, 95 per cent of participants were able to find one shared statement they could support: 'The government should leverage this opportunity to challenge the taxi industry to improve their management and quality control system, so that drivers and riders would enjoy the same quality service as UberX.'

This reframing of the issue was the breakthrough: by the fourth week of the process, there was a new agenda beyond banning or permitting, one which took the desires of customers and the needs of drivers on all sides into account, and which gave regulators a practical, middle way forward.

'vTaiwan is not just a consultation process. It's a meta-process that generates more consultative processes,'

Audrey says. From my perspective, when I sometimes see frictions arise in these kinds of industry or community negotiations, it sounds like a dream to have a process that actually unifies individuals and stakeholders from different communities or places, enabling them to find allies, organise around issues and work together on solutions.

While the ride-sharing case stands out because it's a relatable global issue, in Audrey's view the best use cases are those without established advocates, like unions or industry associations, but situations where there are no clear groups to stand for and against. Audrey gives me two examples. The first is remote working. 'There is no union of teleworkers because we're all in different industries,' she says. The second example is Taiwanese companies that register in the Cayman Islands ('It's just a tax device or a governance device'). In both cases, there aren't the usual peak bodies or representatives ready (or perhaps willing) to assemble and argue their cases.

'In cases in which there are no obvious top-down hierarchical organisations, that's where the vTaiwan approach shines. It enables people who don't have a voice because they don't have an organised presence that has a protocol dealing with the governance. It enables them to discover each other, form a kind of ad hoc stakeholder coalition, and even maintain that relationship afterwards.'

As a country, Taiwan is the epitome of the underdog. Their big, powerful neighbour wants to undermine their sovereignty, and as China's global influence grows, entities like the World Health Organization and trading partners, like Australia, bend over backwards to dodge officially recognising Taiwan. And yet, despite these challenges, Taiwan is emerging as a global leader in the new, people-powered democracy, expanding access to information through technology and lifting the bar when it comes to transparency and public participation. So, how have they done it? Why are they so far out in front?

'I think, first of all, Taiwan is really having a couple unfair advantages,' Audrey says. 'One is that we offer broadband as a human right because of our geography. Anywhere in Taiwan, even remote islands, if you don't have 10 megabits per second, it's personally my fault. You can talk to me. If anyone wants an unlimited 4G access plan to deliver such broadband, it is less than $20 US per month from all major telecom operators.'

Audrey beams at me: 'This is really unfair, right?' She laughs, then continues:

[In Taiwan] with more social media accounts than citizen population and free broadband – not really free, but almost free broadband access as a human right – I think that enables us to basically provide a full context of policymaking. So that anyone who wants to know any bit of the budget can just drill down to the budget item and have a real-time conversation with public service on that particular budget item for all of our national budgets, for example.

People usually are just curious: 'How is my neighbourhood doing?'

and things like that. It is just an informative piece, just like a Google map that people would like to explore. If something occurred to them at that time, then of course they just leave it on the platform or they start an e-petition or things like that. It's all part of the flow. They don't have to specifically go to a town hall on the specific Sunday to do something specific. It's all kind of an ongoing process.

There's also another kind of model that we're following: is that we bring the technology to the space of people rather than asking the people to come to the space of technology. Once there is an e-petition with 5000 signatures, for example, then we make sure that, if it's a local matter, all the relevant ministries are summoned into that locality and to have a real face-to-face conversation – that is still amplified through 360 live-streaming and so on.

Because of that, for everybody, all these decoders involved, they can minimise the personal cost to them to participate in this process. They're always met with at least an equal kind of contextualising benefit that makes sure that if they put in one hour of time, it can save at least one hour of reading, because people are contextualising for each other.

Access to these online tools is important, but Audrey is adamant that the other crucial element is a good kitchen, ideally one with a kick-arse chef. She believes people need a place to meet to shape the kind of society they want and food to fuel the conversations. This is why the Social Innovation Lab in Taipei is part of the open-government process, a drop-in space where people can meet, talk, work and eat, that operates from 7am to 11pm every day. 'I think with these three elements – that is to say, excellent food, a relaxed atmosphere with no deadlines and timing, and a recurrent record-keeping culture – anything can happen,' she says.

On Wednesdays, Audrey has open office hours at the Lab: anyone can book in to meet with her between 10am and 10pm. She also tours regional cities on a regular basis. She takes me through her schedule for the next day. She's meeting with the BLab on connecting benefit corporations with the Asia Pacific Social Innovation Partnership Award, Taiwan's action to promote the United Nations Sustainable Development Goals. Then she's meeting with a group called Crossroads, working on expanding international knowledge of the diversity of Taiwan's cultures (another of Taiwan's recent moves towards inclusion is translating all government information and correspondence into the 16 indigenous and regional languages, rather than solely using Mandarin, as in the past). After this, she'll be talking with a team using AI to analyse biometrics about how to shift regulation to make advances in telemedicine and telediagnosis law.

Can you imagine being able to schedule a meeting with a government minister, at a convenient time after work, to talk about your social project or business idea, to get connections and advice? What kinds of creative outcomes could we gain if our government processes were this open, accessible and inclusive? We might see government policies that keep pace with our changing world, more closely reflecting our values and priorities.

Engage beyond elections

If there's one thing that's becoming more common in this fractured political age, it's the decline of the major parties who have traditionally dominated parliaments. As the share of votes for team blue and team red (and it's always blue and red teams, for some reason) have declined, around the world we've seen the rise of minor parties and independents, and of disparate coalitions forming government. Where some might see fractures, I see cracks to let more light into the political process.

Belgium is a country divided along the lines of its three language groups: autonomous zones serve each of these communities in their own regions. But it gets even more complicated than that. In the German-speaking Eupen region, the governing coalition is currently made up of five different political parties, a compromise position that has become quite common around the world. Sometimes, diverse coalitions can be brilliant ways to interrogate policies and ensure different perspectives are considered; sometimes the coalition can lack direction, be consumed by internal tensions or have difficulty gaining consensus among its members.

To overcome that, in early 2019 Eupen began an experiment in a new kind of citizen-powered decision-making, creating a Citizens' Council to sit alongside their parliament. Australian deliberative democracy advocate Luca Belgiorno-Nettis was in the room as the Citizens' Council was shaped in 2018, and his newDemocracy Foundation are helping to deliver the outcome. 'Having this complementary parliament, a Citizens' Council which is randomly recruited, avoids having those tensions and at the same time, brings in this direct citizens' voice, if you like, and provides a legitimacy,' he explains.

Every year, after the parliament determines its legislative agenda, the Citizens' Council reviews that agenda and says, 'We think it's great' or 'We think there are some shortcomings here, and in those areas where it's got shortcomings there should be further analysis.' That analysis is done by a separate citizen jury, called the Citizens' Assembly, on the specific topic. Both the Citizens' Council and the Citizens' Assembly are made up of people drafted by the drawing of lots. The proposal is to have up to three citizen juries operating every year to address whatever might be the topics that the council has determined needs to be addressed.

The Citizens' Council and Assembly system is designed to bring ordinary citizens into the political decision-making process, to add a layer of scrutiny and to give people a platform to raise the priorities that are relevant to a more representative section of the community. Over the last ten years, Luca and the newDemocracy Foundation have been championing the role juries can play through deliberative democracy projects, in a range of global contexts, and covering a wide array of issues.

Luca continues:

I see these citizen juries – and I say this quite openly – these are Trojan horses for me. These are meant to demonstrate the capacity of everyday people to deliberate on public policy issues and to actually *be* the political representative class.

What as deliberative democrats we are trying to get away from is this reliance on the elected politicians.

I think the way we envisage political representation today has no other way of thinking about citizen engagement other than through an electioneering process. How do we create a much more collaborative political parliament? You've got to do it in a way which is not divisive from the outset and continues this process of elections and campaigning, which is divisive right through the process.

'Hang on a minute, Luca,' I say, only slightly miffed at his disdain for elected officials and definitely not taking this personally. 'By cutting elected representatives out of the picture, aren't you just handing more power to the unelected parts of government? The bureaucracy are the ones who would then frame the issues the juries would discuss, present the evidence they want the jury to see, and so direct the outcome.'

Luca sees things slightly differently:

These processes are not designed to hear just from bureaucrats. These processes are designed to hear from all the stakeholders: yes, the executives often provide the basic information to start with, but if the process is designed properly, they're not determining the information sources. On the contrary, the jury at the end of the day actually get to hear from whoever they want to hear from.

We had a jury here in the very early days. In 2011, the Public Accounts Committee of the New South Wales Government was looking at options in respect of the energy futures for the state. The jury wanted to hear from the actual contractors. So, they asked [publicly listed energy companies] AGL and Origin Energy to present – not just the state government energy operator at the time. In fact, we got responses from the AGLs and the Origins that questions they were getting from this process were more informed than the questions they got from the select committee from the parliament. This is why my colleagues and I encourage anyone who has not seen a jury to actually come in and see the jury. Because I think more often than not, people are swayed by that – by the capacity of that process, by the real ability of that forum and that process to really come to grips with complex matters and come to sensible decisions.

There's a lot to agree with in Luca's view. Elections and the party systems are divisive; the very nature of our Westminster system is adversarial, us versus them, and that can be extremely hard on the people involved and damaging to our discourse. But I don't go as far as Luca does in seeking to replace the elected officials entirely. I think we need both: I want to inject more opportunities for the kind of citizen-led oversight and direction that the newDemocracy Foundation generate through their citizens' juries but I also want to see governments elected that are more representative.

Meanwhile, I'm interested in the factors that are central to the newDemocracy Foundation model of deliberative democracy. The first is random selection. This is to avoid recruiting people with vested interests in the topic or an agenda to push. It also ensures that every decision reached might more closely represent the community's view. We've already discussed all the ways our elected parliaments look nothing like the broader population, but in deliberative democracy, the jury is a mini public.

'We do so-called "stratified demographic cross-check" and you can do it on three or four criteria,' Luca explains. 'Firstly, on gender: if a community has 50:50 male–female demographics, you represent that. Then the bell curve of age: we usually take people from the electoral rolls, so it's from 18 onwards. And then we do it in terms of income, using a proxy which is renting or ownership. So, if the renting or ownership is 50:50 in the community, we want to make sure that there is 50:50 representation there as well.'

The second major factor is time: jurors have to have an extended period to read, reflect, stew over issues and for the full range of witnesses to be called to provide the evidence needed to reach a decision. One or two days won't do it. In the newDemocracy model, each jury requires a minimum of 50 hours, and they do this by locking themselves away on alternate Saturdays over 12 weeks. Importantly, they are paid for their time, allowing more people to be able to afford to dedicate time to this form of community service.

But what on earth would compel ordinary people to spend such an extended period of their leisure time to throw themselves into processing complex information, debating and deliberating with strangers? I ask Luca what motivates people to participate, and what incentives if any the newDemocracy Foundation have to offer.

'The only thing that really is attractive to them is: will they have authority? Will their voices be heard? So, that's why the commissioning authority needs to be government. It can't be a quango [a semi-public administrative authority], because people think, "Well, do I really want to invest my effort into this and then *Where does it go?*" Whereas, if they know that it's going to be at least heard by government, not necessarily taken up holus bolus but at least heard by government, then people are more prepared to invest their time,' he says.

The third important factor is the ability of the jury to call their own witnesses, manage their own deliberations and write their own final report. Good facilitation is important to the process, but the most crucial element is letting the jury (usually a group of 50, who then break into groups of five or six for discussions) find their way through the issue.

'You get to hear, of course, from all the stakeholders, the pros and the cons

– [from] the zealots and the academics and professional sector experts. And just as in a jury, they weigh up the evidence themselves; and they don't necessarily need to have advocates assisting them on one side or the other. They're perfectly capable of deliberating amongst themselves and finding the capacity within themselves to actually write the report themselves at the end of that day.'

In late 2019, I got to see one of the newDemocracy juries in action at the City of Sydney, providing us with direction and feedback on our guiding plan for the next decade: Sustainable Sydney 2050. As part of an extensive, 18-month long community consultation process, we'd gathered more than 2500 ideas from the people of Sydney, and 50 randomly selected Sydneysiders generously gave up six Saturdays over 12 weeks to go through these suggestions and develop their synthesis of these ideas, with their own thrown in. Watching spokespeople from the group present their final report gave me goosebumps on my goosebumps: they went so far beyond the day-to-day issues that we usually see raised in community consultation, and they genuinely engaged with the idea of what our city could be in 2050 in a visionary way.

They asked us to create a city that isn't just sustainable but that is regenerative: one that cleans the air and the water, that gives back more than it takes. They put culture, creativity and nightlife at the heart of their vision, knowing that you have to feed the soul of a city, not just its belly or its wallet. We already pride ourselves on being courageous and pushing well beyond the usual domains of local government, and we're already well ahead of our state and federal governments when it comes to renewables (we're powered by 100 per cent renewable energy, with our energy buy coming in part from community solar and wind farms in regional New South Wales to help bring in a just transition), water, and much else besides, but this citizens' jury process showed us we could be even more ambitious.

They set us goals to aspire to which were even further beyond anything we could have imagined or, more accurately, what we could have imagined that the public appetite was ready for. I sat next to Luca as each speaker presented and I could feel his pride at seeing the model in action. The way we do politics today underestimates the altruism and big-picture thinking of the average citizen. A process like the citizens' jury reminds us that we need to trust that people are willing to be brave, to make sacrifices and to embrace change. But they have to be part of the process of setting that vision and they need to take part in telling the story of what we all get from being part of that change.

Another successful example of deliberative democracy in action took place in South Australia over a public policy issue that was so contentious it was – literally – radioactive. The question posed was this: 'Under what circumstances, if any, could South Australia pursue the opportunity to store and dispose of nuclear waste from other countries?'

The South Australian state government seemed to be in favour of the idea and had already launched a Royal Commission into it. Understanding that there would be community concerns, they called on Luca and the newDemocracy Foundation to run one of the biggest juries ever convened. In the event, 350 jurors representative of the state deliberated over a compressed period of six days to determine if there was social licence for it to go ahead. Although Luca considered the process suboptimal because of the political conditions and urgency, the final report, penned by the jury members themselves, gives a heartening picture. The big ideas were explored very thoughtfully in that short time; there were many witnesses called in concurrent sessions; and the jury arrived at a consensus not often present in political debates. The result? 'Two thirds of the jury do not wish to pursue the opportunity under any circumstances and one third support a commitment to pursue under the circumstances outlined in this report.[6]

As for the newDemocracy Foundation, it's gone from facilitating citizens' juries on nuclear waste to redesigning democracy in the developing world: they're now working with the United Nations Democracy Fund. They've produced a handbook, *Enabling National Initiatives to Take Democracy Beyond Elections,*[7] to help more cities and states adopt the jury model. They're also running three demonstration jury projects – in Papua New Guinea, Peru and Rwanda – and producing a documentary to capture the process.

Those are highly challenging contexts and they couldn't be further away from the beautiful newDemocracy Foundation office we're meeting in, at a wharf on Sydney Harbour. Luca's family is one of Australia's wealthiest, his late father having co-established one of the biggest engineering and construction firms around. Given that Luca could really do anything he pleased with his time, I ask what compels him to take on this fight. His explanation is frank:

> I had the good fortune to be involved in a big infrastructure family company, Transfield. I got

to see government in action, I got to see how big infrastructure projects come together. I suppose I got to also be lobbied by political parties for campaign funding and so was kind of pretty close to the political action, if you like. And I was not very impressed.

I didn't think that one party was necessarily more deserving of campaign funding than the other. I thought that a number of infrastructure projects were being compromised by political expediency – where people were basically wanting to have a project done in that electorate because it helped their particular electoral outcomes.

We're sitting in one of the most privileged places in the world, and it's still somewhere that could benefit from more direct participation from more of the people, and a more representative group of decision-makers, something that deliberative democracy can offer. I'd love to see this model spread everywhere there are disconnects between the governed and governments.

Raise different voices

These tools and participatory pathways are all part of the solutions required to refocus our politics: we have to try it all to fast-track the future we need. One of the fastest ways to get results has got to be expanding the pool of people elected to represent us and claiming the power to get the change our future needs.

If you think about 'Andrew', the typical parliamentarian described earlier, you get a sense of the gulf between communities and representatives. I roll my eyes when people talk about 'diversity', when what they really mean is reality. When we see leaders from different backgrounds we see a wider field of people stepping up to lead in their wake, and we start to see approaches being tried and issues being aired that are usually left on the margins.

The political leaders who are inspiring optimism and admiration right now don't act like the usual suspects, in large part because they aren't the usual suspects. They're often closer in age and life experience to the people they represent, and it's not just a breath of fresh air, it's a competitive advantage when you're dealing with rapidly and radically changing times.

Over the last couple of years, the generally peaceful country of New Zealand has been rocked by a string of unimaginable tragedies: from a racist massacre to a volcanic eruption, followed by the COVID-19 pandemic. Through it all, Prime Minister Jacinda Ardern inspired the world with her compassionate and forthright leadership. She's a warm and genuine communicator who has taken to social media with an ease and skill few other leaders can muster (maybe because she's under 40, and it's second nature) to share the achievements of her government as well as to provide comfort during extraordinary times. Her decisiveness and resolve are also striking. After the Christchurch massacre, she refused to say the name of the perpetrator, denying him notoriety or a platform for hate. Instead, she elevated the names and stories of the victims.

Prime Minister Ardern acted swiftly to move New Zealand to the highest level of containment possible as the pandemic spread, implementing the world's strongest lockdown, with an ambitious goal of elimination of the virus. She provided the kind of clear, direct explanation to the community that those of us over 'the ditch' watched with envy. She hosted regular online Q&A sessions with the nation – including special ones for children – to dispel misinformation, and inspired New Zealanders to make sacrifices in the spirit of kindness. And then her government did the same, announcing they'd be taking a 20 per cent pay-cut in solidarity with everyone doing it tough. Jacinda appealed to the best in people, trusting her community rather than using threats of force or fear. This is leadership using empathy, not enforcement, as the guiding principle.

Now, I'm not saying Jacinda is doing a better job than most purely because she's a woman and mother to a young child, but simply highlighting the gulf between her style of leadership and the types of response we've seen from leaders in the usual mould – in countries like Australia, the UK or the USA. She's showing that there's another way to lead, and she's showing women across the globe that the world needs our voices and skills. In September 2018 Jacinda made history as the first world leader in history to take their child to a meeting of the United Nations General Assembly: I still cry when I see that picture of Jacinda and her baby, Neve, in that hallowed chamber. She has thrown open the door of what is possible for all of us who might walk in her footsteps. With her response to the pandemic and the transformative mindset of the Wellbeing Budget we discussed in the last chapter, Jacinda has shown that when you change the leader, you can change the politics.

Sanna Marin was 34 when she became Prime Minister of Finland, one of the youngest world leaders in history, and she leads a governing coalition of five political parties, all of which are led by women, most of them under 40. When she rose to power in December 2019, critics mocked a cabinet made up mostly of young women, calling them the Spice Girls or the Lipstick Cabinet, but they proved themselves more than capable when the crisis hit. When the COVID-19 pandemic hit Finland, the Marin government took a decidedly Millennial approach to communicating the need for physical distancing measures: they enlisted 1500 social media influencers to help get the word out, providing them with the facts on the health crisis, but leaving them to tell the story in their own ways.[8] It meant that a generation of people who might not be reading newspapers or watching the nightly news got the right information, from sources they already listen to and trust. While not everything in their COVID-19 containment approach was as successful as their take on communications, Sanna's government secured an 84 per cent approval rating from Finns for their handling of the shutdown.[9]

These leaders inspire me to believe that another kind of political leadership is possible, and that a shift in who leads will help bring change. I'm not that young – I'm 39 as I write this – but that puts me closer to Australia's median age of 38 than most political representatives. As a first-generation Australian from a non-English-speaking, less privileged background, I'm also highly representative of Sydney, a city where over 49 per cent of us come from families in which both parents were born overseas. While I did study law (classic pollie move), the fact that most of my career has focused on the creative world makes me an atypical elected leader. I'm uniquely fortunate to have joined the team of a progressive, independent Lord Mayor in Clover Moore, who in her 16 years in the role has been a powerful force for change in the areas of climate action, social justice, and investment in culture and a creative city. As well as supporting the important work that has come before, I've been able to champion a generation of new causes, such as local procurement policy, a citizens' jury process and the introduction of participatory budgeting, and for Sydney to become a signatory to the Declaration of Cities Coalition for Digital Rights,[10] which enshrines our right to sovereignty over our data in our digital public realm. I've focused on nightlife and creativity, and trying to help my city recover from damaging venue-lockout laws and this more recent crisis that has disproportionately impacted the creative and entertainment ecology of our city. I've worked towards new approaches to affordable space and housing through innovative mechanisms like co-ops and community land trusts (more on that later in our story) inspired by the ideas and talented people I've discovered in researching this book. I've been so proud to contribute to a team that fights for the most marginalised, defends the vulnerable and redirects local government to be an enabler, to help more people access opportunities to contribute and feel valued.

In my experience all the ways I am not an 'Andrew' has had immediate, positive and tangible impacts for the people I serve as well as for those I work with. Different priorities and concerns get raised when you raise different voices. The prospect of more politicians who resemble the people they represent is something that energises me. We're about to meet some exciting change agents who have claimed political power and built channels to change the faces and focus of politics.

Model the future

The revolution will run on caramel and be staged in a nightclub? Now that sounds like my kind of party. That's what they've found in Rosario, Argentina's third largest city.

It's late and here I am stumbling over my Spanish with Rosario city councillor Caren Tepp via video link. We've been talking over each other in excitement for an hour and a half and have decided I need to go visit her. The party she's a member of, Ciudad Futura (Future City), is the embodiment of so many of the solutions I've encountered that give me hope that a new path for politics is possible.

The Ciudad Futura mission is evident in their name: they want to create a tangible experience of the future we need through projects, and then use political power to scale them up and embed them beyond the energy of the moment.

'We say that we dedicate ourselves to the future *before* it happens,' Caren says, 'We can imagine that we have a clear and present criticism of now, the moment in which we live; that we can offer and build a desirable and realistic vision of a different future, in which people can feel part of the society we want. At the same time, the most important thing is to be able to plan a strategy, an organisational approach that helps us answer: how do we make these future images to be able to live them today?'

Ciudad Futura arose from a social movement that used worker-owned enterprises and direct action to address inequalities in Rosario. Now that the party has begun to claim political power, they have no intention of changing their bottom-up approach. They're taking action in the *barrios* – the low-socioeconomic settlements where most of Rosario's inhabitants live – on the streets and through new ways of doing business, not just the corridors of power.

First, about that revolutionary caramel. In 2010, the progenitor of Ciudad Futura, Movimento Giros, was fighting against gated estate developments because they were pricing poor people out of the fringes of the city. Organising and amplifying the protests of the most marginalised communities in the city against powerful property developers, the movement had an incredible win: they managed to have new gated communities banned in Rosario.

'At that moment, we generated an unprecedented political event in the city, which was that a social movement gets institutional forces to approve a project that has practical effects and touches specific interests,' Caren recounts. 'What you have to do now, once you have killed one of the most iconic symbols of neoliberalism in cities [gated communities], what we have to do in those lands that we are defending, is show and start projects that can give an account of what we want in those areas. We do not want private neighbourhoods; we do not want 50 houses in 500 hectares with golf and tennis courts because it seems obscene, with the levels of inequality that the city is experiencing. What [other] things can we imagine in those places?'

The answer was unexpected: a dairy co-op.

In Argentina, inflation had been driving up the cost of living, resulting in a lack of employment opportunities for the urban poor, so people were suffering. By setting up *El tambo La Resistencia* (The Resistance Dairy), at a stroke the movement created jobs, access to affordable nutritious food and a productive alternative use for hotly contested land.

'There arose the project of the defence of the *tambo* and the possibility of demonstrating to the city as a whole that it's a lie that the peripheries of the big cities can only be private or informal housing,' Caren says. 'Instead, in these margins, sustainable life projects can be integrated, integrating decent housing with production in the peripheries and the margins of cities. Food can be produced, which generates work that generates value, which allows then to bring these products in a much more economical and healthy way to the whole city.'

Thanks to the dairy, 900 litres of milk a day are produced on land that had been slated to become swimming pools, tennis courts and golf courses for the wealthy few. Each month, some of that milk is also processed into hundreds of kilos of cheese and dulce de leche (the caramel that we Latinos consider as much a basic necessity as bread and water). These products are sold below market price through the Anti-Inflationary Mission, a food co-op that serves six hundred Rosarino households.

The movement didn't stop there. Realising there were 1500 families in the area without access to any educational institutions, the movement also set up a school and a kindergarten.

Where jobs, food and education had been needed on the city edge, it was creative production and performance space in the contested city centre. Next, Ciudad Futura used the tools of the co-op to build social infrastructure in this context too. Run as a co-operative, Distrito Sie7e (District Seven) is a social club, performance venue and multi-purpose space for social activism: nightclub by weekend, workshops and community gathering space during the week.

'It was Rosario's first cinema, and we were also defending it because, with the urban growth in that place, they wanted to demolish it and build garages. Until Distrito Sie7e appeared, singers and local artists had to rent spaces in bars, theatres and elsewhere to be able to present cultural production. What we have done is to start making more associative links with these producers, so they do not have to pay to give their cultural presentation there, but instead they can take part of the proceeds of the profits of a cultural show for their own group,' Caren explains.

'There are 28 workers, from security to cleaning staff, who are part of the co-operative. The space works from 7am to 1am every day, and also on weekends has shows until later – live shows – and other workshops: hip hop, salsa.'

Rosario might be a very different context to Sydney, but this rings true here too: there's a need for creative practitioners to find fresh ways to work together to collectively manage cultural space, setting up bulwarks against the gentrification and rising costs that push them out of the inner city. Caren says the Distrito Sie7e model has also become a reference in Rosario for forms of co-operative management of cultural spaces, replicated by others at different scales.

Argentina is a global leader when it comes to worker co-ops. Their most dramatic economic crisis pre-COVID-19 was in 2001, and when foreign investors and the wealthy withdrew from the country, suddenly unemployed workers decided to take control of their workplaces and start worker-owned cooperatives. These are an important part of the solutions I've encountered in different parts of the world: there's more on worker-owned enterprises, co-ops and Argentina's history later in our story.

The big evolution from the original Argentinian worker co-op movement, and what's happening in Rosario today, is that Ciudad Futura are now translating this social mission into a political platform. In 2015, they stood for the municipal elections and won three seats. A couple of weeks before Caren and I spoke, in April 2019, they stood again, received over 11 per cent of the vote, and increased their representation to four seats. This is how we make politics vital, tangible and connected to daily life for more people: working within the political system while also building a community-driven, social movement with real-world projects providing proof that another way is possible.

'We say we're operating with a logic of social movements, a form of construction of social movements: much more democratic, horizontal, participatory, feminist,' Caren says. 'In addition to this practice and in this logic, we are turning it into a political instrument that fights for institutional places – the party is for us today the instrument that allows us to present ourselves to elections – but the dynamics and the form of political construction that we preserve is the one of the social movements.'

They're a young political party that has quickly ascended to be the fourth force in politics in their region, but gaining elected office is not an end in itself. A word Caren uses over and over in our conversation is *herramienta,* meaning tool. Ciudad Futura are using elected office as a tool for social change, yes, but also with the goal of re-tooling what politics concerns itself with, who makes decisions and how. Ciudad Futura are part of a global radical municipalist movement, a term that loosely describes how grassroots organisations are rising up to claim City Halls and local governments as tools for social change, environmental action and fighting inequality in cities. It's sometimes called the Municipal Spring, borrowing from the Arab Spring of 2011, and you can see the vanguard in cities from Spain to the UK, the USA to Latin America.

Now, I'm pretty biased, as a massive cheerleader for the role of local government, but hear me out. We usually have major constraints on our powers, having limits set by state or national governments, and we're not able to make structural economic changes. But we have advantages the big guys lack. We're closer to the people we represent and more able to counter apathy with direct, inclusive and participatory action. Importantly, radical municipalists are using the tool of urban planning to construct fairer cities, something we'll explore in our story too. At a local level of politics, we have some control over how we plan and build our cities and whose voices are heard in that process, and in my opinion city-making can be one of the most powerful tools we have to build in equity and pathways to sustainability for everyone.

Caren says:

We say we do not handle the price of the dollar or certain economic variables that are established at the national level, but we do have the possibility of having this tool in our hands, which is that of urban planning. Land-use planning can allow us to generate a distribution policy, a policy that goes towards a much more equitable and integrated and less fragmented city.

The wishes and economic interests of corporations make our cities: they understand it, and that is generating wealth, without doubt. If we can recover that, it is what allows us to give back to public life and put on the agenda the issues that have to do much more with the needs and desires of the citizens. We can then put in the centre in the agenda taking care of the things that a person or a family needs to live and to develop fully in a city. It has to do with changing the perspective in which government agendas are constructed.

If we want to bring politics much closer to the citizens, [there's] nothing better than the local governments to be in that contact. The problem we have is that, historically, what we feel is that the problems of the 21st century are being resolved with 20th-century institutions: the market clearly already has moved forward, but the state and the public have been left with tools of the 20th century, with which it can never solve those problems.

This is a profound insight. It's late, and my Spanish is less than stellar, but even at this moment I sense that Caren and her movement have hit on something major here. This could be one of our most effective shortcuts in accelerating positive change: ensure the forces of equality have access to tools that are at least as good as those of the market. There's an echo of the work Audrey is doing in Taiwan, and Robert and the Citizens' Foundation in Iceland. Until now, civil society have been left using an old operating system while business has raced ahead. It's time for an upgrade.

***

I started setting down my ideas for this chapter what seems a lifetime ago, while Australia heaved through the 2019 federal election campaign; COVID-19 was nowhere in sight. From inside my bubble it seemed like we were being presented with an easy choice: on the left, Labor offered a climate policy that, while not perfect, positioned action as a priority. They offered a narrative about fairness between the generations, cutting some of the generous provisions to wealthy retirees and landlords in exchange for a better deal on child care and affordable housing. While not executed in a perfect way, it was a story about needing to rebalance the scales. On the right, the Liberal–National Coalition offered tax cuts for corporations and the biggest earners, and demolished the narrative of the left by appealing to people's fear of change and suggesting that tax money was 'better off in your pocket' than applied to the works of government. It was big government versus small; older generations versus younger; business as usual versus change.

It was meant to be the election Labor couldn't lose, and they lost it. Stunned, they immediately went to water, back-tracking on their moves towards fairness, deciding that policy ambition had been their downfall and that they had to slide to the right to match the self-interested mindset that had won the day. Big-picture thinking was off the table again.

The day after the election, the internet burned with the disbelief of progressives, raging at those parts of the country who'd seemingly let down the rest of us. Images abounded of Australia with pro-mining Queensland sawn off; more rips in the fabric of our society, more fracturing into us and them. Conservatives clapped back, saying effectively, 'If you don't like it, leave.' It was hard to resist falling into a camp. I cried more than once.

When I revisited the story I've told you so far it felt inadequate, insubstantial. Participatory, deliberative democracy is great, but how can it stand up against a tidal wave of disillusionment with democracy in general? How do you appeal to generosity and solidarity, when many are falling into debt and precarity and want to put up walls to protect what they've got? How do you tell a story that includes everyone, that transcends the fearfulness and gives people hope that they have a role to play in a sustainable future?

I needed to see how transformative political ideas could be made real and relevant in people's lives: made only more urgent now by the way the pandemic and the rush to contain it had destabilised the employment and security of millions of people, and made their future more uncertain.

The next set of leaders I set out to learn from offer visions that prove that politics can improve everyday life: and that you get the biggest impact precisely when you dare to be more inclusive and radical. They're mobilising young people and excluded communities to be agents of change; they're implementing holistic alternative systems; while some are scaling up to shape a different kind of politics.

Elevate the local

Often, when people talk to local government, they're telling us to stay in our place. As a progressive, active (some would say activist) council, at the City of Sydney we're often advised to 'stick to our knitting' and to concentrate on the three Rs: rates, roads and rubbish. That's certainly what I hear from a handful of people who aren't afraid to demand that we take a smaller world view and have less ambition. While they are few, they're angry, vocal and aggressive, and they're always online. These people think we should keep out of environmental policy, affordable housing, addressing inequality and the impacts of bad state and commonwealth policies.

I think that's a load of rubbish.

We might not have legislative power or budgets in the billions but in local government we're closest to our communities, have the most immediate knowledge of the issues they face, and – when not hamstrung by higher levels of government – we can have direct impact on people's lives. Cities, in particular, are becoming more and more important socially, environmentally and economically – and so many city governments are breaking out of the old managerial mindset and instead choosing to be transformative in transitioning their cities towards sustainable, locally focused economic models.

Preston, a city of about 400,000 people in the north-west of England, is one place showing the world what genuinely transformative leadership can achieve.

Like Liverpool and Manchester, Preston boomed as a textile town in the Industrial Revolution, but over the 20th century, Preston found itself bearing the brunt of each wave of globalisation, financialisation and wealth extraction. During the GFC the City of London, one of the world's most bullish financial capitals, partied too hard, and cities like Preston copped the hangover. The town had been counting on a big shopping-centre redevelopment to revitalise their town centre and provide construction and retail jobs, but as capital coursed away from the real economy, it was scrapped. Then, austerity hit: after bailing out the banks, the UK central government slashed spending on social infrastructure and local government. From 2011, Preston's grants from the UK government were almost halved. How could local government continue to deliver basic services, let alone help their community to regenerate and build new opportunities, when they had to do more with less?

The situation called for a radical rethink.

Councillor Matthew Brown is one of my local government heroes – someone who has led the way in combining and implementing many of the big ideas we're exploring in this story. Matthew has been a Labour councillor on Preston City Council since 2002, and when his party won a majority in 2011, he decided to try something different. It was time for this city to save itself.

The first order of business was to make sure the people who were in work were being paid a living wage, going beyond a minimum wage to what's required to live a dignified life in this part of the UK. Aside from making the commitment within the city council, this became a reason to negotiate with major 'anchor institutions' in the city, like colleges, universities and the Lancashire County Council, as well as some big private employers.

'We're quite small in the council. We couldn't really have the effect we wanted just by ourselves, so we were really inclined to go to the head of the anchor institutions and say: "Well, we're doing this. We're going through our books increasing our local spend and paying the living wage. Do you fancy doing it with us?",' Matthew tells me.

'They pretty much said yes. I was quite surprised by how easy it was, with organisations that are much bigger than what we are, to be honest. I mean, well, we've got legitimacy in that we're elected city government, in that sense, but it's amazing how supportive they were.'

Matthew and his team built on these newly strengthened relationships with anchor institutions to have even greater impact, by encouraging the council, university and hospital to preference local suppliers when they buy products or services. That doesn't sound like a big move, but more often than not, big organisations have procurement policies that equate the 'best value' with the lowest price for a product or service. This means multinationals and major corporations often undercut on price to win contracts, rather than local suppliers. But what if you redefined 'best value' to prioritise the value of that money staying in the local community rather than flowing out and away? We'll explore the flow-on effects of keeping money local later in our story, with a success story from the island of Sardinia, but in Preston's case that benefit added up to tens of millions of pounds being retained in businesses and for workers close to home: not bad for a little local government.

'We started going through the books, doing spend analysis; the Centre for Local Economic Strategy, CLES, did that for us. It's fascinating how much wealth there is within these institutions, within our communities, and that we obviously managed to, over a period of years, repatriate it. It's about £75 million we brought back in 2017, which is a lot of money, isn't it?' There's a bit of wonder in Matthew's voice.

A lot of this went into SMEs [small-and-medium enterprises] that have grown in the community, in construction especially. That's gone to so many locally based businesses. It's not gone to the big corporations, like Carillion and Balfour Beatty and Robert McAlpine; it's gone mainly to locally based companies, family businesses. Now, some of them might only have a couple of hundred employees, but it really does ripple through the supply chain. So, they subcontract between three, four, five small companies – often family businesses – and these individuals contract to supply the larger companies, and they're getting lots of opportunities. So, it's been fantastic.

By interrogating their buying practices and introducing a local-preference policy across local government and major players, Preston was able to more than double the proportion of its local procurement spend, from 14 per cent to 30 per cent, with local businesses, social enterprises and co-operatives benefiting.

Even though it's become famous among advocates of new approaches to politics and the economy as 'the Preston model', Matthew, ever humble, is surprised by all the attention, and points out that Manchester City Council have subsequently applied the same approach and had an even bigger impact, increasing their local spend from about 51 per cent to about 73 per cent. 'But we were the first [to do this in the UK], which is why we're getting all the fame, I think,' he says.

The lesson to learn here is to start with life, not politics. People need to feel and see the benefits that locally focused, practical and people-centred politics can provide in their everyday lives before they're likely to get engaged in a political system that has failed them for decades. When you're broke it's hard to care about teams blue or red. When leaders focus on improving people's day-to-day lives by influencing wages and conditions, improving access to credit and generating local economic activity, citizens can begin to see the benefit of political engagement or the difference between the ideologies on offer.

Still on the money, it was evident to the Preston community that the mainstream banks were failing them: branches were closing, and loans to the real economy were contracting. How do you rebuild trust in democracy when governments seem to be working exclusively on behalf of the big end of town, like the banks, and yet they're the first to flee town when times get tough? When I put this to Matthew, he makes some pointed observations:

It's dreadful, because we bailed out the banks [after the GFC] with 1.2 trillion of our money: I think it was about £20,000 per family in the UK. And now, even though all that money was released to bail out banking systems, small businesses find it difficult because there's evidence now that the large banks would prefer to lend 20 million quid to another large bank or to another financial institution rather than investing in what could be described as the real economy.

So, from their perspective it becomes the standard. It's much easier to lend 20 million quid to another bank than it is to, say, lend 10,000 lots of £10,000 to small businesses. So, there's a real gap in the market.

Sure, redesigning banking is outside the remit of local government, but that didn't stop them trying to fix things in Preston. You can't rebuild the local economy if no one can get a loan to run their business, so Matthew and the council stepped in. They invested in supporting a neighbouring credit union to expand their operations to include Preston: as credit unions are co-operatives, or mutuals, they have a community-benefit purpose, not a pure profit motive, unlike high-street banks. That initiative got money flowing to local businesses again. It's not obvious, and it can be complicated to explain the benefits of local ownership, co-ops and the like, but the Preston model is starting to bear fruit in the form of visible signs of a healthy, locally centred economy.

'The eternal problem we have is that people are beaten up by neoliberal economics. If you try to inspire people from working-class communities, they just don't believe you as politicians. And rightly so, in many ways. They have their doubts. It's going to take time,' Matthew says.

'You're beginning to see people get this. We've refurbished our city markets, they're really good, and we've got lots of independent local businesses in there. I think people really like it. You know, they love the idea of, you know, buying local – supporting local businesses that employ local people.'

Supporting the co-operative economy, which is all about direct benefits to members, workers and the community, was another key move for Preston. Here's how it works: a coop cafe sources their produce from local farmers, uses their kitchens to train staff who might not otherwise find training, and are now gearing up to apply for the government catering contracts that would otherwise go to big firms from the south of England or beyond, but now, thanks to local procurement policies, retain that spend at home. Preston is considering how they might support community renewable-energy projects, and how they can support new co-ops in building businesses that give back and keep money local.

I was inspired by the Preston model to introduce a local procurement policy for the City of Sydney in 2019. Even though we have limitations – thanks to national competition laws and the state Local Government Act, which has been interpreted to have a very narrow reading of 'best value' – we're working on putting social and community value into the frame as a factor when we're buying services, materials, catering – you name it.

Throughout our conversation, Matthew expresses a lot of pride about what has been achieved in his city. Still, there's also frustration in his voice, and he explains that there's still far too much to get done to be able to indulge in back-patting. Turning local politics into an engine of radical change isn't easy, and the job is never done, so I can understand when he has more to say about the things that they've been held back from achieving than the big wins he can claim. But this is the relentless energy and ambition needed if we are to rehabilitate politics and re-engage people with democracy. People who make change refuse to 'stick to their knitting' and let economic forces and the policies of other levels of government disadvantage their communities. If we want people to have faith in politics, we have to show them what government can do for them when it puts them first.

Set more seats at the table

When I was ten, my family went on a holiday to my mum's homeland of Chile, and we ended up staying for two years. Pinochet, the dictator who'd ruled for 17 years after leading a military coup in 1973, had finally left office, and it was safe for my mum and many others to return.

Like Australia, Chile was founded as a colonial outpost (of Spain, in this case) and started off by displacing Indigenous peoples and importing a rigid class hierarchy from Europe. Inequality was built in from day one, which may explain why Salvador Allende's socialist government was elected in 1970. In the midst of the Cold War, there was no way the USA was ever going to let a socialist government flourish so close to home: they backed a bloody military coup in 1973 that killed thousands and sent tens of thousands more into exile.

Under Pinochet, Chile became a laboratory for the experiments of American economists, particularly a group called the Chicago School, who put all their most extreme neoliberal theories into practice. They cut public spending, went wild with privatisation (including privatising the pension system, education, healthcare, water, you name it) and state services, and removed tariffs and protections for local producers. On paper, Chile got richer and richer, becoming the economic success story of Latin America. But we know measures like GDP reveal little about the experiences of most people living in a country. Inequality skyrocketed while a privileged few got richer and richer. There's a standard measure of inequality, the Gini co-efficient, which measures relative wealth: it tells us Chile is the 26th most unequal country in the world, the widest inequality gap of any country in the OECD.

Even at the age of ten, I could feel it. My mum's cousin lived with her parents in the house where she'd been born in Santiago, and they walked several blocks to access a telephone: not a pay phone, but a phone you paid to use through a window in the front room of someone's house. Mum's uncle worked as an ambulance driver at the local public hospital, and visiting him at work was an eye-opening experience: people had to bring their own injections and supplies to get treated by medical staff. It was the '90s, but not the way it looked at home.

We ended up living in a coastal resort city, Viña del Mar, where my sister and I went to a private school and hung out with kids whose houses definitely had phones: they looked like the kinds of places we'd seen when we toured Beverly Hills in California. Meanwhile, across the valley from our house was the twin town of Valparaíso, a much more working-class port city. Our house faced onto a hillside of shanties, and to deter any unwelcome guests crossing the gully and clearing out our place, my grandma carried a small pearl-handled revolver in the pocket of her apron, which she fired into the air every couple of weeks. If ever tradies arrived to work on our house, they came without cars or tools; most labourers lacked the capital to be able to purchase the tools of their own trades and had to wait for the *jefe* to unlock the toolboxes and materials for the day. This seemed odd, coming from Australia, a place where tradies were small business owners in their own right. In the space of one day, sometimes I'd go with my *tia* to the *matadero* and the *feria,* the fresh food markets where poorer people did their shopping, and then visit the glamorous malls of Parque Arauco or Alto Las Condes. Even to a child, the gulf between the two Chiles seemed impossibly vast. When I returned as an adult, and by chance found myself swept into the world of Chile's more privileged artists and actors, I could see the division had only gotten more extreme. Arch neoliberal economist Milton Friedman had crowed about the 'miracle of Chile' but this success story of a nation was still ringed with the blue tarps and corrugated iron of shanty towns, a staggering level of personal debt in the population, and heavily privatised basic services.

By late 2019, the gulf had continued to grow and people had finally had enough: a 30-peso increase in the price of subway fares was 'the drop that spilled the glass', and the resentment of years of neoliberal extraction exploded into massive protests. Protesters chanted as much, saying, 'It's not for 30 pesos, it's for 30 years.'[11]

My friends and relatives posted daily videos of protests. Then, after a state of emergency was declared with curfews locking them indoors, they shared videos of people leaning out their apartment windows, banging pots and pans like in Iceland – a *cacerolazo* – a peaceful, persistent, loud way of saying, 'We're here, we're angry, we're not going away.'

The message sprayed on walls and protest signs was *Chile desperto* – Chile awakened. People began to come together to voice their dissatisfaction with the way the system is designed for only a handful to profit, while the cost of living skyrockets for everyone else.[12]

Protesters had a range of demands, from raising the pension to investment in healthcare, but for their biggest ask they didn't fuss around the edges: they demanded constitutional change. During the protests, the Chilean constitution soared to second place on the non-fiction bestseller list as people coalesced around the fact that their constitution was imposed in 1980 by the dictator and it fails to include many basic rights that Chileans deserve to expect from their country. The 1980 constitution was deliberately set up that way by its architect, arch-conservative Jaime Guzmán. Prior to his 1991 assassination, he went on the record saying it was designed such that should 'our adversaries govern, they would be constrained to follow an action not so different from what one would yearn for.'[13]

By November 2019, billionaire President Sebastián Piñera's position was shaky. His government agreed to a referendum in October 2020 on constitutional change, asking if Chilenos want a new constitution (according to polls, 78 per cent have said they do) and how they'd like it to be drafted.

One of the reasons Chile's protests were more effective than most was that this leaderless uprising included a broad coalition of social forces who gathered together under one banner as *La Mesa de Unidad Social,* the table of social unity. The groups included about two hundred organisations: student federations and teachers unions; organisations representing the people who live in informal settlements and First Nations; workers in the mines, ports and financial sector; transport and health workers; representatives of former political prisoners and those who 'disappeared' during the Pinochet years; and feminists, LGBTQI+ and climate activists such as the young local Fridays for the Future climate strikers.

One legacy of a repressive dictatorship and a neoliberal era in a country is the erosion of civil society institutions – organisations outside of government representing a diversity of experiences and making calls on behalf of their communities. This means that

Unidad Social is a powerful step forward in offering a bottom-up counterpoint to the government for the wealthy, by the wealthy that dominates Chile. Unidad Social have organised *cabildos* (community discussions) in cities and towns the length of the country to bring citizens together to ask big-picture questions and have the conversations that will shape the demands of Unidad Social on their behalf. But really, everyone is encouraged to run their own sessions, using a suggested format and questions on their website:

- What is the origin of the current conflict? What has generated the citizen malaise? What opportunities does this national mobilisation offer?
- How is it possible to advance in greater social justice from this juncture? Are there priority demands for citizenship? Is a Constituent Assembly needed to transform Chile?
- What kind of actions can citizens and social organisations carry out to achieve their objectives?

It's exciting to see such broad, reflective questioning being brought out among citizens across a diversity of communities. The lesson I take from it is about the power of building allies, and then drawing on a rainbow spectrum of networks to dive deep into communities and ask them, 'Why do you think we got here, and where would you like to go from here?'

Not everyone agrees that the demands were so clearly articulated. I trade messages with my school friend Mauricio, who says that on the ground it felt like there was a lack of focus and too many competing agendas, and so he thinks there'll still be people protesting for some time to come. He writes:

I think one of the biggest problems is that the protestors are all over the place with their demands, and there is no political party or person or politician leading the movement, so no one is coordinating the protestors to say 'This is what we will settle for.' My personal choice was to stop protesting because we got constitutional reform. But for many people that's not their priority.

Pension reform was their priority. Or health reform. Or education reform. Or judicial reform ... the list goes on. That's why we are now approaching three months of this shit [in early 2020] and those people have not stopped protesting.

I believe people won't stop protesting until the government manages to come out with some kind of holistic long-term plan to address all these things ... But they are just too incompetent. So, we are in this weird equilibrium where people go out and peacefully protest, violence starts, the police repress, they just barely manage to maintain public order, the government does nothing, next day the same thing all over again. We have become weirdly desensitised to the chaos, especially in Santiago.

Many in Chile are cynical about a requirement that there would have to be a two-thirds majority of parliament to support each constitutional clause. For their part, Unidad Social aren't satisfied with the models proposed for the constitutional review and are pushing for a 'Democratic Constituent Assembly, free, sovereign, joint and plurinational', and so they've managed to get 41 local government municipalities to vote on and raise this demand in the national consultations process. They're living their catch-cry of 'We get tired, we get united!' It's something we could all adopt when we feel worn down and exhausted by our own battles.

Chile's quest for fairness isn't over, but with the tension having reached a boiling point, there's now a sense that change is in the air and a renegotiation of the social contract is inevitable. And that's an achievement in itself. Mauricio tells me that one of the biggest shifts has been opening the floodgates and redefining what kinds of conversation are possible. For the last 30 years, the country has been divided into those who hated the coup and the resulting dictatorship and those who believed it had some positive impact on the country. Even within families like my own there are people in both camps. The protests and the questioning of the *cabildos* has been a big step forward.

Jess, the social conversation that this has spawned is AMAZING! I am sitting back and watching an entire nation jump ahead one generation. From literally one day to the next, it was okay to talk about politics. The throwback of the dictatorship is still really big here. Politics was a really taboo subject – obviously because that inevitably led to a conversation about the dictatorship, and that wound is still healing – so, people in general here did not talk openly about politics. Now, you cannot have a day where you don't talk at some point with someone about what is going on.

Unidad Social are continuing to organise and agitate, bringing citizens together to discuss alternate models for constitutional review and to train people to be election monitors. Chile's protests continue – as I write this, they're in day 80 of the protest movement – at least 24 people have been killed and thousands more injured and arrested. Chile's citizens have made serious sacrifices to bring this change into being, and they should never have had to pay such a heavy price for equality. Yet there is much to learn from the way Chilenos have realised that, if they have deeper conversations, raise their voices, are persistent and focused, work together and aim at the fundamentals of their system, governments have to respond.

Let society lead itself

One of the most inspiring stories of political possibility arose in one of the most unstable and conflict-torn places in the world.

In 2011, as the Arab Spring swept the Middle East, Syrians rose up against dictator Bashar al-Assad. While the Arab Spring uprisings resulted in social progress in places like Tunisia, unfortunately Syria plunged into a civil war that's still boiling over today.

Syria had its own long-held tensions and problems, but the war became even more complex and the conflict more intractable as the country became a battleground for proxy wars between global forces like the USA and Russia, Iran and Saudi Arabia. It's a war in which there are now not two sides but at least five different warring factions. There have been flare-ups of ages-old regional conflicts, such as that between Turks and Kurds, between the forces loyal to Assad and those seeking to overthrow the regime, and the rise (and fall) of violent militants like ISIS as another terrible factor that emerged from the war and devastation in neighbouring Iraq.

In among all this chaos and carnage, hope blossomed in the North and East of Syria: a radically new and active form of community-led social organisation was realised. Variously called Rojava or Kobane or – more of a mouthful – the Autonomous Administration of North and East Syria (let's just call it Rojava for our purposes), is home to between four and five million people (it's hard to get accurate stats with many displaced people), comprising seven districts spread across this stretch of Syria bordering Turkey and Iraq. In Rojava a new kind of politics is being developed that puts planet first, embraces difference, elevates the status and role of women, and brings democracy into daily life, to build shared prosperity and security despite the horror swirling all around.

The Kurdish concept of 'autonomous administration' most closely translates to 'society leading itself', which I love. Rather than top down directives coming from a distant capital, Rojava operates a system called democratic confederalism, with decisions made on a street-by-street, village-by-village level. While first established by Kurds, Rojava has expanded to welcome in many more oppressed people from the region and is feminist and multi-ethnic at its foundation. At least 50 per cent of leadership roles are required to be held by women, and Kurds, Arabs, Yazidis, Christians and other religious groups are invited to share in decision-making roles. This is unique in a part of the world that has been riven by holy wars and patriarchy.

The dream of Rojava originated in the writings of Abdullah Öcalan, a Kurdish leader who's been a political prisoner in Turkey since 1999. Öcalan explained his vision for democratic confederalism like this:

In contrast to centralized administrations and bureaucratic exercise of power, confederalism proposes political self-administration, in which all groups of the society and all cultural identities express themselves in local meetings, general conventions, and councils. Such a democracy opens political space for all social strata and allows diverse political groups to express themselves. In this way it advances the political integration of society as a whole. Politics becomes part of everyday life.[14]

The context in which Abdullah developed his innovative, unconventional political philosophy is the oppression of the Kurdish people – an ethnic group of over 30 million people whose traditional territory disappeared when the British and other victors divided up the Middle East after the First World War, sowing the seeds of many subsequent conflicts. The Kurds found themselves split across Iraq, Iran, Turkey and Syria. Since then the Kurds have suffered genocide, been branded terrorists and many forced into exile. Obviously, there's a long story here, and it's not a simple one, but democratic confederalism was developed in this crucible.

Of note, while some Kurdish groups have continued to fight for their own nation state (and there's a province called Kurdistan in Iran), from the mid-2000s a new line of thinking, drawing on Öcalan's vision, began to prompt a different approach.

As the Syrian civil war began and a power vacuum emerged, some Kurdish communities took advantage of the moment, created their own defence forces (now called the SDF, Syrian Defence Force) and claimed territory in the North and East of Syria. The SDF won some stunning victories against ISIS and have a major claim to having defanged this brutal force. Images of their women fighters became iconic symbols of defiance towards the regressive, oppressive forces that had festered in the region.

Unique as these gender-inclusive fighting forces were, what was most transformative here was that the SDF created room for a new form of social organisation to take root in cities like Afrin, Raqqa, Kobane, Manbij and Taqba that had been liberated from ISIS and other oppressive forces. By pushing the invaders out, and in the absence of central rule from Damascus, the potential of democratic confederalism began to be realised by way of a new social contract. This isn't a metaphorical one like the one Burke wrote about in the 1700s but a literal, real social contract that's regularly updated and has been negotiated among at least 50 different political parties, organisations and communities. At the core of the social contract is a commitment to gender equality, democracy, and environmental, youth and social rights.

Here's a glimpse of it, from the Social Contract of the Democratic Federation of Northern Syria, 2016:

The consensual democratic federal system guarantees the participation of all individuals and groups, on equal levels, in the discussion, decision, and implementation of affairs. It takes ethnic and religious differences into consideration according to the characteristics of each group based on the principles of mutual coexistence and fraternity. It guarantees the equality of all peoples in rights and duties, respects the charters of human rights, and preserves national and international peace.[15]

Here's how it works, in brief: 'communes' of around two hundred households (communes range in number from 150 to 1500 people) are the central forum for decision-making, much like councils of elders in traditional Kurdish tribal life. In every neighbourhood or village there's a 'people's house', open to everyone 24 hours a day, which is the local home for politics and social services. It's the place you go to get access to social services or raise issues; a distribution point for any resources that might be scarce; and also where the boards and committees that manage the community meet. Examples are the economics commission, which helps coordinate agriculture, business needs, construction and supply chains (a hefty challenge in a place surrounded by war) and the peace committee, which is a community-managed conflict-resolution and justice system. When bigger decisions need to be made that impact on a larger population or area, these communes connect upwards to councils: on neighbourhood, municipal or district levels, depending on the size of the town or city. Co-operatives, unions and other civil organisations also send delegates to participate in councils, so you have worker and specialist representatives making decisions alongside elected community members. These councils feed up to bodies for each region, with the Autonomous Administration co-ordinating across the board wherever necessary. The kinds of decisions made at a higher level are those that can't be solved closer to home, like ensuring the supply of energy; preventing price gouging; planning for education, health or roads; and broader security questions.

There's a political stream of life too: the Syrian Democratic Council, which is more outward facing and addresses the conflict all around Rojava. As well, there are opposition parties within the system – even ones that are opposed to confederalism and advocate for statehood. This isn't about creating a one-party state but rather a society in which parties and national control is less important because decisions and power flow upwards.

Zozan Hussein, co-chair of the Legislative Council of Manbij Region, has commented:

Before, society and the state were really distant from each other. The state would make decisions and society would not really apply them. Now the society makes decisions by itself and applies them. If you give value to society, the society has more agency – they will take ownership of their decisions. This is something really positive, so we want to spread this democratic system across all of Syria, the Middle East, Europe, and the whole world.[16]

Rojava isn't your usual separatist state. First of all, it's not one territory but several areas dotted across the region, with enemy positions still separating them. Secondly, the people of Rojava have no intention of declaring themselves a country. As the traditional nation state has been a source of pain for many Kurds, there's a reluctance to recreate it: Rojava seeks to be a self-governing region within Syria, and the hope is that they'll be left to their own devices within a future peaceful country.

By opting out of the battle for statehood and embedding decision-making into everyday life, Rojava aims to be a society that's run by civil society, rather than by an elected political class. Observers have flocked from all over the world to document the experiment, and many have remarked on the absence of NGOs – non-governmental organisations such as charities, which carry a lot of the load of community support in much of the Western world. They don't exist in Rojava because *everything* is considered the work of civil society.

It's easy to see why Rojava has attracted so much admiration. In the most difficult of circumstances – with sanctions and roadblocks, warring armies on all sides and international aid cut off – people have come together to be visionary and ambitious, generous and inclusive. These communities have overcome hundreds of years of divisive politics that have sought to pit people against each other based on their ethnicity or religion. Instead, they have learned from the systems that oppressed them and opted to create a secular society in which every group has their voices heard, and no one group conspires to lift themselves up at the expense of others. Prompted by a scarcity of resources and an ecological aspiration towards self-sufficiency, a circular economy is central to the functioning of Rojava, and worker-owned business models like co-operatives have flourished. There's also a strong focus on education. Schools are free, and lifelong learning and training is encouraged for everyone – in history, language, self-defence, philosophy, construction, digital security, 3D printing, you name it.

It's not perfect. Organising any human society is hard work, even in much less dangerous and precarious circumstances, let alone when there's been deep trauma and a history of oppression and distrust. But enough good stories have come out of Rojava to inspire hope: the story of the first 'national park' being planted near Dêrîk; the establishment of an Ecology Academy to help people build food security; rehabilitation and retraining academies for injured veterans; and the thoughtful way women's institutions are being built up and feminism is being embedded while maintaining sensitivity towards more conservative communities. It's especially heartening to hear how marginalised groups like the Yazidi, who had their language and even their names banned under the Assad regime and were targeted by ISIS, have been coming into their own as they are liberated. There are Yazidi houses of gathering in every city in Rojava, and the level of inclusivity on offer has not been experienced for generations.

For those following the story of Rojava, it was devastating to see it come under major threat in late 2019. President Trump declared ISIS 'defeated' and ordered US troops to withdraw from Syria – despite the fact that the SDF had really been the ones on the ground fighting ISIS and holding thousands of fighters as prisoners of war. Trump's announcement came not long after the USA had struck a big missile sale deal with Turkey. The withdrawal of the few US troops in the region was roundly condemned, and as predicted, Turkey considered that a green light and promptly invaded North and East Syria, determined to cut short the experiment in Rojava and replace the communities there with refugees and Turkish settlers. It's part of an anti-Kurd expansionist mission of the authoritarian Turkish President Erdogan, and a huge step backwards for freedom in the region. There are reports of terrible repression and civilian attacks as Turkish-allied forces move forward and displace the communities of Rojava.

As we go to press, it's hard to know what the future holds for the people of North and East Syria. I'm constantly looking up Rojava news for promising signs amid the reports, hoping that some of the people I'd read about and reached out to have survived this terrible setback. So far, much of the damage has been contained, but the more of us who bear witness, the more we can help these communities in their courageous stand.

The story of Rojava reminds us that we can sometimes have a very limited political imagination. We don't just have to choose between capitalism and communism, the nanny state or libertarianism, authoritarianism or anarchy. Decentralised, devolved forms of decision-making are possible, even in places where life is most challenging, and even in times of dire crisis and fear, we shouldn't underestimate the human capacity to lead in a way that serves the common good.

Demand a new deal

So far our story has taken us from Taiwan to Syria, from Iceland to Chile, from a dairy and nightclub in Rosario Argentina to a market hall in Preston in the UK. We've spun the globe and entered vastly different contexts, yet many of the solutions we've encountered so far keep repeating themselves – shared realisations reached through unique struggles.

That's a theme you'll see emerging as we work our way around the world and through this story. There are ideas that come up time and again – like valuing the care we provide each other and our planet, giving more people a stake in our politics as leaders and the world of business as owners, and recouping the benefit of the things we create together as a society – and I find that enormously reassuring. It means that we're not all off on our own tangents, each out reinventing the wheel, but instead that there's something about these solutions that's proving to be enduring and worthwhile.

A lot of these ideas are already finding a home under the banner of the Green New Deal (GND).

You've probably heard the term, but it's likely that you've encountered it as a rather vague, catch-all concept. Today's GND is inspired by the shift to the war economy in the UK during the Second World War and the recovery efforts afterwards, and by President

Franklin Delano Roosevelt (FDR)'s New Deal in the USA.

To give you a bit of background on that, as Depression hit the USA in the 1930s to fend off the appeal of communism, FDR introduced an ambitious national reform and works program called the New Deal. As a first step, the government regulated the financial markets, to try to avoid another boom and bust. A slew of workers' rights were proposed by Labor Secretary Frances Perkins: banning child labour, setting a minimum wage, introducing social security support and unemployment payments, and establishing the 40-hour work week (which, by the way, Australian unions had secured for skilled workers almost a century before).

Then a whole host of new national agencies were established, such as the United States Housing Authority and the Works Progress Administration, which employed millions of people directly for construction projects: to build dams to provide electricity to rural America; roads; airports; housing and public buildings; along with state parks and much more besides. The Public Works of Art Project put thousands of artists to work creating artworks and murals that documented a significant moment in history, while the Federal Art Project also provided community centres where art could be made and exhibited, the birth of arts institutions that continue to provide cultural infrastructure in the USA. A good deal of what you might recognise as the heroic, epic American aesthetic of the 20th century was built at this time: icons like the Hoover Dam came about because of this national push to get people working.

As Naomi Klein points out in her book *On Fire,* the original New Deal didn't just spring from the generosity and vision of politicians: unionists and activists had fought for years for many of these moves, and yet many were excluded, particularly African Americans, Native Americans and women.

On the positive side, the solutions weren't simply devised in Washington and rolled out around the country. In most New Deal projects, although there was a large proportion of federal funding, or workers employed by a federal agency doing the work, it was local authorities who determined the projects that were needed and a multiplicity of architects, artists, designers and technical experts delivered them.

This background is important because, even if you've heard of the New Deal, like me you might have thought it was all about major infrastructure, big buildings and large-scale public works. As it turns out, that stuff matters, and projects like those form a lasting physical legacy of what it looks like when a government invests in infrastructure. But what we don't see so much, looking back, is how the New Deal made a significant investment in people, in regulation to improve lives and provide certainty, in artists and storytelling to lift spirits and bring people together, and the foundations of community support in the Social Security Act. When we think about a GND for our times, we should remember that the social, cultural, human software – how people are treated, and how we return rights and dignity to work – will be every bit as important as transitioning to a zero-carbon building, transport and manufacturing sector.

The GND was first formulated in the UK in 2008 as a way for governments to make a genuine shift to a zero-carbon economy and to confront the antisocial impacts of the bloated financial sector. Economist Ann Pettifor and the UK's brilliant New Economics Foundation championed it as a way to get the renewable energy, efficient buildings, public transport and sustainable production we need, along with the decent, secure and human-centred jobs we want.

Then the 2008 GFC hit. The GND was just emerging and gaining support, and it became another victim of austerity, to all our detriment.

In its aftermath, as country after country bailed out the banks and slashed public spending to pay for this lavish corporate welfare, the looming climate and inequality crisis got pushed onto the back burner. But eventually, the GND rose again and pre-COVID-19, it was gaining momentum around the world. It's possible that the GND will be derailed once again by this new crisis: or we can fight to make sure we have a plan for post-pandemic reconstruction that centres sustainability, care and fair work like the GND can do.

In 2018, US House of Representatives rising star Alexandria Ocasio-Cortez (aka AOC) made the GND part of her platform as she offered a radical progressive alternative to the Democrat status quo. Subsequently, the prominence of the GND was boosted as AOC and her fellow Justice Democrats – a new generation of political change-makers – started getting traction with voters. More on this in a minute: let's talk about what would actually be in the deal.

The US GND talks about mobilisation – echoing the language of a wartime response – but instead of making munitions and enlisting young people in the armed forces, the GND would give everyone who wants a job access to employment in making preparations against climate change and a great, green transition to a climate-adapted society. Physically, that could mean building defences against rising waters or securing people's access to clean water, expanding renewable energy to be a decentralised grid providing all the power needs of a nation and upgrading existing building stock to be energy efficient. There would also be a shift in what would be incentivised through subsidies and tax breaks in order to encourage more sustainable small-scale farming practices (as opposed to the draining practices of industrial agriculture) and investment in manufacturing zero-emission vehicles and public transport infrastructure.

Care for the planet is also part of the vision: investing in projects to regenerate natural ecosystems, for their own sakes and for ours, and for their value in sequestering carbon and purifying air and water.

Naomi Klein put it really well when she said, 'There was finally a big and bold "yes" to pair with the climate movement's many "no's", a story of what the world could look like after we embraced deep transformation, and a plan for how to get there. ['17]

The GND doesn't include every move I've seen in the glimpses of a fairer future but it's a damn good start. Here's why I find it appealing: in the GND, social justice is at the foundation of environmental sustainability. It's a plan designed to benefit the many by protecting natural landscapes, providing transport and better quality housing (more on this later), lowering costs of living while also giving more people pathways into work that actually creates value in the real world.

Professor Robert Hockett, an adviser to AOC, emphasises the interconnectedness of the GND's social and ecological agendas: 'Prosperity, planetary survival, participatory democracy and distributive justice go hand in hand. These are not separate values haphazardly thrown together but are deeply and mutually interconnected – to pursue one of them intelligently is to pursue all four of them simultaneously.'[18]

***

If there was a positive theme in the last few years of dramatic, chaotic change, it was the rising power of young people, the generation being handed a burning planet, coming into their power and refusing to let business as usual steal their future. Sunrise Movement are one of the most inspired examples of the influence that can be achieved when you ignite the passion of those who've been left out of the conversation across a nation.

In the USA, a group of young climate activists united as the Sunrise Movement in 2017, and in the short time since they've created a groundswell through distributed, nationwide cells of young people terrified about the threat of climate change and outraged at having their potential cut short by inequality. The Sunrise Movement were the conscience of the Democratic Presidential primary, compelling candidates to not only endorse a GND but to refuse fossil-fuel donations, because to make change, we need the distorting power of fossil fuel money out of politics.

Young activists waited for their representatives outsides their offices with novelty-sized cheques showing how much each rep had received from the fossil-fuel lobby. To make sure climate change was on the agenda, they sat in for three days at the Democratic National Committee headquarters until the DNC Chair agreed to a climate debate.

Aracely Jimenez-Hudis, Sunrise Movement's Digital Media Manager, explained their approach to me like this:

As a movement of young people, we hold moral authority when it comes to questioning and confronting political candidates about their finances. Back when we first launched Sunrise Movement in 2017, we quickly found that when we not only confronted politicians in public spaces about their campaign contributions from fossil-fuel billionaires, but also recorded those interactions and posted the responses online, we were able to grow our movement exponentially. These were easy viral moments to recreate between Sunrisers and candidates all across the country. Every single person who watched one of those interactions was confronted with a key question for themselves: whose side are you on? Are you with the young person fighting for the future they deserve or with the politician who values cheques more than their constituents? For many, it's an easy choice to make, and for candidates watching who hadn't been confronted yet, it was an easy incentive to sign on fast and keep their pledge over fear of bad press.

Their tactics have been overwhelmingly successful: over 1900 candidates standing for election in 2020 at multiple levels of government have signed their No Fossil Fuel Money Pledge, including all but one of 25 Democratic Presidential candidates who contested the Democratic nomination.

While of course online organising is a crucial tool, particularly for a movement of digital natives, the Sunrise Movement show us how important gatherings are for political change. In April 2019, their Road to the Green New Deal tour kicked off in Boston and then spread across the country, with major rallies in eight cities across the country and over two hundred smaller town hall events in 46 states. They had more in the works for the intensely contested 2020 United States Presidential campaign, but like so much else, it was cut short by the pandemic. Prior to that, nurturing face-to-face relationships and the energy of real-world gatherings was a key part in building community around the Sunrise Movement. Aracely explains:

> One part of our three-prong strategy is people power, an active base of public support that is consistently taking action to build the movement, organise our communities and engage in mass moral protest. We know that without this level of face-to-face organising and action-taking, we won't win transformational change the Green New Deal promises. Any campaign we run is always run with the intention of getting young people to learn how to organise and build the movement in their communities.

As the COVID-19 pandemic cut a swathe through the USA, and talk of an economic rescue package arose, the Sunrise Movement expanded their message to call for a 'People's Bailout', one that prioritised human health and provided direct economic aid to people, not corporations. They demanded that the billions, trillions being spent in the name of recovery be directed to fund a regenerative economy that would make their nation more resilient in the face of future crises.

It's a message that each of us need to advocate for in our own communities and nations. As we recover from this global trauma, we must be mindful not to recreate the mistakes of the last recovery, and instead that we're spending money to lay the foundations of the fairer, sustainable society that we need for the next century. It's one of the reasons why we need to dive into a better understanding of how we use funding and finance to shape the world, in the work we reward, the resources we share and the places we construct, and to be able to properly diagnose the drivers of inequality that brought us to this point: that's where our story takes us next.

4

Redesign work

Some people have a knack for being in the right place at the right time: my career suggests I've got the opposite of that. You name an industry that's been 'disrupted' and there's a good chance I'll have some entry about it on my CV.

While I studied journalism and law at university in Sydney, on the side, I threw myself into editing (painfully niche) creative publications – so much so that I never quite got around to graduating. Whoops. From the early 2000s, just when I started my full-time media career as a magazine editor – running publications celebrating design, fashion, music and social issues – media started to feel the effects of the digital age. More people were consuming content online. While the demand for interesting content to click on seemed to be growing, revenue from advertising or subscriptions kept shrinking, which left publishers less and less to spend on generating that content. The business model of indie mags always seemed to rely on creatives providing their content for free to get their foot in the door – it was always to 'build up their portfolios'. Less scrupulous publishers asked me to cut off writers, photographers, illustrators and contributors once they'd had sufficient 'exposure' and had the nerve to ask to be paid for their work. Those publishers knew there were always more people out there, willing to provide their work for free in order to break into the industry – an industry which was moving steadily away from permanent, paid jobs and towards the gig economy, years before Uber or Airtasker appeared.

In the course of the last two decades, I've seen a contraction of career opportunities and income prospects for people working in the creative economy, even as our sector has grown in reach and influence. The creative industries were the canaries in the coal mine of the digital age: we were the first to see our content set 'free' by the platforms of the internet giants. This resulted in more content, yes – don't get me wrong; I know a lot of incredible opportunities have been generated too – and I'm glad that more people than ever are able to make music, find audiences, or share their images or stories. But the advertising dollars generated by this content have been funnelled to an ever-diminishing pool of winners, the big-name tech platform owners, while creators and the industries around them have lost out.

Over the last 20 years, that trend – ad dollars bypassing the funding of media production and, instead, going to the tech platforms – has only intensified. Today, between them Facebook and Google swallow up 50 per cent of all advertising revenue worldwide and don't produce a single article or video, story or photo essay. In allowing content to be 'free', we've let the channels consume all the value, with terrible outcomes for creative content and more crucially for our democracy, for journalism as a profession and safeguarder of democracy. Rather than paying, say, the *New York Times* or *National Geographic, Colors* magazine or *The Guardian,* enabling them to pay the writers, photographers and content producers, most of the ad revenue goes to aggregators that gather that content and platforms that simply point at it.

Yes, that's been the model for the first few decades of the internet, but it doesn't have to be this way: we'll dive into alternatives to our digital dystopia a little later.

Back to my career and my experiencing first-hand the digital disruption of the media and creative industries. Launching a music publication in 2004 was the business equivalent of buying shares in the *Titanic.* The radical makeover of the creative industry started in music with peer-to-peer file-sharing platforms like Napster in the early 2000s and expanded to a generation listening to music on YouTube. Consequently, the price we paid for recorded music fell to zero (a situation which has improved only marginally with the more recent advent of streaming services). It wasn't a good time for a bunch of young would-be publishers to be sourcing advertising from the music industry for a print magazine. While the old business model was failing, great music kept on coming: the music was there, the audiences hadn't gone away, but the profits now went to the platforms (like YouTube or, later, Spotify) that hosted the content, rather than the makers or the labels and managers that fostered them, or the critics, photographers and publications that once helped them find an audience.

After this experience (and many more just like it, in art, fashion, design and other creative-content publications), I realised that every creative industry was facing the same sorts of challenges, and I started working on mentorship and development programs to help creators reskill to build businesses for this new era. I was trying to equip these creative Davids in a battle against the new-economy Goliaths: helping them learn how to use these channels to build their own audiences to take back some control, or to develop strategies and side hustles that would diversify their incomes.

Eventually, I set up a festival that brought together people across industries to share knowledge and collaborate. I ran Vivid Ideas for nine years, and I'm still proud of the connections made and the conversations we started. Many were about the new skills creatives – and increasingly, all of us – need to develop as we confront life in the new world of work. Today, the creative industries are finally being recognised as a key part of the knowledge economy that we're shifting into. Here, ideas, learning, human ingenuity and imagination are the key resource rather than manual labour or fossil fuel extraction. Potentially, this embrace of creativity will spread through – and change – the economy at large.

Similarly, we'll likely be seeing many more examples of the kind of disruption I've seen in my working life with creative content. This isn't just about designers, filmmakers, journalists and musicians. We were the first to feel the effects of this new digital age, but the same experience is being replicated across industries that, until now, have seemed solid and secure. Taxi drivers didn't see Uber coming; hotel workers couldn't have predicted the rise of Airbnb. Will lawyers, accountants, builders and teachers be luckier and be able to pre-empt the changes ahead for them?

All this rapid, radical change to the world of work has been packaged up and sold to us as 'digital disruption', but there's another phrase for it: 'creative destruction'.

The economist who made that phrase his own, Joseph Schumpeter, was under no illusions that creative destruction was a blip or a phase. It's built into the architecture of the economic system we live in: utterly predictable and to be expected. He wrote:

> The fundamental impulse that sets and keeps the capitalist engine in motion comes from the new consumers' goods, the new methods of production or transportation, the new markets, the new forms of industrial organization that capitalist enterprise creates.
>
> The ... process of industrial mutation ... incessantly revolutionizes the economic structure from within, incessantly destroying the old one, incessantly

creating a new one. This process of Creative Destruction is the essential fact about capitalism. It is what capitalism consists in and what every capitalist concern has got to live in.[1]

To translate Schumpeter's 1940s language to the terms of the tech world, creative destruction is a feature, not a bug, of capitalism. In real-life terms, what that means is that as more and more industries have their revenue models 'creatively destroyed', there are fewer jobs or sustainable careers in these sectors. This is what has happened in the media and creative sector and is now occurring in other fields that have also seen the digital players invade their turf, from retail to taxis.

Of course, change this profound has happened before – such as during the shift from an agricultural to a manufacturing economy, and then from manufacturing to services – and new jobs were created in new industries to compensate. Schumpeter said capitalism generates a 'perennial gale of creative destruction'. In the past, it might have been true to say that gale blew away some of the dangers and disadvantages of old industries: often, the new jobs that were created were safer, better paid and offered better benefits. Unfortunately, that's not what we're seeing on the business-as-usual path right now. Work is becoming more precarious and unsafe for many: just think about all those gig-economy workers, Uber and food-delivery drivers, left to find their own protective equipment and without any kind of compensation or income during the COVID-19 pandemic.

Over the last few years a job that is a solid foundation for life has become less and less common, while Schumpter's gale blows a tidal wave of change sweeping across the planet, pushing people from industry to industry in its wake. If you feel like you're barely keeping your head above water, this is why: we're all caught in a rip, pulled this way and that by invisible forces eroding the certainty and protections that previous generations had around work. As whole industries are erased or redefined, career options and pathways disappear. It doesn't feel great when you're churning inside the wave, and it's not clear right now what comes next or where this wave will deposit us. In the past, change happened across decades and generations, and it happened at different paces in different parts of the world. Now, it seems like that wave is moving much more quickly, and it's swirling us around in the global north and south alike. It's also feeling, increasingly, like jobs themselves are being washed away.

But this is not happening just because of technology. Those apps we've come to depend on, artificial intelligence, machine learning and automation: sure, they're accelerating the shift to the gig economy, but in the story of my career, you can see that was already in the works. There's a different set of innovations, much less discussed than those robots supposedly coming for our jobs, that are removing security and purpose from the work lives of millions around the world. There are three I'll explore in this chapter: monopoly power of platform capitalism, the fissuring of work from jobs and the financialisation of industry. These are exacerbating the impact of this 'perennial gale': combining into a perfect storm to reduce the number and quality of jobs and reframing the nature and power dynamics of work like never before.

The COVID-19 pandemic and global shutdown have only accelerated these trends. Within the first few weeks, 26 million Americans had lost their jobs, with at least an extra million added to the dole queue in Australia, and many more besides saw their incomes and job prospects eroded. But the Great Reset could be our chance to stop and reassess: what kind of work do we need and conditions do we want to see on the other side of this?

Thankfully, there are people showing us better ways to organise our working lives to make sure Schumpeter's gale doesn't blow away hard-won gains for working people.

Expand ownership

What if you were the boss as well as being a worker? Your business would likely be more profitable, more productive and more stable than most: better able to weather recessions with fewer layoffs and fitter in the face of uncertain economic headwinds.

That's not just because you'd be a great boss (though if your reading choices are anything to go by, I'm sure you would be): I'm talking about the tangible, measurable difference it makes when workers are empowered and given a stake as co-owners in companies. Redesigning business to be better for people and planet is not just a nice idea: it makes sense from a cold-headed capitalist perspective too.

The secret isn't giving executives generous stock options as part of salary packages. Having broad-based ownership – across hierarchy – by the people who work in a firm has multiple benefits. In their research and writing on US companies, Rutgers School of Management and Labor Relations Distinguished Professor Douglas Kruse and University of Massachusetts Amherst Associate Professor Fidan Ana Kurtulus found that companies with employee stock ownership had only half as many layoffs as other companies during the last two recessions.

Kruse and Kurtulus observed that when the goals of the owners and workers are more closely aligned, everyone benefits from higher productivity. There's evidence of less absenteeism, lower staff turnover, more positive signs of functional workplaces like people staying in their jobs for longer and being more proactive employees, and that the effects of this are especially strong when there's employee participation in decision-making. If people aren't simply owners on paper, but in practice, firms perform better and survive longer, even in the face of recessions.

A higher level of worker ownership and participation – also known as inclusive, or democratic, ownership – can take many forms. Today, Kruse and Kurtulus estimate that 22.9 million Americans – about one-fifth of the workforce – own stock in the companies they work for.[2] One of the most common in the USA is employee stock ownership plans, in which, typically, employees gain an ownership stake through their pension fund. Another is the employee stock purchase plans, which may offer discounts on company stock to allow employees to choose the extent of their investment. Then there are co-operatives, which aren't popular in the USA but have an enormous membership worldwide – much more on them later. This isn't effective only for small concerns or not-for-profits: there are some extraordinary companies, global leaders in their fields, with employee-ownership models at their foundation. One example is Arup, an engineering, design and planning firm, a company that has played a major role in building cities and icons since the 1940s, from the Sydney Opera House to London's Barbican, to Beijing's Water Cube and Birds' Nest.

The example of Arup shows how business-as-unusual can work better for everyone. Arup is owned by a trust, not shareholders, and the company distributes annual profits among past and present employees (and there are a lot of them): currently, Arup has 14,000 employees in 34 countries. Arup's employee-ownership model contributes to a culture of investing in its employees through its own Arup University, a mechanism for training and knowledge-sharing within the organisation. Arup also offers secondments into other companies or international placements across its global network of offices. Sounds like a pretty great place to work, right?

Another iconic employee-owned business is Germany's *Der Spiegel,* a weekly news magazine that's one of the most respected publications in the world, renowned for its investigative journalism. Founded in Hamburg after World War Two, *Der Spiegel* was restructured into a majority employee-owned enterprise in 1974. After three years with the company, employees are granted a stake in ownership and a say in electing the management committee. This employee leadership is more common in Germany, in the form of works councils, or *Betriebsräte.*

Workers in Germany chart the right of employee representation back to the medieval guild system. It was formalised in 1976 though the Codetermination Act, which gives workers in companies with more than 2000 employees the right to elect up to half of the supervisory board: even in publicly owned companies, workers and shareholders share the right to appoint the board of directors. It's hard to draw a direct link between worker empowerment and Germany's renowned productivity and strong economy, but it's a formula that's worth exploring. Two of the UK's most well-known retail brands, Waitrose and John Lewis, are wholly employee-owned: their parent company is the John Lewis Partnership, owned in trust by their 83,900 partners, otherwise known as employees. Employee ownership has been at the foundation of the company since 1919, embodied by principle one of the company constitution: 'The happiness of all its members, through their worthwhile and satisfying employment in a successful business. Because the Partnership is owned in trust for its members, they share the responsibilities of ownership as well as its rewards – profit, knowledge and power.'

These employee-owned businesses are living proof that inclusive ownership models can power resilient companies that are best-in-class globally. They're places where people can do their best work while sharing profits equitably, re-investing in research and training talent. This is the very opposite of the extractive, exploitative models that have got our society and planet into the mess we're in. It suggests that business isn't the problem, but to make it part of the solution, we need to build up more generative businesses – that is, businesses that give back more than they take from their employees and the communities they're in. It also suggests it's possible to reshape the priorities of firms to align with the interests of workers, society and the places we share. So, what does that look like from the inside?

Form businesses that care

After years working as a case worker and care worker, Robyn Kaczmarek was frustrated by every aspect of the business of care in Australia. The cocktail included the isolation of working alone day after day in different people's houses, showing up without an introduction and only having a written care plan to explain this person's needs, then not staying on one job long enough to build relationships with clients or to best understand their needs. When she worked as a care worker for agencies, she wasn't allocated any travel time: she tells me about having to cut 15 minutes off one client's care hours to race across the city just to arrive 15 minutes late to the next. She hated short-changing the clients, who needed her companionship and care, and she hated the stress being shunted onto her as a carer, just so the agency could squeeze out a profit.

Positive there had to be a better way, Robyn started searching online to see if anywhere in the world had got care work right. She found Sunderland Home Care Associates in England, a social enterprise owned by its 300 employees, and Home Care Associates in New York. Robyn had come across a model that was fundamentally different to the usual corporate care agencies: both these award-winning businesses are co-operatives, owned by the carers who powered them, and focused on providing a better quality of life for everyone involved.

'I'm like, "Why don't we have one?" And so then I went and tried to meet anybody, everybody that knew about cooperatives. I was going to the lecturers at Sydney University who know about labour law and talk how wonderful it is, and I said, "Yeah, but I want to start a co-op. How do I do it?" And they said, "Oh, I don't know about that."' Robyn laughs, 'So we just did it, didn't we?'

She looks at her co-founder Margaret Ciarka, another lifelong carer. I'm sitting at a boardroom table in Waterloo, Sydney, with Margaret, Robyn and almost their whole in-office team, enjoying some of the delicious cakes and biscuits they've laid out. This is already much more like a house visit with friendly neighbours than a meeting with a health-services corporation. As women in their 50s, Margaret and Robyn aren't your typical start-up founders, and I love this. They're true experts in their fields and passionate about their mission to make care better for everyone.

The two women met via the internet back in 2011. Margaret found Robyn's writing about care work online and, identifying with the frustrations she described, decided to reach out to a total stranger (although one with a familiar Polish surname) to see if they couldn't find a way to improve this work they both loved doing.

'When we had that conversation on the phone the first time, Robyn said, "You know what? I have an idea. So, let's meet and talk."' At the face-to-face meeting they organised, at a pub, Robyn arrived with a full folder of research. 'And that's when she mentioned the worker-owned co-operative. I'd never heard of that,' says Margaret. 'So, she already was quite into that.'

'That's my obsessive–compulsive heart coming out,' Robyn concedes.

Together, Robyn and Margaret have created Australia's first employee co-owned social care provider, The Co-Operative Life. They kicked off in 2013 with one worker (Robyn) – and Margaret working when they could afford it – with zero capital (just a small overdraft from a mutual bank, Bank Australia, which they've never touched) and one client. They pretty much had to forge their own path. Apart from some advice on setting up a co-op from someone who'd managed a fishing co-operative on the south coast – this was before the establishment of the Business Council of Cooperatives and Mutuals – they found little support or co-op knowledge elsewhere.

Today, The Co-Operative Life have 85 staff members and big plans for the future, having shifted to a distributing cooperative model with share capital – which basically means they're now set up to make the workers co-owners in the business, sharing in decision-making and the profits. Getting that working well is the next step, a challenge when there's so much change in their sector, good and bad. In Australia at the moment, there's a huge shift taking place in disability care with the introduction of the National Disability Insurance Scheme (NDIS), and a similar shift happening in aged care. Essentially, the NDIS moved from funding organisations to deliver care to providing each person needing care with their own budget, which they can then allocate to the carers they believe will help them achieve their personal goals. While enormously disruptive to the sector, and particularly challenging in regional areas, there's a window of opportunity for niche providers like The Co-Operative Life to emerge between the cracks of the corporate care sector and forge a new offering. Robyn says that when a similar shift took place in Germany, the care sector flipped from 90 per cent corporate and 10 per cent niche, to the exact opposite within five years.

The transition to a buyer-led 'care market' isn't always smooth – in particular, in places where the market can't provide for unique needs, like rural and regional areas – and there have already been care providers who've had to shut up shop. In early 2019, The Co-Operative Life were called on to provide a lifeline to a care provider in the New England region of New South Wales which was about to fold and leave 26 people without jobs and several dozen people without care. It was a big leap for Robyn, Margaret and their team, but they decided to take over that business, turning those employees into co-op members and co-owners overnight. They're clearly very proud of being part of a solution that preserved care for a community and created better quality, secure jobs for workers.

Robyn recalls how the transition worked:

> So, it was something like the 11th of May that it ended services with that organisation, the 12th of May we took them on, and there was not really a disruption. I mean, it did move and shift, and people left and came back and whatever,

but they're going really well; they're really strong there. I think they're limited [in growth] in the small population, but we are looking at how we're going to expand them into other areas.

That's the issue, I think, with the rural and remote areas. If the big funded organisations go over, then that means that there's going to be no service, and those people are all going to be looking for jobs. But wouldn't it be great if they could all just say, 'We'll become a cooperative. And we'll work on our own', you know. And so we've got to figure out how they do that.

I'm so excited to see a co-operative care worker-owned enterprise take off right in my backyard, grow from nothing into a thriving business, and now be part of the solution for even more vulnerable communities in the regions. This is a just transition in action, in care and democratic ownership – and it couldn't be more timely. The demographic shift that will see the Baby Boomer generation retiring also entails their requiring aged care – at a time when the economic models that used to provide socialised care are rupturing.

NDIS is sort of the starting point, but it's really a bit of a pilot compared to what's coming for aged care. And I don't think we even know what that's going to be like, you know: the Baby Boomers, which is my parents' generation, haven't even started yet [to fully shift into needing aged care]. And they're going to be demanding; they have very high expectations. So I've said to them, start making noise. Start making noise because it's going to be you guys that have problems. And it's going to be the people that will shift it, you know; then things will happen.

While co-ops have been around for a long time, right now may be the moment when the principles of co-operative ownership applied to care could transform the world of business into a force for good, and to make care fairer for everyone.

Throughout our conversation Robyn has quoted 'the seven co-operative principles' time and again: these are the historical Rochdale principles from the first officially recognised cooperative. A small co-op grocery was established in 1844 by weavers in the north of England who'd been left out of work by the industrial revolution and needed an affordable way of feeding their families. The guiding principles have evolved but have endured ever since. Essentially, they say co-ops need to be voluntary to join, with non-discriminatory membership that's open to everyone, democratically controlled by members, and with concern for the community built in from the outset. The Co-Operative Life are beginning to find their co-operative values are providing a competitive advantage in building their worker community.

'So, I have just employed three people recently,' Margaret tells me. 'And the three of them actually said the same thing: "I checked your website before I applied and I like your values." One of them said, "I'm not here to make a dollar. I'm having passion to help people, to work with people." So, you're thinking, "Okay, that's the same thinking we all have." So, people start recognising our values – that they are probably different from many others.'

Robyn adds, 'Co-operatives make you do that, because you've got your seven co-operative principles. The values of a co-operative are self-help, self-responsibility, equality ... you know, we're beginning to live those.'

It's a long chat, and by the end of it I've worked my way through quite a few of the cakes (there was an upside to being heavily pregnant while writing this section). Listening back to the recording, I can hear the excitement we all share in this model as the conversation bounces around the table. Robyn, Margaret and the team are all passionate about making care jobs good jobs, and the path they're forging shows us how business can be turned into a force for empowerment across more industries and parts of the world too. So, why doesn't it work like this for everyone?

***

There are a couple of f-bombs you could drop when it comes to the state of work today, but these two might not immediately come to mind: fissuring and financialisation. They're a bit obscure, but you've probably felt their effects in your career without even knowing it, and they're some of the factors Robyn described earlier when she told me what isn't working in care work.

Fissuring describes the way work and jobs have been separated from each other. Today, less than half of Australians in the workforce are in permanent, full-time jobs.[3] More and more of us have moved from being regular employees to being contractors: responsible for providing our own equipment, paying our own superannuation and managing quarterly tax payments, without the sick leave, maternity or annual leave entitlements employees get. The lure for this has been flexibility, but in many industries the offer of a secure employment contract simply isn't on the table anymore. Think about the workers at Telstra, Australia's telecommunications giant. In the past, the people laying the cables, installing phone lines or testing your connections were usually employed by Telstra. Today, they're more likely to be 'independent contractors' supplied by a company like Tandem, an 'end to end workforce management' firm ... though just how independent, is now a question to be decided by the courts. In late 2018, 4700 technicians launched a class action against Tandem (still ongoing as we went to print)[4] claiming they were encouraged to borrow tens of thousands of dollars to buy vehicles, equipment and set themselves up as contractors, only to earn less than minimum wage and to have almost no control over their 'flexible' working arrangements.[5]

Meanwhile, union membership rates have fallen, workers' rights have eroded and wage growth has stalled, leading to a decline in 'real wages' (that is, the buying power of wages). With fewer jobs out there, more people are vulnerable to bad deals or accepting reduced rights. This isn't just happening to the blue-collar workforce. At Google, half of their workforce are 'TVCs', their label for temporary, vendor and contract workers, second-class citizens when it comes to workplace rights. These workers don't have access to the same healthcare, stock options or even complaint mechanisms for reporting on sexual misconduct, even as they work alongside 'Googlers', employees that do.[6]

The other f-word impacting the world of work is financialisation. In the traditional story of capitalism, owners of productive enterprises would reinvest business profits back in the business in the form of better machinery, higher wages or more employees. They might also spend those profits on research and development, training their workforce or in new technology. The theory was that you've got to spend money to make money. Profitability would lead to better conditions for workers or enhanced skills, allowing them to be even more productive. Developing new product lines or innovative services to sell would lead to a higher quantity or quality of output from the business. This remained true for some time. In Australia, productivity and real wages last kept pace in 2001, meaning that's the last time workers' pay packets grew at the same rate as employer profits, but since then, wages stopped growing even as owners' returns increased.[7] In the United States, between 1973 and 2016 productivity increased by 77 per cent, but wages increased by only 12 per cent. The percentage of profits going to workers – described as 'workers' share of income' – is at a 50-year low, and this trend is being played out around the world.

So, where are those profits going instead of into workers' pockets or improving business performance? This is where the financialisation part of the story comes in.

For companies listed on the stock exchange, we tend to assume their profits are either reinvested in the company (in one of the ways listed above) or distributed among their shareholders in the form of dividends. Instead, in many listed firms, the majority of corporate profits are being sunk into share buy-backs – that is, using profits to buy shares in the company, which serves to keep the stock price high without product innovation or a better performance by a company.

Canadian-born economist William Lazonick has focused his career on tracking this trend: he found, from the late 1970s, more and more corporations shifting from a 'retain and reinvest' towards a 'downsize and distribute' model of operations that extracts value from businesses, using profits to inflate stock prices so a business looks good on paper, rather than increasing a company's productive value.

It's happening at a staggering scale. From 2003 through 2012, Lazonick studied the S&P 500 index, a collection of 500 companies listed on US stock exchanges. In that period, 449 of the 500 companies used 54 per cent of their profits to buy back their own stock. That equated to $2.4 trillion being invested in shares, rather than in innovation, technology, staff or new products. A further 37 per cent of their earnings were given to shareholders as dividends. As Lazonick notes, 'That left very little for investments in productive capabilities or higher incomes for employees.[8]

Why should those of us without a stock portfolio care if corporate executives decide to sink their firm's quarterly profits into share buy-backs? In short, because this impacts us all. This practice is contributing to the disturbing trend of workers' share of income falling to record lows. There's no incentive to pay workers more or deliver better services or products, and it's a clear case of benefit trickling up, widening that inequality divide. Since share options are a large part of executive pay packages, when the profits that historically funded wage increases or other forms of reinvestment are instead spent on boosting the value of the firm's stocks, executives are effectively increasing their own take-home pay.

Another way this trend towards financialisation is playing itself out is through investing in speculative instruments: in a nutshell, betting on whether or not there's demand for a certain product or betting against that industry. You might achieve a return on investing your capital in production, sure: but if you can make double that by betting on speculation, isn't it just sound management to bet rather than produce? It's risky, but if you hedge your bets, the rewards are real and lucrative. We'll dive into this later, when we look at the tug of war between the real economy (where you and I live and work) and its shadow, the realm of FIRE (finance, insurance and real-estate speculation), which is swallowing up and abstracting productive capital, with real-world impacts for us all.

Unify the precariat

There's a big difference between worker-owned business and the 'flexible' gig economy model we're seeing eating the world of work. Today's union-busting, wage-shrinking monopolies have a shiny, participatory gloss to them: in their telling of the story, they're not ripping workers off or causing a race to the bottom in standards and wages, they're allowing everyone to make money on the side in a flexible, easy way.

German columnist Sascha Lobo is credited with coining the term 'platform capitalism' way back in 2014. Then, many people were optimistic about the potential of the new digital platforms to open up new markets for makers and writers (you could sell to the world on Etsy, Amazon or eBay), help people make some cash from their spare room or holiday house (everyone's a hotelier on Airbnb) and make or save money getting around town (as a driver or rider on Uber).

'Platforms do not want to be the best in the game, they want to determine the rules of the game,' Lobo wrote.[9]

Lobo pointed out that for all their talk of innovation, these new icons of platform capitalism are old-fashioned middlemen cloaked in tech and the language of flexibility and empowerment. Despite their colossal size and brand domination, they're not actually profitable: instead, they're backed by seemingly endless venture capital money that allows them to rapidly outpace any competition, to become market giants with unchallengeable monopolies over their sectors. All that liquidity (translation:

cash) has come thanks to more money floating around the financial economy, far from the real economy, and we see all these destructive trends rolling together at the expense of people in their working lives.

Uber has still never had a profitable quarter: in three months in 2019 alone, they lost US$5.2 billion. They're spending big to claim market dominance, and then, as Sacha Lobo points out, they'll be able to change the rules of the game.

So, why should this bother us? Aren't we all benefiting from these companies providing cheaper prices, greater convenience and more options? Maybe. But those savings come at a big cost down the line. Whether we work for them or not, the platform giants are also playing a major role in redesigning the world of work, shifting expectations and conditions.

A recent study from the Australian National University splintered Australians based on economic, social and cultural capital, and it identified six class-types. These are more nuanced than the working/middle/upper distinctions we're used to: 'precariat', 'ageing workers', 'new workers', 'mobile middle', 'emerging affluent', and 'established affluent'. In this study, 13 per cent of the respondents were classed as part of the precariat.[10] The term 'precariat' (a blend of precarious and proletariat) was first used in France in the 1980s to refer to agricultural workers, but it has leapt into headlines in the 21st century as more and more people around the world have found themselves sourcing their income through apps from Uber to Freelancer, Deliveroo, Foodora, UpWork and Airtasker, or working in traditional workplaces, but as contractors rather than employees, thanks to the fissuring process we explored earlier.

Amazon claimed the mantle as the world's most valuable company in early 2019: their profits skyrocket as they bank on the desperation of the precariat in their distribution chain. Head to ama zondeliversjobs.com and look up CamperForce, their recruitment tool for the people who roam the United States in campervans. CamperForce offers this nomadic precariat free campsites, $15 an hour and insurance in return for three months of their labour: picking, packing, stowing and sorting in their massive 'fulfilment centres' for the big Christmas shopping rush.

In her 2018 book, *Nomadland,* writer Jessica Bruder trailed the rolling precariat from desert campsites and distribution warehouses around the USA, and found the vast majority of CamperForce workers, are 'grey nomads'.[11] Usually that's a term associated with happy retirees in caravans and mobile homes, wandering the countryside at their leisure. However, this is a cohort of more financially stressed older American workers who now find themselves on the road as part of the precariat. Many of them lost their savings or saw the value of their home and maybe other nest eggs plummet in the 2008 global financial crisis. And so, dislocated by the financial market, these people are scooped up by another arm of the machine to be cheap seasonal labour for the tech-platform monopolies.

At the other end of their supply chain, Amazon Flex draws on precariat workers to deliver packages for their rapid-fire Prime Now service. To secure delivery 'blocks' (otherwise known as a single delivery job), workers have to constantly refresh the Flex app. To give you a sense of the associated anxiety, this has led to the creation of 'block grabber' devices that can automatically refresh and tap the Flex app up to 800 times a minute. The company claims Flex workers can make up to $25 an hour. Reporting suggests very few of these independent contractors do, especially once they've covered all their own car and fuel costs, and of course, they lack the job security, health insurance or other benefits employees are entitled to.

But, the argument goes, aren't these Flex workers and grey nomads just making a choice: flexibility over stability, freedom over security? I've even heard some commentators suggest that 'Millennials don't like commitment' and so are choosing a job-free, gig-based lifestyle. Are those workers making conscious, empowered trade-offs or are they being exploited? Who can say? Isn't the opportunity to choose your own work hours or seasons opening work up to more people, who might have been excluded by the old ways of working?

Guy Standing, a British professor of development, has pointed out that there's a tension in how the precariat view themselves and are portrayed in media: 'between the precariat as victims, penalised and demonised by mainstream institutions and policies, and the precariat as heroes, rejecting those institutions in a concerted act of intellectual and emotional defiance'.[12]

He says the precariat isn't just made up of backpackers delivering dinners to fund their gap year or retirees who need a little extra income. The precariat is diverse: it includes highly educated sessional academics who can't get permanent positions at universities, and therefore can't apply for research funding or further their careers, while at the same time including manual labourers, new migrants, the under-skilled or those left behind by industry-scale shifts, as well as those left out by language or age. Increasingly, whole swathes of generations are finding themselves in the precariat as the traditional career pathways evaporate for the young or older workers find themselves pushed out of jobs and unable to land new roles thanks to ageism. Young and old, educated or not, the ranks of the precariat are swelling: Standing estimates that in some countries, a quarter of working-age adults are in the precariat.

Standing points out the significant challenges of the precariat experience: the low incomes and the need to manage costs of living while relying on irregular, insecure work. But, he says, the biggest challenge is emotional: the deep sense of vulnerability and alienation. There's the lack of social support networks and work-based identity that you get from being part of a team, and the rumbling, continuous anxiety that comes from not knowing if you'll get enough gigs to pay the bills. Standing also suggests that many in the precariat harbour a simmering anger, a feeling of being denied the progress and upward mobility of a 'career ladder' that previous generations have taken for granted, 'leaving people hovering between deeper self-exploitation and disengagement'.[13]

The precariat are likely to be those most impacted by economic contraction through the COVID-19 shutdown, with very few workplace rights and protections and outdated industrial relations frameworks that render them invisible.

Here's what we've lost as work has fissured from jobs and careers have become more precarious. *New York Times* writer Neil Irwin compared the career trajectories of two cleaners, each working for the tech giants of their day: one who worked for Kodak in the 1980s and the other who cleans the Apple offices today. Gail Evans, the 1980s Kodak cleaner, progressed through the company and had career development opportunities offered to her by managers who noticed her interests and capacity. This led to college study, and Gail eventually becoming chief technology officer of the whole company. While hers is clearly an exceptional story, the comparison with Marta Ramos, today's Apple cleaner, is stark. To begin with, she isn't employed by Apple, but by a contract cleaning firm, in keeping with the fissuring and outsourcing trends discussed earlier. She has little contact with employees at the tech giant, despite cleaning their headquarters daily. No career progression is open to her other than being promoted to a team leader at the cleaning services company, which would secure her an extra 50 cents an hour.[14]

There's another big trend operating here: the business giants of this century are employing fewer people than their counterparts of the recent past. Irwin compares the direct workforces of Apple, Alphabet (parent of Google) and Facebook today, who collectively have 205,000 employees worldwide, with their 1993 peers, Kodak, IBM and AT&T, who between them employed 675,000 people. Not only do today's giants employ three times fewer people, they're doing so while making 30 per cent more revenue than their 20th-century equivalents. In 2016, those 205,000 employees earned Apple, Alphabet and Facebook US$333 billion of revenue combined.

Many of these platform giants go to extraordinary lengths to avoid having employees on their books. It's a battle they recently lost in California: after concerted campaigns by drivers and workers' rights advocates, Assembly Bill 5 was signed into law in September 2019. Also known as the 'gig worker law', this law attempts to have delivery and rideshare app drivers classified as employees, not independent contractors. But the exploitative Uber, Lyft and food delivery business model is so seat-of-the-pants it would collapse if they had to treat their drivers like employees by actually paying minimum wage and offering health insurance and other benefits to drivers. It's estimated a workforce of employees would cost them 20 to 30 per cent more than a workforce of contractors under the conditions they currently impose. Assembly Bill 5 is a great step, though the battle isn't over yet, and you can expect that these companies will throw all the cash they can at this threat. At the time of writing, Uber, Lyft and DoorDash had sunk US$90 million into a fighting fund for a ballot initiative in

2020 to ask voters to give them an exemption.

Almost all the benefits and protections workers enjoy have been hard-won by unions, fighting over decades: but the trend toward fissuring at the heart of the platform giants meant that, almost everywhere, precariat workers are seen as independent contractors, not employees, and haven't traditionally been represented by unions. We're seeing the first few steps towards change. In September 2019, Norway's 600 Foodora riders did what unionised workforces have done for decades to achieve change – they went on strike, then proceeded to negotiate a collective bargaining agreement to secure better wages and for some of their essential equipment expenses like bicycle maintenance and smart phones to be covered as part of their employment.[15] In October 2019, 17 of Japan's 15,000 Uber Eats delivery riders gathered together and began the process of unionising, demanding better conditions such as workers compensation insurance, more transparency over their payments and a clearer process for being suspended from the platform.[16] In early 2020, Foodora delivery riders in one Canadian province were given the green light to begin to create their own union, as the Ontario Labour Relations Board ruled that the riders weren't independent contractors (as the platforms always argue), but actually dependent workers. It's a good start, but having been ruled eligible, now the riders need to get at least 40 per cent of the Foodora workforce to sign up, a major challenge when the platform is holding a lot of the cards and the power differential is significant.[17]

Change is rising in the precariat beyond the platform, too. There is a new trend of 'upstart unions', unions representing contract and precarious workers that slip through the cracks of traditional unions, from hospital cleaners working for subcontractors to sex workers.[18] The UK's United Voices of the World has fought for precariat workers to be paid the London Living Wage[19] and for access to personal protective equipment during the pandemic, and they've got an inclusive approach that includes sub-branches such as United Strippers of the World[20] (who supported workers to form an online coop strip club during lockdown) and Designers and Cultural Workers.[21] This is exactly the kind of union I wish we had here; I would have joined it: they advocate against unpaid internships and endless uncompensated overtime, among many other poor workplace conditions that are considered par for the course in the creative industries. They argued for rent freezes on studio space, for example, or for income support during the pandemic, when almost 50 per cent of UK creative workers found themselves ineligible for support because they operate in non-traditional ways:[22] something I and many others experienced in Australia too.[23]

These are hopeful signs that the precariat are organising to reclaim some of the workplace rights that have been fissured and lost, and to make sure the new world of work has some of the protections that thousands fought to secure in the past.

We need to tell a broader story when we talk about work. The rise of the precariat isn't solely about individual career choices and a result of personal preferences. Nor, as is sometimes suggested, is it about a generational shift in the way people want to work. This is a broader structural shift in the work opportunities that are open to people, resulting from a combination of technological change, the incentives to 'efficiency' that come from financialisation and globalisation, and the fissuring of work from employment.

So, what can we do about it?

Transition to the democratic economy

The alternative is the democratic economy.

The democratic economy entails putting the idea of common good – which is supposed to be at the foundation of democracy in politics – into the way we run business and manage the economy too. It means seeing more employees have a stake in the places they work, and for businesses to have a positive obligation to establish models that are socially as well as environmentally responsible. In other words, not voraciously consuming the resources and energies of your community.

It sounds basic, but so many of the fundamentals of the business world lack this sense of fairness or consequence. The 'fiduciary duty' (or ethical obligation) of a company director, for example, is often construed as being a responsibility to maximise profits for owners and shareholders by any means necessary. This could mean spending money to lobby governments to cut environmental protections that might increase costs or cutting workforce numbers or employee pay so as to squeeze out higher returns. The owners and shareholders who are the beneficiaries of this effort might live a million miles away from the business. Their personal involvement – transacted on paper or online – might last only for the heartbeat length of time of a flurry of stockmarket trades. This is in stark contrast to the daily experiences of the people who power the business with their ideas and time every single day, sometimes for years or whole careers.

People and planet are costs to be cut in the business-as-usual model, while the democratic economy recognises the reality that there is no business without them.

You can't atone for cost-cutting, resource-guzzling or employee-squeezing by adding some feel-good bunting to your business's front window. The Corporate Social Responsibility manager isn't going to be able to do this by organising fundraisers and internships, and the marketing department won't be able to do it with clever sponsorship deals or woke social media comms. If we want to see this model change, and for business to be a force for good, we have to get down to the foundations and embed real, human-centred values at the heart of the businesses we run, work in and support.

The Democracy Collaborative is a research and advisory group based at the University of Maryland in Cleveland that helps communities unlock their own latent potential. Marjorie Kelly and Ted Howard from the Democracy

Collaborative have outlined seven principles of a democratic economy: community, inclusion, place, good work, sustainability, democratic ownership and ethical finance.

This rings true to me as I've seen it in action time and time again, and you'll notice many of these principles threaded through the stories in this book. When you put human values and valuing humans at the core of business, people share in prosperity. Individuals who've been excluded from today's mainstream are invited in to contribute and be counted. When you're rooted in and belong to the place where you base your business, your business is likely to be a mindful environmental consumer and performer and attempt to leave the lightest possible footprint around you. When people do work that helps others, and have a say in how their companies are run, strong social ties result and workers enjoy multiple benefits.

Ted and Marjorie write:

'A democratic economy designs social architectures around what we value, with community and sustainability the alpha and omega, our interrelatedness and interdependence at the center. It involves the development of what ecologists call symbioses. As conservationist Aldo Leopold once put it, "Politics and economics are advanced symbioses" in which free-for-all competition is replaced by structures for co-operation.'[24]

They've helped organisations put these ideas into practice by working with Councillor Matthew Brown in Preston, UK, and in cities across the USA, most famously in Cleveland, Ohio, in an ecosystem of co-operation around the Evergreen Laundry.

Powered by Evergreen Energy Solutions, a solar energy company, and connected to Green City Growers, an urban vegetable farm, this network of co-operatives is employee-owned and focused on drawing out the talents of people who've been excluded from the economy, particularly people who've been caught up in America's toxic criminal justice system. They're committed to place, and have grown steadily, secure in serving 'anchor institutions', large for-purpose entities like hospitals and universities, which also have deep roots.

The Evergreen ecosystem keeps money circulating locally rather than being extracted for distant shareholders – at the end of the year, the over 200 employee-owners are entitled to a share in the value they create, which in 2018 saw them take home a $4000 bonus. Worker–owners even benefit from a home-renewal and subsidy program that has supported 21 of them to purchase their own homes at an affordable price, and to pay for it through a salary sacrifice mechanism.

I can imagine what you're thinking: if these worker-owned and co-operative models are so great, why aren't there more of them?

Well, there are a lot more than you'd think. Ed Mayo, the Secretary General of Co-operatives UK, takes me through a list of transformative co-op powered projects around the world, from coffee co-ops with gender equality committees in Nicaragua to affordable housing and First Nations economic development co-ops in Vancouver, Canada, 15,000 renewable energy communities in Brussels, Belgium to Unimed, Brazil's health co-operative that serves 20 million people.

By Ed's calculations, one billion of us around the world are members of a co-operative or mutual enterprise: there are three times more member owners of co-operatives than individual shareholders worldwide.[25] Often, we don't even know we're in a co-op or benefitting from a mutualised form of business where benefits to members are the primary goal: you may be a member if you're part of an industry superannuation fund, for example.

'They tend to be the business models for social change. There are a huge variety of organisational forms for commoning, but the key characteristics for voice, accountability and collective action mean co-ops are the model to do that,' Ed says.

I mean, he would say that: he's holding a co-op slogan mug and wearing the T-shirt as he says it. But he's got the research to back it up.

Co-ops and mutuals tend to provide better conditions and less hierarchical organisations, which boosts fairness within businesses, but they're also a positive contributor to the communities around them, as they tend to be connected to networks of local suppliers, keeping money doing good locally as we saw in Preston. 'It's up-close rather than distant ownership,' he says.

In his research, Ed points to the Emilia Romagna region in Northern Italy: 'Co-operatives generate close to 40 per cent of economic production [GDP] in Emilia Romagna and notably, it is the region of Europe with the lowest social-economic inequality between the rich and the poor.'

Ed tells me the biggest stumbling block to the growth of these democratic, inclusive business models is access to capital: banks tend to see the least risk in lending to one owner or a more traditional corporate form, which is why we see so many Pty Ltds rather than more businesses taking a democratic form. That's what our next change agent is enabling.

***

Sometimes people say a movie changed their lives. In Brendan Martin's case, that film was *The Take,* the 2004 documentary by Avi Lewis and Naomi Klein. Its exploration of the rise of worker-owned business in Argentina showed Brendan an alternative to the dominant system.

'That's what I was driven by when I wanted to study economics: what would be a system that would be different, that wouldn't put property and profit in the centre, but that was good for people and planet or other things that should be sacred?' he explains.

'Within a few months of seeing the film and meeting [filmmakers Avi and Naomi], I was on a plane with Avi flying to Argentina to meet people down there to open up The Working World, to try and see if we could replicate a commons-owned financial source that would help generate these worker-owned co-operatives.'

In the 1990s, Argentina had received the same inflate-debt-and-strip-assets treatment many corporations have experienced in hostile takeovers: except applied on a country-wide scale by the International Monetary Fund (IMF). Arriving in Argentina with Avi Lewis,

Brendan witnessed the resulting devastation. The IMF policies had encouraged Argentina's government to take out massive loans to fund projects to be delivered by big international infrastructure, accountancy, logistics firms. When the big winners left town, Argentina was left holding the debt. Suddenly, working Argentinians found the owners of their workplaces stripping and selling assets, leaving them without employment while public spending contracted. Workers created their own solutions by running the businesses themselves, but they lacked a line of credit to either buy reluctant owners out, pay for upgrades or cover cash-flow shortfalls. Even today, worker-owned businesses are viewed by lenders and investors as out-of-the-ordinary and too risky to back. That's the problem Brendan set out to solve by creating The Working World, a new form of finance for worker-owned enterprise, one that seeks to be 'non-extractive finance'.

In the loans they negotiate, The Working World ensures that the borrower gets paid a living wage, can put aside capital for replacing their equipment, and generally benefits before the loan is paid off. 'So you'd say that at least half the wealth creation stays with the labour.'

Since 2005, The Working World have connected co-ops and worker-owned businesses with millions in patient capital – money designed to generate benefit in the real world, for real people and communities, which can often take longer and yield more modest returns. The Working World helps businesses convert from traditional models of one owner to many workers, to worker-owned business models, by stepping in to offer lines of credit and start-up capital, loans to buy equipment and cover cash-flow shortfalls, and even the initial loans that help workers buy out business owners and convert their operations to a worker-owned model. As non-extractive, patient lenders, they've made loans between $5000 and $1,000,000, on average providing about $100,000 to each business. The model has been highly effective. Encouragingly, The Working World have a 98 per cent repayment rate and have expanded their operations to include Nicaragua in 2008 and the USA from 2012.

Brendan took inspiration from the world's most celebrated co-operative ecosystem, Mondragon. Named after the town in northern Spain where it's based, Mondragon is shorthand for a network of worker-owned co-operatives which have transformed the region since the 1950s. The Mondragon Corporation has an annual turnover of €15 billion (about AU$24.4 billion) across 250 co-operatives and linked organisations and more than 80,000 workers.

While Spain's economy suffered for several years after the 2008 global financial crisis and the public sector austerity that followed, Mondragon co-ops tightened their belts, cut profits and wages but avoided layoffs; they had only one closure.[26] They had the resilience across their network to move workers around to meet new demands and to cushion against the impacts of the crisis. With their shared sense of purpose and common stake, it made sense to take a temporary hit for the sake of long-term viability.

As Brendan sees it, at the heart of the Mondragon success story is access to finance that prioritises the real, local economy. When finance is there for public benefit, not private shareholder (or executive) profit, the benefits flow outwards and there's more stability as a result.

They have a source of finance that was not a 'for profit': it wasn't a profit-maximising bank. It was a bank that was there solely for the benefit of the community to use that property to make a worker-run co-operative or make co-operative insurance or a co-operative grocery store. So, it was a resource: like a community that had water that they shared based on rules of the commons, on governance of the common for the general benefit. Obviously, those things are always contested and talked about and debated about and voted on. But that was the overriding goal of this bank: which never went bankrupt, never had a run [on deposits], never needed government assistance, always was profitable but never became outsized in the economy, never began to swallow most of the benefits, which continue to spread out [across] the rest of the town of Mondragon and that financial region around it.

Through The Working World, Brendan is providing that resource to worker-owned enterprise in the Americas, helping businesses transition to democratic models of ownership at a moment of great demographic change that's sometimes labelled the 'silver tsunami'.

The generation we call the Baby Boomers, born after World War Two, have benefited from an economy, finance and social welfare system that worked more fairly (more or less) than the current one. Many Baby Boomers established family-run businesses that are still operating today. As these business owners retire, there's an opportunity for employees to buy the founders out and create a new generation of fairer, sustainable worker-owned businesses on these foundations.

This demographic transition is an opportunity to convert the (literal) business-as-usual model to a democratic form of business that gives workers a better deal.

Brendan explains:

The possibility of conversion is one that we believe in pretty strongly ... You don't have to be a start-up [to benefit from being a worker-owned business]. But there are challenges conversion has: it's hard to change the culture of a 30-year-old business. So, it's more of a cultural problem, whereas if a start-up, it's more of a marketing problem: how do you gain market share?

We're not just trying to create a whole new economy one by one; we want to [also] take the existing economy and change it. So, conversion is a good idea, especially given the silver tsunami opportunity.

So, we've done about ten conversions so far. A lot of them are on the small side ... and we're looking out to do much bigger ones with a few million dollars per business range. We're really trying to explore it and grow it as a potential avenue of work beyond the start-ups or working with existing co-ops and grow them.

According to Brendan, by their nature, worker-owned co-ops tend to have broader ambitions than just 'the immediate bottom-line interest'. They're embedded in their communities, rather than distant and removed, and therefore the people involved are predisposed to being more conscious of the environmental and social impacts they're responsible for.

I don't know any co-operative we work with that didn't have some sense of a broader impact – beyond just increasing the workers' salary – that didn't have some kind of cross-community benefit of people learning from it or having some awareness of the ecology – things like that.

The idea of a co-operative is: the workers run it so they can bring all their values to the table ... the workers can do whatever they want with it. And if they decide that they only need to work five hours a day and it makes enough money for them, they can do it. If they decide they shouldn't pollute the river, even if it costs them a little more, [then they don't pollute the river]. They very frequently will balance the desire for a greater amount of money with other things: like quality of life, but also better impact on their neighbourhood, their local ecology

...You have people – usually from the local ecology who are around there – and their families, and staff who can represent them. What you put in the river, you kind of see it in your face – it's not owned by outside investors that are far far away and never see it: they have to think about the concrete impact they're having.

In 2020, The Working World is on target to have distributed US$20 million of loans since its establishment. From the start, they've sourced their capital from philanthropists, foundations and people investing their retirement funds, but now they're hoping to also source investment from impact investment funds, which are pools of capital dedicated to prosocial ends. By funding democratic ownership models, The Working World is doing the structural work of making business benefit people and planet. But, warns Brendan, they're not the silver bullet solution: 'It's a starting point. It's a good place to organise from and try to build community around, not a finish line. It's a starting point by changing where the power is held.'

5

Reward the human

Does your pay packet bear any relationship to your impact in the world? In 2019, Oxfam reported that the 26 richest people in the world own the same amount of wealth as the 3.8 billion poorest people.[1] The year before, 43 people owned as much wealth as half the world's population – making it clear that trickle-down economics is a myth. The reality is that abundance and wealth are trickling up. Over the course of 2018, the wealth of billionaires (there are 2200 of them) grew by $2.5 billion a day: their wealth increased by 12 per cent while the wealth of the world's poorest half shrunk by 11 per cent. According to projections by the UK House of Commons Library, if we continue on our current trajectory, the richest 1 per cent of people will hold 64 per cent of all wealth by the year 2030.[2]

So, why is this happening? Why are the astronomically rich getting richer, at a breakneck speed, while the poor are getting poorer, and the rest of us feel like we're frantically working harder than ever simply to make ends meet?

As discussed in our last chapter, wage growth has stagnated across the developed world as the f-word trends result in incomes becoming more constrained and precarious. At the same time, returns on wealth (whether that's real estate, shares or other investments) are growing at about 5 per cent a year.[3] Yes, automation and new technology has played a part, as has the shifting of work to the developing world through globalisation. But the bald fact is you just cannot earn enough by your hard work to match the returns that people receive merely for owning stuff: shares and property for the most part. If it feels like the rich are getting richer and everyone else is struggling just to keep their heads above water, that's why.

In researching this book, I've gathered that it's really common to have a version of this conversation – you may have had it yourself, with friends or family – 'Well, you know, capitalism isn't perfect, but it's the best system that we have, and it has lifted millions out of poverty' or 'I don't mind things being a bit unequal: if some people are working harder than others, they should be able to earn more.'

I can understand that. Historically, capitalism has played an important role in accelerating development and expanding people's quality of life in many parts of the world. Yes, some people do work very hard, make big sacrifices and deserve to be paid well. But if we take this line of argument seriously, we have to decide: what does hard work look like? What kind of work deserves big rewards, and what kind of value does it have to deliver to earn them? Who's decided this in the past and how should we decide for the future?

Here and now, in this moment of massive change and growing unfairness, we have the opportunity to confront the fundamental fact that our society doesn't properly reward a lot of the most important work that humans do today. Further, this undervalued work – caring – is exactly the type of employment that we're going to continue to need, even after the robots have come for our jobs. As well as being highly resistant to automation, caring jobs generate the lightest environmental footprint and the lowest negative externalities while providing the most essential services to producing healthy, happy, resilient humans and a working ecosystem.

By caring jobs, I mean educating children, caring for infants, children, the elderly and people with disabilities, caring for our planet and restoring natural ecosystems. The more I learn, the more I realise the deeply human and crucial work of the caring economy needs to be at the foundation of a fairer future. Philosopher Eva Feder Kittay puts it beautifully:

'People do not spring up from the soil like mushrooms. People produce people. People need to be cared for and nurtured throughout their lives by other people, at some times more urgently and more completely than at other times. Who is available to do the labor of care and who gets the care they require is contingent on political and social organisation.'[4]

None of us spring up like mushrooms, are born fully grown or stay in the independent prime of our lives forever. So, if we've all been cared for and know that we're all likely to need care in the future, we must at some deep level know that caring is fundamental to society and productivity. Ai-jen Poo from the US National Domestic Workers Alliance calls it 'the work that makes other work possible',[5] and she's absolutely right.

So, why do we tolerate a 'political and social organisation' that undervalues or erases this work?

Anthropologist David Graeber has written about the rise of what he calls 'bullshit jobs'[6] and the historical disconnect between the social utility of a job and how it's valued in our economy. He draws the distinction between *value* (which is something we can put a price on) and *values* (the unquantifiable, desirable, altruistic and socially useful). This distinction is one of the reasons why, as a society, we tolerate useful tasks being unpaid or underpaid: we've allowed ourselves to swallow the line that 'moral benefit' – feeling like your work matters and is making a difference – is its own reward. But warm fuzzy glows don't pay the bills.

In Australia, the 'health care and social assistance' sector employs the greatest number of people of any one sector – almost 13 per cent of workers, or about 1.5 million people – but those workers are likely to be paid between $800 and $900 a week, about half the full-time weekly average for the country, which is $1811 per week for men and $1516 for women (yes, the gender pay gap is a real thing). Many of the jobs in this sector are classed as 'low skill': something that doesn't ring true if you've ever had to care for a toddler or an elderly relative with dementia. Many of these jobs take a high physical and emotional toll on workers, require patience, compassion and love, and span hours well beyond the nine to five.

There's a highly gendered reason for this pay disparity and low regard: caring is considered women's work. In Australia, more than 95 per cent of child-care workers and 75 per cent of nursing support workers are female,[7] but they earn about half the hourly rate of a metal fitter, an industrial worker with the same level of qualifications. Back in 2013, unions United Voice and the Australian Education Union launched an equal pay case for early childhood workers with the Fair Work Commission, using the metal fitter as a comparative case. Unfortunately, in 2018 the Commission dismissed the case, refusing to see the correlation between the skills required in both roles. Their conclusion reinforces the structural devaluation of caring work as low-skilled work, mostly because it's carried out by women, and our society is used to getting it for free.

Feminist Gloria Steinem put it like this:

> The truth was (and still is) that in the United States as in almost every country, categories of work are less likely to be paid by the expertise they require – or even by importance to the community or to the often mythical free market – than by the sex, race, and class of most of their workers.

Work is valued by the social value of the worker. A category of work is paid least when women do it, somewhat more when almost any variety of men do it, and much more when men of the 'right' race or class do it.[8]

Plainly, there's a long way to go to transform the way we see and reward the care economy. It's not something that should solely be done out of a sense of duty either. Even if you use the limiting metrics of economic growth, it makes sense on paper too. A study by the UK Women's Budget Group (more on them soon) of seven OECD countries, including Australia, found that if governments invested 2 per cent of GDP in the care economy, it would yield an increase in employment that would be double a similar investment in construction. That's worth repeating: you'd get twice as many jobs and you'd reduce the gender employment gap by investing in the care economy over the construction economy.

This research is out there, yet whenever governments pursue big 'nation-building' projects, the focus is always on the hardware of our society: roads, rail and ports are seen as infrastructure and investments in our economy, while hospitals, schools, elder and child care are seen as costs. The reality is that investments in our caring economy yield more long-term jobs and have multiplier effects across the economy, unlocking more productivity and improving people's quality of life.

In this chapter, we'll meet leaders who are reframing care work as the most essential work for social and environmental wellbeing – contributing to our common wealth – and finding new business and tax models to reward these most human and nurturing of the professions and vocations. Can we reconnect the generation of wealth with the creation of value to society, rather than rewarding the fields that enhance private wealth, damage the planet and exacerbate inequality, as we do now?

Invest in social infrastructure

If we want to – need to – change course, we have to ask: how did we get here? This stuff falls squarely under culture, not nature. Humans set up this system, so let's ask why it's built this way and take charge of changing it.

For a long time, we've been told that some parts of our society are economically productive, generating income and fuelling GDP, while others are socially useful but classed as expenses. In this worldview, you have the business sector who are the 'wealth creators' – particularly those visionary entrepreneurs and the daring investors who back them – but never the academic researchers or public servants who generate and invest in long-term innovation. At the other end of the spectrum is the slow, lumbering public sector, including all those high-cost high-touch services, like education and healthcare, and the altruistic not-for-profit sector. These sectors are seen as well-intentioned but inefficient: all outgoings and no revenue.

This extremely narrow view of the world is currently the invisible, unchallenged foundation of our decision-making. Philosopher Hannah Arendt unpicked the trail of what work is considered 'productive' and 'unproductive', and laid the blame right at the (kitchen) doors of the two grandfathers of our economic system: 18th- and 19th-century political philosophers Adam Smith and Karl Marx.[9] Neither of them had any respect for the domestic sphere (Arendt says their attitude to domestic work bordered on contempt), and so they categorised all work in the household (cooking, cleaning, care and often at that time, education) as unproductive work, contributing only to the economy as a source of consumption.

Arendt maintains that Marx had transposed the Ancient Greek ideas of the division between the public and private sphere into a contemporary context, recreating a gulf between household activity and the broader economy that simply didn't exist anywhere, except in theory.

She wrote: 'In the modern world, the two realms indeed constantly flow into each other like waves in the never-resting stream of the life process itself.'[10]

That's a lot more like the world we live in. In unrelated news, Adam Smith lived at home with his mother for most of his life (she died when he was 61), who helpfully provided all the 'unproductive' care that allowed him to write his economic theories. After she died, his cousin Janet took over his care. (Read *Who Cooked Adam Smith's Dinner?* by Katrine Marcal if you'd like to get really mad about that epic blind spot.) As for Karl Marx: his wife, Jenny von Westphalen, gave up her aristocratic privilege to follow her own passionate political beliefs in socialism and women's rights and wrote about the marginalisation of women even within the radical left, something she experienced first hand. She was instrumental in all of Marx's writing and activism, transcribed his ideas into manuscripts, fought to hold their family together through bankruptcies, exiles and that time Karl impregnated their housekeeper. Forgive me if I'm sceptical of how these two guys viewed the role of care in the economy.

In the early 1970s, economist John Kenneth Galbraith called out how reliant the economy was (and still is) on the unpaid, invisible labour of care in the household and beyond. His characterisation of the housewifely ideal as a 'crypto-servant class' will give chills to anyone who's found themselves bearing the mental load in managing a household. He also called out those 'convenient social virtues' (those warm and fuzzy feelings I mentioned earlier) that are designed to replace actual payment for providing the public goods of care and compassion. He wrote:

> The conversion of women into a crypto-servant class was an economic accomplishment of the first importance. Menially employed servants were available only to a minority of the pre-industrial population; the servant-wife is available, democratically, to almost the entire present male population. Were the workers so employed subject to pecuniary compensation, they would be by far the largest single category in the labour force. The value of services of housewives has been calculated, somewhat impressionistically, at roughly one

fourth of total Gross National Product.[11]

Okay, I'm off on a tangent – but the point I'm making is important. Just as the natural environment has been labelled an 'externality', and polluting it a cost that doesn't appear on a company's balance sheet, the entire world of care is classed as 'unproductive', an expense and not an investment, based to a large extent on the biases and blindspots of a couple of flawed guys from different times. Thankfully, the world has changed a lot since the days of Adam and Karl, but we've built their biases into the foundation of our economy, and that's no basis for a functional, fair future. This has major repercussions for how we reward care, who gets paid for it, and how we include it in our future plans.

None of this is new: there's a reason why there's an entire field of feminist economics, a philosophical field called the ethics of care, and – since at least the 1970s – a call for wages for housework.[12]

While the battle has raged for a long time, the moment has caught up with the movement. Could this be our chance to change how we reward some of the most valuable contributors to our society, without the biases of yesterday, and with a greater understanding of our planetary limits?

Properly valuing care work has compound benefits for society, the planet and the economy. The International Labour Organization, the United Nation's 100-year-old advocacy and research arm in the world of work, is championing care work as one of the key drivers to help the world reach the targets of the Sustainable Development Goals (SDGs), close the gender pay gap, and deliver more decent wages around the world.[13]

While jobs are contracting in other parts of the economy, care is a growth area: by 2030, an estimated 2.3 billion people will require care, and to meet that need, there's the potential to create 269 million new jobs.

To get there, we'll need to increase, not reduce, what we invest in the care economy. All those 'budget-saving' and 'efficiency-dividend' measures cutting health and education budgets have to stop. Governments must be convinced of the benefit of investing in their human capital and care economies, and to double their investment in the care economy to about 18.3 per cent of GDP by 2030. It sounds like a big shift, but consider this: the United States already spends 17.9 per cent of their GDP on healthcare,[14] a very high percentage considering the uneven, unfair coverage that country is infamous for.

If we do this the right way, it's a win–win scenario: more stable, decent jobs are created; countries can meet their SDG obligations; more people can enter the workforce (with more child care, aged and disability carers unlocking productive potential, particularly for women); and we're more educated (the highest number of care-sector workers globally are in education) and healthier (as this expanded workforce helps to achieve healthcare for all). Care workers are then likely to spend their increased, decent wages in their local economies. This would be fiscal stimulus – that's the spending governments make to jump-start the economy – with substantial positive flow-on effects.

The UK Women's Budget Group, together with the Scottish Women's Budget Group – collectively known as the WBG – are among the economists and advocates leading the charge towards a new way of valuing care and transforming the economy. Researchers from the WBG examined seven wealthy OECD countries around the world – Australia, Denmark, Germany, Italy, Japan, the UK and the USA. They looked at public and private spending on care, as well as employment and earnings in the care versus the construction industries, then modelled the impact of government investments in these two sectors. Essentially, they did the maths on what it would mean for governments to direct fiscal stimulus policies into social or caring infrastructure – education, social care and health services – rather than physical infrastructure, the usual 'nation-building' approach we see in times of slowing growth, such as building roads, railways or school halls (as Australia did as a stimulus measure after the GFC to the tune of AU$14 billion[15] on primary school halls).

Modelling by the WBG showed that a 2 per cent investment of GDP in the care economy would increase employment by between 2.4 per cent to 6.1 per cent across the countries they studied. They estimate up to 13 million new jobs could be created in the USA, 3.5 million in Japan, nearly 2 million in Germany, 1.5 million in the UK, 1 million in Italy, 600,000 in Australia and nearly 120,000 in Denmark.[16]

That's mighty significant: under normal circumstances about 5 per cent of the Australian population are unemployed: that's about 700,000 people. Post the COVID-19 shutdown, those numbers are much higher.

An investment in social infrastructure would generate a lot of jobs and growth at a time when stable, reasonably well-paid jobs are in decline. Care is needed everywhere, which means these jobs could be created in precisely the kinds of regional and outer-urban communities that need solid, valued work the most.

It's not that the usual approach taken by governments in times of economic downturn, investing in physical infrastructure, doesn't result in jobs. What the WBG found, however, was that the same investment would result in half as many jobs and would increase rather than decrease the gender gap in employment. Sure, care-sector jobs would generate fewer shiny new projects with ribbons to cut, but there'd be more long-term jobs with ongoing tax and consumption benefits to show for it. It's easy to see where you'd get the biggest bang for the public buck.

Professor Sue Himmelweit is a feminist economist from the UK, a member of the WBG since the 1990s, and one of the authors of 'Investing in the Care Economy', the remarkable study into the impact of investments in 'hard' versus 'soft' infrastructure, comparing construction and care. I think it's one of the most forward-thinking pieces of research I've read: it sets out the opportunity for an economy that enhances the human experience and demonstrates that social spending on care isn't a hand-out but an investment that pays multiple dividends. While the opportunity that investment in care presents is massive, unfortunately we've been seeing the opposite from governments. After the GFC, many governments cut public-sector spending in austerity moves to pay for the financial-sector bailout, and there's a big risk that we'll see more of the same after the COVID-19 crisis. We need to be vigilant because care is often the first victim of austerity, and the sword doesn't fall on everyone equally. Sue explains that, shortly after the first austerity budget, a female MP asked the House of Commons Library to determine how gendered the impacts were, 'to say how much of it was paid for by men and how much for a women. And it was staggering. It was something like 81 per cent was paid for by women. And this is not to do with public services. This is simply the taxes and benefits side of it.'

This research found that, disproportionately, budget cuts made in the name of austerity took more from women than men, and then whenever moves were made to stimulate spending (such as through tax cuts or lifting the tax-free threshold, two classic conservative-government moves that are very familiar to us in Australia), women lost out again. Tax cuts reduce the available pool for government spending on social infrastructure like care, and hand more money back to higher earners, who are much more likely to be men.

In response, the WBG have championed PLAN F, a long-term feminist economic plan to invest in creating a caring and sustainable economy that prioritises care for people and for the planet. Funding care properly is at its core, with a brilliant source of income, the 'Maid Marion Tax'. This is a financial transactions tax that attacks the root cause of austerity, the speculation and greed of the financial sector, which is a tremendous social drain in the UK in particular.

By imposing a tiny 0.01 per cent tax on speculative financial transactions, the Maid Marion Tax would raise a staggering £20 billion (close to AU$40 billion) a year in the UK alone. In the WBG's proposal, this revenue is hypothecated (that is, gathered for a specific use) towards funding services that counterbalance the negative effects of austerity on women, and which increase women's economic empowerment, like social and child care.

Imagine the ways that kind of investment could change lives, enhance the quality of care and reward some of the most meaningful and lasting of the work we do as humans: caring for, educating and healing each other. It'd also have a bigger economic impact in the real economy than putting it into the pockets of the wealthy or, based on the WBG's research, than putting it into 'nation-building' construction projects. We've got to put this story on the agenda and refute the received wisdom when we're designing our way out of the inequality and climate crisis we're in.

Formalise domestic work

To build the fair future we want, we need to wrestle with the realities that care workers face all over the world. There's a host of problems to tackle, but thankfully there are also committed activists making progress against the invisibility and undervalued nature of care.

Since the 1970s, India's groundbreaking Self Employed Women's Association (SEWA) has been leading the way as a trade union that advocates for the vast numbers of 'cash-in-hand' women who work outside the official workforce. According to some estimates, as many as 93 per cent of women in India's labour force come under this category. There are no small numbers in a country as populous as India, but SEWA's are truly staggering: they have 1.5 million members across the subcontinent, and run co-operatives with over 300,000 members delivering services from child care to insurance.

Working outside traditional contracts or workplaces, SEWA members self-organise to set and uphold their own standards. They come up against patriarchal conceptions of the value of women's work and also the dehumanising caste system, which relegates whole communities to lower status and reduced working conditions.

Nalini Nayak from SEWA Kerala writes about how they challenged the dominant mindset by holding firm and simply refusing to contemplate client requests for workers of a particular caste or religion. She lists the gains domestic workers have made by working together: setting their own minimum wage (well above the government standard), establishing co-operatives and worker–producer companies and providing their members with access to finance through the SEWA bank, which was created because there was no access to credit for women.

In the USA, the National Domestic Workers Alliance (NDWA) are now trying to achieve something similar using high-tech tools. Starting in 2007, NDWA has identified the connection between domestic and care work, and the precarious conditions of the 'on-demand' workforce that has been enabled by technology. Domestic and care workers have been facing poor workplace conditions for longer than Airtasker or TaskRabbit have been around, but as these new platforms have grown, there have been more ways for workers to be exploited (and more workers to be put on a slippery slope) in the race-to-the-bottom on conditions and pay.

The NDWA are determined to establish a national standard for workers providing care in the home. They drafted a National Domestic Workers Bill of Rights, which was introduced to the US Congress and Senate in July 2019 in companion bills championed by Senator Kamala Harris and Representative Pramila Jayapal. The Act seeks to secure for domestic workers the kinds of workplace conditions most of us would expect, like standard hours or set breaks, overtime pay, a minimum wage, workers' compensation, unemployment benefits or the right to unionise. It's clearly necessary: 67 per cent of US domestic workers earn below the minimum wage.

It's staggering that people who work in other people's homes don't already have these basic protections, yet that's a common state of affairs around the world. But people (and they're overwhelmingly women) who provide child, elder or disability care in the home, or who carry out domestic duties for their work, aren't currently covered by US labour laws. This wasn't an oversight: when the Fair Labor Standards Act was introduced in the 1930s, domestic and farm workers were deliberately excluded.[17] This was a concession to southern states and highlights the racially loaded undertones to the treatment of care workers. Today, the situation is heightened by the US political climate of deportation; as many domestic workers are Latinx, they're less likely to assert their rights about poor working conditions or abuse.

The NDWA is fighting for three key principles for domestic workers: a living wage, a clear work agreement and paid time off. The last is particularly difficult to secure when domestic workers often make up their income by working for multiple employers, cleaning or caring in different households over the course of a week or month. As we've already seen, tech platforms have played a big role in eroding work standards, but what if these tech platforms were built for workers, by workers, themselves?

Through NDWA Labs, their in-house innovation arm, domestic workers have collaborated on the design of Alia, the world's first portable benefits platform, which helps workers accrue benefits like paid leave and insurance. It allows workplace benefits to travel with the worker, by making it easy for multiple employers to contribute to a single worker's account. It also helps gather days of paid leave by aggregating five-dollar contributions for a rainy day.

NDWA's solution aims for a decidedly difficult problem – helping bilingual workers in what has been primarily a cash economy, and where there's often a power differential between employer and employed – to build their own security within a gig economy. But, as NDWA's Ai-jen Poo observes, what happens on the margins soon becomes the mainstream: the experiences of care workers tend to predict where the economy is going in its treatment of everyone. By solving the hardest problem first, and centring one of the most vulnerable communities, this platform is a tool to enable a more equitable economy for everyone.

***

Carers aren't getting the treatment they deserve, even when they're the ones powering a transnational flow of money and labour that supports entire economies. Remittances – money being sent home – play an enormous role in many developing economies. Much of that income flows from domestic workers (and they're mostly women) from countries like the Philippines, Sri Lanka, Bangladesh and Cameroon, working in wealthier countries like Singapore, Hong Kong, Malaysia and across the Middle East.

Farah Salka and I have had a rather transnational correspondence in the lead-up to our conversation for this book. I first learned about her advocacy for migrant workers in Lebanon when I saw her speak at a conference in Austria, and we finally get a chance to video-chat while she's in Dubai at a meeting of the Arab Network for Migrant Rights. Our conversation focuses on Lebanon, but this issue is widespread across the Middle East, Asia and Europe. In the Middle East alone, it's estimated that there are over 25 million migrant workers, many of whom spend years of their lives working far from home, with little to no rights or freedoms.

Farah began her interest in activism and social justice with a strong feminist focus, and soon discovered that there was a feminist struggle in her country that was near invisible: supporting the migrant women working behind closed doors as domestic workers. Farah is now Executive Director of the Anti-Racism Movement (ARM), a collective of feminist activists and migrant workers who've organised to overcome this structural, government-enabled exploitation of women working in care. Farah says it's hard to get accurate figures on the number of domestic workers there are in Lebanon, but she says of the country's four million citizens and two million refugees, ARM estimates about 8 per cent are migrant women working as domestic labourers. She explains:

> The country cannot function for one day without all [the] care

services that they give at home because we live in a dysfunctional country that doesn't provide anything for its citizens. We don't have services for our elderly, we don't have affordable nurseries, we don't have proper public schools. So, there's so much reliance on all of these women doing the work at home. But with all this reliance and all this dependability, there is zero gratitude.

The majority here are always complaining and nagging about these women: that they don't know how to do their job well, that they're not employed full-function for 12 hours a day, that they are always asking for more, that they want to take two days rather than one day off, that they want to seek all the basic rights that any other worker has by default.

Farah explains that Lebanese labour law explicitly excludes a whole class of workers – those whose work could be considered to centre on private or family life. Among them are domestic workers, farmers and staff of family companies. A lack of rights is exacerbated by the *kafala* system (more on that shortly), a disregard for women's work and a deep-seated racism against Asians and Africans. The women who make up the majority of migrant domestic workers are from Asia and Africa.

'We rely on domestic workers – without them hotels won't work, the households won't work, the hospitals, et cetera. At the same time, we don't even consider them workers. We don't grant them the minimum wage, which is anyway very low; we don't grant them all the basic things that come with this: a specific number of working hours, specific numbers of annual leave days, health care, the right to quit decently,' Farah says.

In Lebanon, and in many other countries in the region, domestic workers operate under a sponsorship system called *kafala,* an immigration system that leaves these workers dependent on their employers for their ability to remain in the country, with very few rights or options if anything goes wrong. Many are required to hand over their passports to their employers on arrival, and their immigration status relies on those same employers. Migrant workers may live in a country with this status for decades and have children in the country. They and those children aren't considered citizens – they can often be deported to homelands they've never seen – while, in their workplaces, the power imbalance makes underpayment and exploitation commonplace. It's rare for a domestic worker to have set working hours or more than one day off a week, if that. In extreme cases, they're isolated, vulnerable to violence and abuse, and there are terrible stories of workers who haven't been allowed outside their homes for years.

Despite the entrenched, systemic nature of this problem, Farah and the ARM are making progress in working to denormalise the abuse of domestic workers in Lebanese society. They have created Migrant Care Centres across Lebanon (in Beirut, Saida, Hamra and Jounieh) – places where migrant domestic workers can gather on their precious days off, to meet each other and build social networks, access information on their rights and develop their skills with language and computer classes. Workers can see doctors, obtain mental health care and access legal advice. ARM run case management for extreme cases of abuse and exploitation, but for the most part, ARM's goal is empowering migrant domestic workers to become their own advocates, to help them raise their voices rather than speaking for them.

Have conditions materially improved? Lebanon's domestic workers are starting from a very low base but, tentatively, yes. Recently, two Kenyan migrant workers were assaulted in public. Although the victims were deported and charged in absentia – which sounds utterly horrendous – the upside is that their attackers were fined and received some jail time. This sets a precedent that migrant workers can seek justice in the courts, which can be counted as a win in the world of *kafala*.

'There is a lot to be unlearned and there's a lot to be untangled within these discussions,' Farah Salka says.

One of the things that we need to focus on in this region and internationally is formalising care work and formalising domestic work. It cannot continue to be under the umbrella of informal work.

If you want to hire somebody to do work at your house, whether hourly work or full-time work, then you have opened doors for yourself to have labour inspections. If you insist on having this kind of job done at your house, you need to understand that you have made your house no longer a completely private premise: now it's also public, because somebody is working there and it needs to be formal and there will have to be some changes for this.

We can't have these exceptions on the back of domestic workers.

The end goal for ARM is to abolish the *kafala* system across Lebanon and the Middle East, which is going to take an extraordinary social and cultural shift. Meanwhile, they're also doing the practical work on the ground of improving conditions for the hundreds of thousands of migrant workers in the country today, and creating pathways for legal change by fighting cases and partnering with the La Sagesse University Faculty of Law to train law students in migration law. ARM's migrant-worker members take to the streets for International Women's Day, visibly connecting the feminist struggle with the fight for rights for these women, who are rendered invisible as non-citizens and non-workers.

We've got to acknowledge that the undervaluing of the care economy is intersectional in nature – meaning there are layers of prejudice at play here, a combination of gender, race and class – which makes it a particularly difficult knot to untangle. The international dimensions add to the complexity: if we allow care to be undervalued, for care workers to be exploited anywhere, it impacts on how care is valued everywhere. Sociologist Arlie Hoschschild calls it the 'global care chain': she says there's been a 'care drain' from the global south towards industrialised countries, leaving a care deficit in some parts of the world.[18]

When we think about ensuring that the care economy is an engine for sustainable, dignified jobs for the future, we need to work to improve conditions everywhere, not just in our own hospitals, nursing homes, schools and child-care centres.

Change the conditions of work, improve the conditions of care

When the Oxford Dictionary team start choosing their word of the year for 2020, 'unprecedented' is going to be in with a good shot: it's been getting a workout thanks primarily to COVID-19. There's been no event this all-encompassing and universal in our lifetimes, though it's a portent of the kinds of unsettling and unpredictable crises that are ahead unless there is effective action taken on climate change.

Over March and April 2020, a lot of the world's citizens suddenly found themselves at home, helping to 'flatten the curve' (that's another contender, Oxford), going through this alone in our bubbles but together across the planet. As many parents attempted the impossible feat of working from home while trying to entertain and educate their kids, we began to appreciate the enormity of the task teachers and child-care workers perform for society, as well as those grandparents, aunts or uncles who routinely take on some of that role. Those of us with parents or grandparents in aged care found ourselves cut off from them, nervous about what might happen if their nursing homes became sites of an outbreak.

But not everyone has a nurturing, intact family or a strong network. I spoke with community service workers concerned for kids they look out for who'd been disconnected from the support services providing them with food and a safe place to go or locked down in risky home environments. They worried about the ones who'd be left further behind after schools moved to online learning, when many of these kids didn't have access to computers or the internet at home. It's not what you'd expect to find here in one of the wealthiest countries in the world. There were more stories like this: from priests providing outreach for the homeless, even when many of their regular donations and volunteers stop coming, to disability service workers running out of personal protective equipment and dealing with skyrocketing costs while they try to continue their rounds.

All the invisible, outsourced care that enables society to function was thrown into the spotlight, and much of it was revealed to be on some pretty shaky foundations.

While the pandemic-driven lockdown was – as we all heard repeatedly – unprecedented, unexpected and unpredictable, many of the cracks in our community that it daylighted weren't new. The strains on underfunded health services; the vulnerability of people sleeping rough or with tenuous access to housing; the differential in resources at the disposal of private schools versus public; the risks inherent in a privatised aged-care system; the fragility of child-care arrangements: they were already there, just under the surface, so it's no surprise the increased pressure has turned those cracks into canyons.

The cause of the crisis may have been unprecedented, but we could have seen a lot of this coming. Topics such as our undermined public health and housing systems, the shift from government to charity in social provision and the scandal of education funding in Australia are too enormous for me to dive into as part of this story. But it's striking how many of my conversations for this book have come back to the idea that reinvesting in and refocusing our economy around care is at the foundation of the fair and regenerative future we need. Also, although we are teetering on a knife's edge, I have to tell you I do see positive signs for child care and elder care even in the midst of this crisis.

There's a phrase about care that sticks with me: 'The conditions of work are the conditions of care.' It's a principle articulated by Canadian Professor Pat Armstrong, an expert in aged care, and it rings true for all kinds of care workers. The situations that workers navigate to get to work and pull together a living wage, on some of the lowest incomes in our economy, determine the quality of the care that is provided by those workers. Poor conditions for care workers are a system risk for all of society.

Elderly people living together in nursing homes have found themselves incredibly vulnerable to the pandemic: in Europe and Canada in the first few months of 2020, half of all deaths from COVID-19 occurred in aged-care facilities.[19] Australian aged-care homes also became scenes of tragedy.[20] Yes, many residents were in the most high-risk categories for the disease, but other factors are likely to have contributed. Investigations are underway into how care homes became hotbeds of outbreaks. There are important clues in the findings of Professor Armstrong's research in Canada. Pat observed that care workers often have to work across multiple care facilities in order to make a living. Crucially, being on low wages and insecure conditions, many couldn't afford to stay home when they were unwell, which in the conditions of a pandemic increases the risk of virus transmission.[21]

The World Health Organization Regional Director for Europe, Dr Hans Henri P. Kluge, acknowledged the role a degraded elder care system has played in the spread of the virus in Europe, and flagged that this experience will require a radical redesign of how care facilities operate. Kluge said, 'This pandemic has shone a spotlight on the overlooked and undervalued corners of our society. Across the European Region, long-term care has often been notoriously neglected. But it should not be this way. Looking to the future, transitioning to a new normal, we have a clear investment case for setting up integrated, person-centred long-term care systems in each country.'[22]

The Canadian province of British Columbia (BC) has shown one way. BC was on Canada's frontline. It shares a border with Washington state in the USA, the first state to announce a COVID-19 death in North America and, early on, one of the most impacted.[23] As the virus started breaking out in aged-care homes across Canada, in order to eliminate one source of risk, the BC government took over as employer of all of the aged-care workers in the province, committing to hiring them fulltime, paying them a standard wage and confining their work to one home for six months from April 2020.[24] For many, it resulted in a pay increase as workers in the privatised system saw their wages rise to match unionised workers. Thanks to this intervention, all care workers in the province found themselves enjoying the same conditions, and the certainty of a full-time wage.

At the time of writing, it's too early to say BC's moves to change the conditions of labour transformed conditions of care – and crucially, saved lives in the pandemic – but the signs look good. BC was hit first by COVID-19, acted later in terms of declaring a state of emergency, and didn't implement as dramatic a lockdown as other Canadian provinces – but they did make change in nursing homes where other provinces did not – and by May 2020 it was proving to be a Canadian success story, flattening the curve and beginning the reopening process sooner.[25] The province's most senior health officer, Dr Bonnie Henry, has committed to a review at the end of these emergency measures to determine whether uniform conditions and wages are necessary in the sector beyond the crisis, and whether there needs to be a shift away from the subcontracting model of services in care.[26]

It was brought in as a short-term solution, but if it were applied long-term, BC might show the world how targeting and improving the security and wages of care workers flows on to better outcomes for people receiving care, and even has a flow-on effect across society. How much might these measures have saved the province in lost economic activity, enabling the process of reopening ahead of more impacted provinces like Ontario and Quebec? It would be a wasted opportunity if all that happened in the wake of this stress test was that the wage bill of private providers was underwritten by the public purse: this is a moment to redesign care to the benefit of everyone.

As Professor Armstrong writes:

This crisis offers us the opportunity to learn about how to create a new normal, to think through how we design, structure, access and organize long-term residential care. Indeed, it allows us to reimagine nursing homes as rewarding places to work, where life is worth living for residents and where visitors feel comforted about the care.[27]

***

When the pandemic first hit Australia, large numbers of parents pulled their kids out of child care to protect them from the virus – and also because they were suddenly confined to home themselves – and the business models of many centres crumbled. Some parents, worried about losing their places in centres (a common cause of anxiety as demand outstrips supply in a lot of areas), continued to pay for their places even while keeping kids at home. The federal government stepped in with some funding guarantees, but the layers of rebates, subsidies and fees holding up today's system are so complex that there were centres that needed much more help in order to survive. A couple of centre operators I spoke to said they were on the verge of closing because their international student and non-resident workforce weren't eligible for government support.

In Australia, child-care costs have doubled in the last 20 years.[28] Sadly, the increased costs haven't given parents more security or seemingly improved conditions for carers, who are still some of the lowest paid workers in society. My friends with kids have patched together care schedules from different providers and grandparents, and those who work unconventional hours run up massive bills or turn to in-home help (a model that also fractured during the crisis).[29] On average, Australian families spend about 27 per cent of their income on child care,[30] often as much as they might spend on rent or a mortgage. In the UK, it's even worse: OECD data estimates child care would cost a single parent on an average wage up to 37 per cent of household income.[31] In the UK, 84 per cent of child-care services are provided by private entities, and public subsidies are flowing into private profits in an increasingly dysfunctional market-based approach. It's one of the most expensive child-care systems in the world, but it ranks near the bottom of OECD countries in quality, undercutting the usual narratives about competition and choice providing better outcomes.[32]

One of the most commonly cited cautionary tales about the corporate provision of child care is the collapse of ABC Learning in 2008. ABC Learning had expanded aggressively (aiming to open four new centres a week) and was responsible for providing 25 per cent of all child care in Australia.[33] If achieving scale really provided for the most efficient model for delivering child care, then ABC Learning should have been a success story: instead it proved that a corporatised, profit-maximising approach to caring for kids is a system risk. Even before the business-model risks became public knowledge, think-tank The Australia Institute published research focusing on ABC Learning and made the observation that 'corporate chain centres provide poorer quality care on all quality aspects surveyed compared to community-based centres',[34] at a time when the corporation was receiving over $200 million a year in government subsidies.

When it crumbled, ABC Learning was considered 'too big to fail' and the federal government had to bail them out: spending $22 million of public money to keep centres open before this corporate care monolith was rescued by the community sector. A coalition of purpose-driven organisations – The Benevolent Society, Mission Australia, the Brotherhood of St Laurence and Social Ventures Australia – created Goodstart, a not-for-profit organisation that took over and now runs more than 650 former ABC Learning centres. It's a story that has a happy ending, in this one instance, but the structural problems remain. In every analysis of the collapse of ABC Learning, much mention is made of the directors' aggressive expansion and taking on debt, driven by a cowboy-hat-wearing bad-guy CEO. Years later, however, it doesn't really look like there was much meaningful policy change as a result. Australians are still paying too much for child care, which is delivered by workers who aren't as supported or rewarded as they should be, and there is a risk that the sector may crumble again in the volatile environment post-COVID-19 shutdown.

Finally, taking the lessons from the ABC Learning experience and seeing where the cracks have been daylighted through this crisis, this could be our moment to enhance the resilience of Australia's care sector for the long term by providing a pathway to alternative operating models for those child-care operators who struggle to make it through the shutdown. To improve the care options we have in the future, we could call for a transition to worker- or parent-led models, using the approaches we saw earlier in our story from The Co-Operative Life and The Working World. Could we craft a future for child care that offers better outcomes for kids, parents and carers, using the almost $10 billion we spend annually on early childhood care and education now?[35]

There are other pathways to provide great care for kids beyond the binaries of government and corporate: Universal Basic Services (UBS) advocate Anna Coote pointed me towards Grasshoppers in the Park, a 'co-production' model of child care in Hackney, East London.[36] This model asks parents to contribute in any way they are able, supporting the centre's four paid professional staff members, either in the classroom or with admin, repairs or laundry, in order to reduce operating costs and give parents a closer connection to the world their kids inhabit while they're at work. Co-production is a niche approach now, and co-operatives have a long but not widespread reach into child care. Still, these are models that are worth exploring.

In the UK, the New Economics Foundation (NEF) have made a series of useful recommendations.[37] NEF call for 'A Charter for Child Care' setting minimum standards for affordability (such as rate capping) and access (in terms of locations) for parents, and accountability from providers, in order for them to be eligible for public funding. They say that funding should be delivered to the providers themselves, rather than being given to parents in the form of vouchers or rebates, to give governments more direct influence over worker and centre conditions. It goes back to the advantages we explored around the UBS, and the greater bargaining power that we have when society operates collectively, rather than sending individuals out into the market and expecting us to have the access and control to negotiate our own deals.

The most resilient approach would be to have a distributed and diverse set of child-care models – from co-ops and parent co-production models, to not-for-profits, council and privately run providers – which could be accredited to form a system that offers more genuine choice. NEF authors Miranda Hall and Lucie Stephens write:

'Instead of ushering back top-down control of services, the aim should be more ambitious: public–social partnerships to support a process of democratisation from the bottom up, led by parents and child-care professionals who know what needs to change and have a strong interest in changes being effective.'[38]

***

One of the greatest advances of the 20th century was the expansion of access to primary-school education all over the world. Today, even the most market-oriented governments in the world provide some level of free public education. There's an enormous amount of research that documents the importance of early childhood education in personal development, and access to quality early-childhood education is even one of the UN's Sustainable Development Goals.[39] But for some reason, many countries draw a line somewhere between 'early childhood education', 'child care' and 'public education', and demand economic arguments about unlocking the workforce productivity of women, for example, to justify spending on care and education of kids under primary-school age.

Dr Jen Jackson from Victoria University has called out this counter-productive distinction and the expensive inefficiencies it's generating.[40] In Australia today, it's estimated that we're spending, per child, about the same on early-childhood education and care as we spend on primary school, with the difference that families pay a much larger share of the former.[41] There is an alternative: the Swedish model of Educare explicitly combines early learning and care and makes it accessible and universal.[42] Its list of attributes sounds like fantasy to any parent in Australia or the UK who's had to navigate an expensive, inflexible system: a sliding scale of fees depending on family income, caps on costs, operating hours that go beyond nine to five, and highly educated, well-resourced early childhood educators. There's more spending by government in the Swedish model and more spending by families in the UK and Australian models. This is one of the most important investments we make as a society in our future, so we need a fuller conversation about the models available to us and the quality of outcomes they deliver, for families, kids and carers.

In child- and elder-care alike, throwing more money at the system we have today isn't going to give us better outcomes tomorrow. There's a strong case for both of these essential care services to form part of the Universal Basic Services we explored earlier in our story, and for each of them, the 2020 crisis has presented an opportunity.

If there's one silver lining of this unprecedented crisis, it's that care moved out of the margins of the conversation, out of the list of the things our society takes for granted, expects from women or leaves at the door of charities, and for a moment became something we couldn't ignore. Let's look for the root causes of the cracks to investigate the deeper inadequacies of our care system and design a path forward that improves both the conditions of work and the conditions of care.

Decolonise the economy

We've already explored some of the in-built biases that have prevented the care economy from being taken seriously. Well, things get even more strained when we consider the colonial mindset that's blocking a shift to the care economy. The people we'll meet in this part of our story have modelled First Nations approaches to caring for country and community that are part of the solutions we need.

Stephanie Gutierrez is telling me about Pine Ridge Reservation, her Lakota homelands, while I look at the landscape on a map. I'm not great with US state geography, so I'm surprised to find South Dakota is way up north, not that far from the border with Canada. There's a name I recognise – Standing Rock Reservation – just north of there, a name Stephanie's fellow Lakota people have made famous in their fierce battle to protect their sacred homelands from the Dakota Access Pipeline. Like them, Stephanie's people are fighting to protect their community, but with a focus on reshaping the economic sustainability of reservation life by framing it around the Lakota way, centred on loyalty to *Oyate* (people) and *Unci Maka* (planet).

'Pine Ridge Reservation is part of our sacred lands, because we've lived there since time immemorial,' she says. 'It's vast. It's bold and big and windy and the weather is tough but it's beautiful. It can also be very lonely: because it's such open space, it's isolating. It's an hour and a half from a large metropolitan city, Rapid City, which is only 68,000 people. That's the closest area for hospitals, for anything besides a gas station, a small grocery store and churches galore. Winters start in late September and go all the way until mid-April.'

There's a lot of love for the place in Stephanie's voice, but it's clear there are problems Pine Ridge faces too.

'It's a food desert. Even though there are 2,000,000 acres [810,000 hectares] – of which, I think, half or more are farmed, grazed or used for pulling minerals, growing corn, wheat, things like that – the people on the reservation see something like 5 per cent of that coming back to feed the community.'

Geographically isolated and with tough conditions, Lakota lands have always been a place of self-reliance, but Stephanie says that began to change with federal policy in the 1930s, which built a culture of dependency on food rations and government support, undermining traditional lifestyles and creating intergenerational impoverishment across Native American communities. Economically, the First People of the United States are that country's most disadvantaged minority group, experiencing poverty rates of around 25 per cent and lower median earnings than the general population. If Native Americans choose to live closer to community and their traditional lands, official unemployment rates are astronomically high, at around 60 per cent.

After building her career helping Native American students to bridge connections between traditional and urban lifestyles, and to access university, Stephanie says she suddenly had the realisation, 'Hey, I want to do this too.' She went back to college to do her Masters in Social Work at the same time (and at the same college) as her eldest daughter, and retrained with a focus on economic and community development. Her path took her back to Pine Ridge Reservation, her mother's country. There she worked with Thunder Valley's Community Development Corporation (CDC), a Lakota-owned not-for-profit entity, on creating their social enterprise program, finding a way to connect financial opportunity with traditional practices and focus on community and place.

Stephanie's first step was establishing a community baseline: itemising the sometimes invisible assets of her community, 'getting a really clear picture of what is happening within your community not just on financial or economical level'. The strengths that exist are often left off the balance sheet in a transactional, colonised approach.

> So, it's really like putting down all of the resources and assets that are available in your community – I mean everything – not just data that the feds put out, but your own

data. So, I dig deep, putting it all in one place, so that you have this really good picture of what's going on, where your strengths are, where there's opportunity areas, things that are weak things or that need assistance. Also, you can determine who those individuals are that want to be part of a collaborative to make it happen, outside of this sort of hierarchical system. You could include anyone that has an interest in shifting the system.

In her work at Thunder Valley, Stephanie focused on supporting and developing new businesses through the social enterprise development program, and she was part of a cross-country initiative by the Democracy Collaborative to connect Native American businesses and not-for-profits.

In chapter 4, we explored the Democracy Collaborative's community wealth building (CWB) approach, including their work in Cleveland's Evergreen Co-operatives. When Stephanie first engaged with them, she was inspired by their successes and open to their ideas but had concerns about the applicability of CWB in a non-urban, First Nations setting. Elders were suspicious when she put it to them, and she too had her doubts. Was this all 'too white', just more of the same Western, transactional thinking that had disrupted the Lakota way and eroded their sovereignty and self-reliance? Stephanie grappled with these issues in dialogue with the Democracy Collaborative.

> My questioning came from a gut feeling, and this is one of the first practices that I want to share with Native women is listening to your gut, and how it's a practice that many cultures do. What does your gut say? My gut kept saying, 'I don't understand this. It doesn't fit with us. Some of some elements make sense to me but I'm not sure how they fit with our culture.'
>
> They were like, 'We need to get your business plan and we need this or that.' And I was like, 'I can't. I can't until I know for sure.' And also, because I'm speaking for a lot of other people, and there are

certain cultural things with that as well. It's not okay for me to speak out for the whole. So anyway, finally I read it a third time and I had seen in the margins where I had put 'This is similar to...'

At this point, Stephanie pulls out her original CWB guide from a folder on her desk, the one from her initial interactions with Democracy Collaborative. It's fringed with Post-it tags and full of notes in the margin.

It's like, 'community benefit agreements' and I had this big star and a question mark drawn on it, and then two months later I read it again and I went [draws a sharp breath]: 'These are old Lakota ways among our *tiospayes*. This is how we worked with each other.'

Tiospayes were large groups, communities, extended families. We had what you would call a community-benefit agreement. The leaders would come together and say, 'What's in the best interest of our *tiospayes?*'

My identity as a Lakota became much stronger living on the land

and being there and connecting with my relatives. That just really solidified my presence and my being as a Lakota person. So I just went back and I started writing all the notes of how these things connected. [Reads aloud a note in the margins] 'Our way since time immemorial, working collaboratively for the common good, that instinctively makes sense. The real economy of jobs and families always lived somewhere someplace real: the real economy is place-based.'

Those were my 'Aha!' moments. And I don't know that I would have had them had I not been home.

At Pine Ridge, the solution is taking multiple forms. Thunder Valley CDC created the Food Sovereignty Coalition to address the issue of the food desert by creating a localised food system, aiming to retain more of the food production on their land and to try to keep their food catchment within a 300-mile (480-kilometre) radius. They support and connect community gardens, a geothermal greenhouse and a poultry system with 500 chickens.

Another key issue was a lack of training opportunities for young people, and a lack of affordable housing, which they're tackling through the Workforce Development Through Sustainable Construction Program: training young adults in environmentally sustainable home construction.

Using those skills, they're building high-efficiency homes on the reservation, helping to reduce energy consumption and costs for their residents.

These concrete steps towards economic self-determination are important for the quality of life of people at Pine Ridge, but there is something deeper – pride, identity and spirituality – at play here too. In partnership with her colleague Rae Tall, Stephanie worked to decolonise the usual approach to economic development for a more holistic idea of what wealth and success look like within a Lakota frame. It's not just about GDP or employment figures but supporting genuine, far-reaching care for community members and sacred lands.

Stephanie points out a medicine wheel drawing she made in the margins of her CWB guide. It eventually made its way into her own publication, *An Indigenous Approach to Community Wealth Building: A Lakota Translation.* That's how I first encountered her work, and my world view was expanded by her translation of local economic development to align with First Nations' core values. These are called the four Rs: relationship, responsibility, reciprocity and redistribution.'[43]

In the context of Pine Ridge, that looks like a sense of self-determination and pride, skills development, food sovereignty and a return to self-sufficiency. It's finding a way to account for and value care as a source of wealth. Stephanie writes:

'For Lakota, wealth means to live by our virtues in order to have a happy, well-balanced life. The goal is not materialistic things but helping, giving, and taking care of one another. Our wealth is measured in our ability to care for our people and to provide a strong foundation for future generations.'

In the aftermath of colonisation, the traditional ways of the Lakota have been disrupted by historical trauma and dispossession, making this a challenging context for community wealth-building and empowerment. What strikes me are the many parallels between Stephanie's approach to rebalancing the relationship between economy and society and those of other leaders I've spoken to on different continents and in radically different circumstances. All have landed in the same neighbourhood, metaphorically speaking – the understanding that the business-as-usual economy works for a very few and has heavy costs for the many. Also that now is our moment to redesign the economy for people and planet, to change the way we do business to prioritise new values that are strikingly aligned with the values of First Nations and other marginalised groups that for too long have been left out of the equation. Care is central to all of it, glaringly absent in mainstream, accepted economic wisdom. That's why it's got to be at the foundation of our efforts for a new world.

This translation of CWB principles into the Lakota way has had resonance beyond Native American contexts. Stephanie tells me about an African-American community in Minnesota that has adapted her adaptation into their own context; some Bosnian and LGBTQI community groups have done the same. Reframing wealth and economic development around care for people and planet elevates the skills and priorities of communities that have been marginalised and have had their knowledge disregarded for a long time. It acknowledges that they are generating real value – even if the dominant system doesn't know how to account for it – and attributes agency to the informal and social practices of communities that have been left out of the economy. Stephanie says education, generational change and intersectional knowledge-sharing among marginalised people is accelerating the moment of transformation that we need for a more caring, sustainable future.

I think that there's been a humming among young people of colour across the country and across the world: it hasn't just been our communities, we're realising more now than ever we're sharing the same challenges, and so there's been this coming together. There's been more discussion across lines. Also, I think the education piece is added to that, so you have our young people who've gone off to universities and colleges and they're learning alongside the children of Black Panthers, they're learning alongside the Me Too movement, and all these others.

So, they're enriched and empowered to take care of their own people but are also understanding and respecting the challenges of other communities and sharing those resources. I was in Pine Ridge two to three years ago, working at Thunder Valley, and the girl who pretty much started the Black Lives Matter movement, she was on the reservation presenting in a little grade school called Wolf Creek school. And parents and children were showing up to hear her, and I thought, 'How cool is that?'

It really is so cool. Ninety minutes after our video chat began, and about six months after we first started emailing, Stephanie and I reluctantly log off the call. Throughout our interactions, we'd giggled and teared up; shared hesitations, optimism and book recommendations. Conversations like this one are the reason I wanted to write this book: I get to learn about stories like these from people like Stephanie, and to see that – despite all the gloom around us and the bad news that piles up on the hour – there is a global movement rising with shared values and a common goal.

There are so many of us out there making our own version of change, creating our own glimpses of utopia, that I think the tide is turning.

***

In Australia, we've got an image of ourselves as living on land that's wild, dangerous, inhospitable and brutal. The story is that progress has been recent – pioneers scraping back patches of that untamed landscape to allow us to build cities and farms in defiance of an unpredictable environment.

Most city dwellers experience that as news of bushfires raging in locations all around the country every summer. It's nothing out of the ordinary to wake up to a heavy haze of smoke sitting over our cities and the powerful smell of eucalypt. It seeps into everything; you wear the smell in your hair all day. The ash falls like snow and settles on cars, leaves and fences, and on long drives you watch the horizon for the plumes rising up like skyscrapers, totems of the season, like sunburn and ice cream vans.

We think of this as normal, but it's actually a sign of dysfunction, a sign that country isn't being cared for. For tens of thousands of years, Australia's Indigenous people managed the lands, waterways, flora and fauna of this, the oldest continent. They created abundance in places colonists and explorers experienced as food deserts and sustained large, thriving communities in places we think of as remote, harsh and barren.

There's a whole history of the economy, ecology and society of this country that's been actively erased since invasion. We cannot begin to build a mature future for Australia until we acknowledge that fact and elevate the Indigenous knowledge that kept Australia prosperous and peaceful for tens of thousands of years before European colonisation.

I was born in Australia in the 1980s, and as a history buff, I thought I had some idea about this place. I'm the kind of person who studies the plaques and the historical interpretations when visiting landmarks and museums, but reading *Dark Emu,* a book by Bunurong man and author Bruce Pascoe, I realised how little I knew. On every page there was a staggering revelation that shook the assumptions we've made and the stories we've been told about this country and its First People. Pascoe documents large-scale agriculture and engineering works, from ploughed plains of grains and tubers, to the sophistication of the Brewarrina and Glyde River fish traps, complex food preservation processes, wells, architecture and building. He draws from the diaries and letters of early colonists who remark on the park-like nature of the plains, and Aboriginal people harvesting crops and animals, or describe the comfort of houses and towns of thousands of people. Pascoe says that some Aboriginal construction was so complex that colonists concocted stories about earlier European arrivals and even alien visitors – so determined were they to deny the evidence of their own eyes, that the Aboriginal people before them were a civilisation with a highly evolved understanding of how to manage a landscape the new arrivals found mystifying.

This is the story of Australia we don't know, the one hidden behind the myth of Aboriginal culture as being based on hunting and gathering in country that was in a wild state of nature at the time of European arrival. This dishonest narrative denies Indigenous people their true status as active managers of the ecosystem, and it denies Australians today the benefit of Aboriginal knowledge about how to create a sustainable, viable future for this country.

Those potential benefits are myriad, but if First Nations' stewardship was restored, for one thing, we wouldn't have such smoky summers.

First Nations land managers used fire as a tool to prevent just the kind of destruction we've come to regard as natural, a form of environmental management that reduced the incidence of out-of-control blazes, and which limited the accumulation of leaf litter, growth of scrub and understorey species. Pascoe writes:

'Changing the timing and intensity of fires radically changed the nature of the country, so that what had been productive agricultural land became scrub within a decade.'[44]

The park-like, productive plains the colonists seized only looked like that thanks to Aboriginal land management practices, and after a few decades being barred from (and often brutally punished for) carrying out their traditional practices, the land had degraded and out-of-control summer bushfires became common. Today, there are community leaders reclaiming that custodianship and knowledge for environmental, social and cultural benefit, and Rowan Foley is one of them.

Rowan Foley is the General Manager of the Aboriginal Carbon Fund (AbCF), an organisation that's building the tools and approaches needed to re-centre traditional land management practices, using carbon abatement and trading. Rowan is a ranger and an Aboriginal man from the Wondunna clan of the Badtjala people, Traditional Owners of Fraser Island (K'gari) in Queensland.

Carbon abatement, or carbon farming, is an approach to eliminating or reducing the release of CO_2 into the atmosphere by paying people or businesses (usually through an auction process) to change their behaviour: creating incentives to counter deforestation, for example, or capturing gases like methane, produced through commercial animal farming. Savannah fires in the north of Australia contribute 4 per cent of Australia's greenhouse gases,[45] and release a higher amount of carbon when they burn uncontrolled in summer months (so-called 'hot burns'). A return to Indigenous-led care for land through controlled burns can reduce carbon emissions while also generating income for communities through carbon trading.

But for Rowan, and his colleague Lisa McMurray, this is only part of the story. In the Western approach, the carbon impact and return is the 'core benefit' and everything else is a 'co-benefit'. In the AbCF approach, caring for country in the right way by restoring agency and control to traditional owners is the primary focus, and everything else is a bonus.

'There's a philosophical difference,' Rowan explains:

> So, when you say 'core benefits', what we're saying is that these are the core values of the project. And we make a little bit of money. Right? If it's co-benefits, it's, 'We make money, first and foremost, and we also do a little bit of these frilly environmental bits on the side.' Co-benefits puts money first and environmental stuff second. Whereas we put

environmental, social, cultural first and money second.

Everyone wants to make a dollar at the end of the day, you know, I can understand that. And that's certainly part of the reason we're here: it's because we're trying to overcome poverty. Having sustainable businesses on Aboriginal land, that's one of our primary aims. But first and foremost is this – and this is what I say to everyone – we've only got one question to answer. And that is: how should this country be burnt? Full stop. That's it. Let's just figure out what's good for the country. How should the country be burnt? And let's go and do that. Right? And then we'll figure out the carbon credits at the end of the project. Let's not put the cart before the horse. Let's have good land management, first and foremost, according to cultural frameworks.

I had it once reported to me that one of the senior traditional owners on the project said, 'Oh, I don't give a fuck about the carbon project. I'm going out to burn country.' And I was like, 'That's music to my ears. That's what I want. That's what I want to hear.' I want people to say, 'The right way of burning this country is this.'

A key part of AbCF's mindset is that they don't always play by the Western-imposed rules on cool (winter) over hot (spring and summer) burns. Again, the priority is traditional care for country: acting in a way consistent with culture, not just maximising credits. Rowan explains:

The practical manifestation of that is hot burns. People say, 'Ah, so we're swapping over now from the occasional hot burn to cool, so everything's gonna be cool burn?' And I say, 'Well, not necessarily: what's good for the country?'

You know, the occasional hot burn is good. That's the way the country has been managed for the last 65,000 years. You know, it's just that 90 per cent of the burns will be cool, and you should have the occasional hot burn. And you can do that early in the season.

And if you've got your cool burns in, around the patch that you want to do a hot burn on, you can do it late in this season as well. And people say, 'If you do it after the 1st of August, that's the cut-off point. You might lose a few carbon credits.' Well, so be it. Who gives a fuck? Just do what you think is best for country and the carbon credits will flow at the end of the day.

Lisa McMurray has worked in development in the Pacific and across Australia, and is now at AbCF supporting their work on the core benefits verification framework, which is how AbCF is trying to change the game.

'For us, we're like: "Actually, the core benefits are people being back on country." That is the core purpose of why people like these projects, because it facilitates people being employed and being back on country,' Lisa says. 'Indigenous people are saying, "This is our core reason why we do it: the cultural stuff, the social stuff and the environmental stuff." But normally, even if you dig down [into] the environmental stuff, you realise it's actually cultural stuff.'

Putting culture, care for country and community at the heart of the AbCF philosophy gives rise to a host of benefits. Local jobs are created that help people stay on country. In turn, this helps connect upcoming generations with Elders who can pass down cultural knowledge. Indigenous land management can support threatened species and reduce the prevalence of introduced plants and animals, which become weeds and pests that can spread when ecosystems aren't being managed.

Reinstating traditional burning practices sometimes brings unexpected rewards. Some ancient sites have been rediscovered and are now being cared for. And some traditional food sources have been restored, with positive impacts on the health of communities.

The distinguishing feature of AbCF is its Indigenous-to-Indigenous evaluation method. AbCF creates tools to get rangers across different communities to assess and verify the impact of projects based on what matters to the traditional owners. The conventional practice would be to fly in management consultants from the capital cities to score projects against an imposed set of indicators. This is a form of eco-colonialism – a sense of superiority that assumes Westerners know best – which runs deep in environmental and development projects. Rowan says, 'We're not using the coloniser's language. We're not using English, French, German, Spanish, Portuguese or Dutch ... they all have their own way of measuring things; they all have their own way of valuing things. They all have their own colonial frameworks that they bring with them, as well as their legislation, policies and their technology. If you step away from that, you will get something different. We're using a tool that the traditional owner, who may speak English as a fourth language, can use.'

AbCF have developed a training course for carbon farming and measurement, including a verification framework, that engages Aboriginal rangers from different regions. The idea is that they then work with communities to determine impact. Run over five days, the course prioritises cultural protocols and offers participants visual tools to document the outcomes. Rowan adds, 'Where we're really forging the [intellectual property] is in the tools that people use to work together.'

How do you enable a traditional owner who's strong in knowledge of culture on country but only went to grade two [at school]? What set of tools do they need to be able to do a professional verification of environmental, social and cultural values? How do you design those tools – and the training program that comes with it – to enable that outcome to be achieved? That's what we spend a lot of time thinking and working on, is: 'How are blackfellas going to use this?'

The AbCF are running 32 projects across northern Australia, often stepping in and rescuing projects when there's a risk they won't go ahead. Rowan shrugs it off when I try to home in on the number of projects they're running. It's clear that's not the point. They're not interested in competing against other groups to run carbon abatement schemes, but rather on changing the way governments and organisations approach the practice, and providing the infrastructure of a radically refocused, Indigenous-led industry.

It hits me that I'm really approaching this conversation like a whitefella. Have I even been listening? It's not about the number of projects, or the percentage of savannah burns that are run by Indigenous teams ... that's all important, sure. But the real story here is what this can do for people. For how they feel about themselves, for their sense of duty and connection to the places they belong to. This work is truly about people, about caring. The rest is detail.

'The number one outcome we came up with from carbon farming was pride. People's pride in themselves, and the pride that people had in the work that they were doing in the community. It had nothing to do with money, nothing to do with carbon credits, nothing to do with burning country,' Rowan says. He tells me about the feedback gathered in Cape York communities after a pilot program there, and the clarity of it even shocked him.

'I didn't pick it. And I'm very open and honest about this. I was as surprised about this as anybody else when they came back and said: "Oh, the number one outcome from carbon farming, the work that they're all doing up on the Cape is pride." I went, "Fucken what?!" And they went: "Yeah, it's self-pride." That's the thing that was driving people. That's what people thought was one of the most valuable things around the whole project. Of course, there are other values as well. But that was a really strong value.'

I can sense Rowan's passion vibrating down the phone line, as well as frustration at how hard it is to get this across to me. But this is a frequent experience. He tells me about a savannah management workshop he attended in which AbCF couldn't even get a spot in the session about monitoring evaluation, let alone an invitation to present their transformative work. Eco-colonialism puts whitefellas on stage; blackfellas are data points.

It was chock-a-block with university and conservation organisations talking about their monitoring evaluation programs, and not one of them mentioned pride. In a break, an ABC journalist got up, asking if any of the rangers can come over and talk, that would be fabulous. 'You guys have so much pride in the work that you're doing, it's going to be lovely to capture that on ABC Radio. We'll do an interview with you.' And I wasn't planning on speaking but I just clicked. And I stood up and said, 'Look, I just want to let you know, because you just mentioned pride, we ran the monitoring evaluation pilot in Cairns, and the number one outcome that we come out with was pride.' Then the senior ranger from Tiwi Islands, a guy black as the ace of spades, grabs the mic off me and he started talking about pride and how proud the community was in their work.

And then Otto from Arnhem Land, he got up and spoke about it really strongly as well. And I thought, 'Well, fuck me, there you go.' So the blackfellas from the floor are talking about it, yeah, but you couldn't even get into the fucking white podium because it was chock-a-block with fucking universities and conservation organisations, all doing their thing, using blackfellas as the fucking data collection: that's nothing to do with the traditions at all, that's using them to collect data!

AbCF and Rowan are brilliant in the thoughtful, culturally led way they have channelled the incentives of the coloniser – in this case, the market for carbon credits – towards the care that First Nations have given to country and community for thousands upon thousands of years. It's wonderful to see it happening, but as always, we need to connect this solution with other transformative thinking to make it work at scale.

Let's go right to the heart of the most potent structural incentives we have today: taxation and transfers. Can we rethink tax and use it as tool to deliver the world we want, rather than subsidising its destruction?

6

Recoup the investment

Who are the real innovators, risk-takers and inventors today? We hear big claims about the breakthrough innovation delivered by tech giants. But if you look behind the shiny surface, you'll find those tech giants are standing on all our shoulders: a lot of their successes have come about thanks to publicly funded research or infrastructure.

If public investment – by people like you and me, paying our taxes every time we purchase a product or get paid for work – plays a major role in enabling the businesses that today dominate our world, it seems logical that we should get a share of the rewards.

Instead, what we're experiencing is the practice of socialising risks and privatising rewards. We saw the principle at play in the GFC, when billions upon billions in public funds were spent to bail out the losses of banks who'd become overextended as a result of their own greed and mismanagement, destabilising economies all over the world. It's hard to know exactly how much public money this private sector crisis cost. Wall Street watchdog Better Markets quoted evidence from the Special Inspector General for the Troubled Asset Relief Program to estimate that, 'The value of the [US] government's total commitment of support, provided through some 50 separate programs, is estimated at not less than $23.7 trillion.'[1] As explored in our last chapter, the austerity – deep public spending cuts – that followed in much of the world continued the squeeze, with most severe effects on women and those who are already marginalised in the business-as-usual approach.

It's not just the financial sector that's socialising risks and privatising rewards. While popular myths and media celebrate the entrepreneurial spirit of household names like Jobs, Bezos, Musk or Gates, there's a whole lot of public investment backing those 'self-made' men.

Take Apple, for example. It's the largest tech company in the world, valued at US$961 billion in 2019,[2] in no small part thanks to their continued dominance of the lucrative smartphone market with the iPhone. But, as UK economist Mariana Mazzucato points out, all the components that make the iPhone 'smart' – the internet, wireless networks, GPS, touch-screen displays, microelectronics and the tech behind Siri – were generated through public investments in research and development. Take the internet. It grew out of the ARPANET computer network, funded by the Defense Advanced Research Projects Agency of the US Department of Defense, which has as its mission to make pivotal investments in breakthrough technologies for national security. The GPS (aka Global Positioning System) that enables every direction or delivery app on your phone is owned and operated by the United States Space Force and its development was initiated by the US Department of Defense. The now-ubiquitous touchscreen evolved from experiments in universities from Illinois in the USA to Toronto in Canada, to other research conducted in the UK's Royal Radar Establishment and Europe's CERN, all of which rely on funding from the public purse. All of this technology was adapted and advanced by commercial players along the way. Sometimes public investment is indirect, taking the form of funding innovative research, and at other times it's direct, coming to companies as grants, low-interest loans or research and development tax breaks.

The conventional wisdom is that these tech giants and business success stories repay their public investments through the jobs they generate and the taxes they pay. Yet, as covered earlier in our story, there are comparatively fewer and fewer jobs being created as these tech giants expand, and as you've probably read in the news, tech giants are less than scrupulous about paying their tax.

More than groundbreaking products or services, the real innovation we're seeing from these companies is in creative accounting. The European Commission has estimated that tech giants are paying an average of 9.5 per cent effective tax rate, thanks to tax minimisation contortions.[3] In Australia in 2018, Apple made $9.08 billion in sales, but paid only $164 million in tax. That's just 1.8 per cent of their income. (Imagine if your tax bill was 1.8 per cent ... the average Australian would be paying about $1440 in tax a year. I bet you're paying a lot more than that.) That's particularly disappointing when the official corporate tax rate is 30 per cent. We'll look at how they do that a little later on in this chapter. Spoiler: it's a lot to do with tax havens.

In an age of tax havens and accounting loopholes, expecting society to recoup our investments in tech R&D through tax seems naive. When the full-time employee workforce in these dominant companies is shrinking, we're not going to make up the difference through the few jobs these companies create. We're going to need a different approach to make business pay what is due to society.

There are three steps to tackle this. First, we need to be getting a return for the public investment that often underpins big successes and for the data that powers the digital age, which we'll explore later in our story. Second, we need to plug the colossal loopholes that all those corporate tax dollars are leaking out through. It's not impossible but it will take concerted global action. Finally, we also need to reform what we tax – to make it a tool that helps deliver a sustainable, caring future.

Take a stake

You might not know it, but taxpayers often play the role of venture capitalists. We're frequently funding the 'basic research' that generates original innovation, the building blocks that the business world then draws on to create products. This might be through funding university research or in the form of research and development tax credits. Sometimes, governments provide cutting-edge business with direct funding and investment for their products or plant, with the goal of generating more economic activity and ideally more jobs. But unlike venture capitalists, most governments have a less than brag-worthy track record with getting a direct return on our investments.

It's time for us to renegotiate the deal and to make sure that the rewards, not just the risks, come back to us. It has been done in the past, so we already have models to follow that show us how well this can work.

Economist Mariana Mazzucato has been investigating ways of obtaining a greater cut of the rewards for the public purse when technology or pharmaceutical companies strike gold as a result of our support.[4] In her view, we should be charging royalities and reusing the money from successes to fund the next brilliant idea:

> Where an applied technological breakthrough is directly financed by the government, the government should in return be able to extract a royalty from its application. Returns from the royalties, earned across sectors and technologies, should be paid into a national 'innovation fund' which the

government can use to fund future innovations ... A first step towards starting this process is increasing the transparency of government investment – by making it easier to track government expenditures in support of industry and by getting companies to report on the content and value of their public–private collaborations in a way that does not compromise proprietary information. The better the information we can glean from the innovation process, the more effective our policy choices can become.[5]

So, what would that look like if the public secured more direct returns for the investments we make in the business giants of today, rather than waiting to be repaid through job creation and taxation, two forms of indirect return we can no longer count on?

Well, it might look like the US government owning shares in Tesla, the electric vehicle manufacturer led by high-profile CEO Elon Musk. If public investment was valued in the same way private investment has been, the American public would own at least 11 per cent of the company, which as of May 2020 is valued at over US$144 billion.[6] Here's why.

In 2009, Tesla received a US$465 million low-interest loan from the US Department of Energy towards the development of their Model S sedan. The loan, which funded the build of their electric vehicle factory, couldn't have come at a better time. The company had had a shocker of a year, and finding that kind of money in the commercial market would have cost them a ton in interest or equity. Tesla's own estimates suggest they'd have paid 30 or 40 per cent in interest annually if they'd borrowed from the banks or investors – not the 3 or 4 per cent the government offered.[7]

When Elon Musk repaid the loan in full, just four years later, it was touted as a green-energy success story. According to journalist Scott Woolley, however, it was a terrible deal for the taxpayer, as an early repayment clause meant Musk could cancel the stock options the government had in Tesla.

Compare this 2009 government deal (the biggest ever investment in Tesla) with the generous deal Musk gave himself in 2008 when he was playing the role of investor. He loaned $38 million to his own company at a 10 per cent interest rate, with the option to convert the debt into stock. This delivered Musk an 11 per cent stake in the company. Woolley points out that 'the resulting shares are now worth a whopping $1.4 billion – a 3,500 per cent return on his investment. By contrast, the Department of Energy earned only $12 million in interest on its $465 million loan – a 2.6 per cent return.'

He noted, 'Making venture capital-style investments in risky companies – without demanding venture capital-style compensation in return – can end up costing taxpayers even more.'[8]

How might this deal have panned out differently if the public investment risk was properly compensated? There's already a terrific example of what this looks like in practice.

If you're over 30, you probably had a Nokia phone at one point. It was the first mobile phone many of us owned, back when we used our phones for calls, texts and Snake. Finland's Nokia started life as a paper mill in 1865 and 'pivoted' many times along the way through the kinds of industries that made sense in a country where the wealth has traditionally grown on trees. In the 1960s, Nokia shifted into telecommunications, and a government-funded electronics lab took part in a joint venture with them. It was a precursor to Nokia's era of dominance in mobile communications in the 1990s and 2000s, which saw them earning $35 billion a year at their peak. In exchange for their investment through this joint venture, the Finnish government received shares in Nokia. In 1991, the government handed those shares over to Sitra, Finland's sovereign wealth fund, to invest in the country's future.

Sitra is an independent public entity which is focused on funding the country's transition to a circular economy for sustainable wellbeing: that is, moving towards an economic system that produces no waste and minimises pollution. To do that, Sitra has an endowment of €840 million (roughly AU$1.6 billion) – all thanks to those Nokia shares – which it uses to fund social impact bonds for mission-oriented investments, to resource research into threats and opportunities the country faces, and to carry out societal debates in towns across Finland to understand public concerns and to test out potential responses.

Through Sitra, Finland has been able to articulate a vision for the future they want for their country, to have a series of public conversations about it – through art projects and exhibitions for teens, through to global forums for experts – to run competitions to draw out ideas from within the community and to fund experimental projects. That vision is one that gives me chills, the good kind. Imagine living in a country that can make such a confident assertion about its future – and actually have the investment and civic conversation vehicle to deliver it. 'The Finland of the future is based on a fair and competitive circular economy – a society that functions within the planetary boundaries and is therefore also secured for future generations. In such a country, technology will not be a threat that just takes away jobs, but an opportunity that is harnessed to create well-being. The diverse new work created in the transformation of work will provide opportunities for earning an income, but the uncertainty will be softened by reformed social security that everyone can genuinely rely on.'[9]

Our Nokia phones may be gathering dust in a drawer today, but Finland is still benefiting from Nokia's success, long after the boom period of the initial investment has faded. This is what's possible when the public take a stake in return for investment in the early stages of an industry – mobile communications, in this case – to pay for a just transition to an inclusive society and circular economy.

Stop the stripping

When the Panama Papers hit the headlines in 2016, the cat of corporate tax dodging was out of the bag and it was time for a serious reckoning. Finally, we had the receipts.

The Panama Papers had it all – glamorous tropical locations, billions of dollars stashed in shady deals, the biggest brand names in the world and even guest appearances by royalty. The papers were treasure troves of leaked documents exposing information that the wealthiest people and biggest corporations in the world go to considerable lengths to keep hidden: detail on the some of the trillions of dollars stashed in secrecy havens, also known as tax havens. Tax havens are places where the tax rate is pretty much zero, and by having 'shell companies' (essentially, companies that exist on paper alone) registered in a haven, companies and individuals can dodge paying tax in the places where they earn income.

The Panama Papers (and their 2017 sequel, the Paradise Papers) gave us a rare insight into something long suspected: that those who benefit the most from our society are finding ever craftier ways of avoiding paying their share, and global leaders, as well as some of the world's biggest brand names, aren't above using tax minimisation tools that shift the costs of running society onto the rest of us. The world leaders listed included former presidents of Ukraine, Argentina, Ecuador and Sudan, former prime ministers Silvio Berlusconi from Italy and our own Malcolm Turnbull,[10] Iceland's prime minister Sigmundur Gunnlaugsson (who was forced to resign in the public uproar), as well as ministers, advisers and MPs from almost every country in the world. Queen Elizabeth II and the King of Saudi Arabia were in there too – our monarch was found to have £10 million (about AU$19 million) of her estate invested in the Cayman Islands and Bermuda, two notorious tax havens.[11]

Publication of the Panama Papers reinforced the idea that we might see more action on tax loopholes and inequality if our leaders' life experiences (and bank accounts) were closer to those of the average person. Economist Thomas Piketty has proposed a wealth tax on the super rich as a solution, and the call is growing. I agree, but I think it might be easiest to begin with corporate citizens.[12]

On the corporate front, Apple and Nike had their tax-dodging and haven-shopping exposed in the Papers. As did Glencore, one of the world's leading fossil-fuel extractors and Australia's biggest coal producer. In an amazing bit of cheek, Glencore then fought the Australian Tax Office all the way to the highest court in the land to try and have those leaked papers scrubbed from the public record so the ATO couldn't consider the reality of their books when working out their tax liability.[13] Give me the confidence of a tax-dodging multinational, please.

A tiny island in the English Channel, Jersey has a population of less than 100,000. If you'd believed Apple's 'Designed in California' tagline or if you'd stepped into an Apple store anywhere in the world, you might be surprised to find Jersey is the headquarters of two of the business units that dominate Apple's corporate structure and receive the bulk of their international earnings. While Apple has subsidiaries in every country they operate in (Apple Retail Germany, France, etc) the profits roll up to four business entities, two of which are based in Jersey, where the iPhone maker has US$252 billion stashed.

Their creative accounting is highly effective, leaving Apple paying a tax rate of about 3.7 per cent: in 2017, the year after the Panama Papers came out, their accounts showed income of US$44.7 billion outside the United States (that's about 55 per cent of their revenue) but they paid only US$1.65 billion in taxes outside the USA.[14]

How do they get away with it? Their armies of lawyers, accountants and publicists will tell you that what they're doing isn't technically illegal – they're bending the rules, not breaking them. Nevertheless, it's a deeply antisocial practice, and it has a name: profit stripping.

Basically, profit stripping is the practice whereby companies split up into multiple parts so they can shuffle money around in order to maximise their returns (that is, keep their tax bill as low as possible). One way to manufacture expenses and minimise tax is to make 'intragroup loans' within a transnational corporate group, from one subsidiary to another. The (usually expensive) loan repayments can be deducted from the taxable income, conveniently turning a profit into a loss when needed. It's not just tech giants who are masters of this manoeuvre: News Corp Australia, the local arm of Rupert Murdoch's media empire, is also famous for lending money from one part of its global business to another, usually cleverly working currency rates to engineer losses rather than profits. They're so good at it they routinely pay zero tax in Australia,[15] and in some years, they've even received whopping great tax refunds, like their rebate of AU$882 million from the ATO in 2013.[16] That one really stings, because News Corp is one of the main causes of our climate-denialist political culture in Australia, and this means we're actually paying Murdoch to poison our media landscape.

Other companies set up subsidiaries in tax havens that own crucial intellectual property that then charge hefty licensing fees to other parts of their business, creating on-paper expenses to be deducted from the tax bill in the country where they are earned. In one such example, Apple claimed to have made only $396 million in profit on $9 billion in sales in Australia in 2019.[17] The subsidiaries are incorporated in the tax haven of Ireland, but are non-resident companies of either Ireland or the USA for tax purposes, meaning that despite all Apple's global licensing profits flowing to Ireland, they're estimated to pay a tax rate of 0.005 per cent there.[18] When the International Consortium of Investigative Journalists (ICIJ) – the global network of journalists who delivered the revelations – looked into this practice, they found that key patents from companies that are household names – assets like the Nike 'Swoosh' trademark or Uber's app – are assigned to shell companies headquartered in tax havens.[19]

The end result of this profit-stripping is that, on paper, these enormously successful global firms can claim they only have expenses and losses in countries where they generate income, and massive profits in countries that, surprise surprise, have zero corporate tax rates. That's the reason we hear about Bermuda, the Caymans or dodgy corporate contortions like the 'Double Irish Dutch Sandwich' – moves that shuffle money through the tax havens of Ireland and the Netherlands – although places like Singapore and US states like Delaware are tax-avoidance destinations too.

This is hurting every society on the planet. It's estimated that multinational corporations are dodging US$500 billion a year globally: that's billions upon billions of dollars sucked away from the places where the profits were earned, allowing corporations to free-ride on the rest of society. It means we pay for the roads their delivery trucks drive on, the schools their employees study at, the police who patrol the streets outside their stores or for the courts they use to protect their trademarks, while they pay nothing or, at best, a token amount.

Here's the good news. The Panama and Paradise Papers did kick-start the process of change. The arrests and tax bills that followed didn't generate as much fanfare as the initial leaks, but the ICIJ estimate that there were subsequent investigations in 82 countries and $1.2 billion has been recouped so far.[20] It's a fraction of the money that leaks out through those tax loopholes, but it is a start.

We've also seen a growing coalition of advocates organising to change the rules, and mobilising around an alternative approach to taxing multinationals that would make taxes fairer and simpler around the world.

The Independent Commission for the Reform of International Corporate Taxation (ICRICT), an influential group of economists, civil society advocates and even ex-Treasurers like Australia's Wayne Swan, and global advocacy group the Tax Justice Network are among those fighting for unitary tax and country-by-country reporting, and they're making progress.

Unitary tax wipes away the corporate fictions that the various Apple or Nike or Google shell companies are all separate entities for tax purposes.

It's purely an accounting fantasy to pretend that Apple's Irish or Jersey firms are making profit while their other global businesses only make losses or that they're all genuinely independent companies. Instead, tax should be calculated on the income each of these companies generates as a whole. This is so central that it is article one of the ICRICT declaration:

> States must reject the artifice that a corporation's subsidiaries and branches are separate entities entitled to separate treatment under tax law, and instead recognize that multinational corporations act as single firms conducting business activities across international borders.[21]

To figure out where a company's actual economic activity is taking place, unitary tax asks: where is their workforce based? Where are their assets physically or practically held? Which country's resources do they depend on to do business? Based on the answers to those questions, unitary tax allows tax collectors to take the global total revenue and apportion it accordingly.

Sure, you can still have your Bermuda or Netherlands company, but if the majority of products are sold somewhere else and staff are based somewhere else again, then your tax debt is split up in those proportions and due in each of those jurisdictions. It makes sense, right?

While support for unitary tax has been growing over the last few years, there are a couple of hurdles to overcome. First of all, you have to get honest reporting on what these companies are doing in each country: this is known as country-by-country reporting.

In early 2020, there was a significant step forward for country-by-country reporting from an unlikely source. Big business and global leaders congregate at the World Economic Forum in Davos, Switzerland early each year. A discussion point over many years has been the unfairness of profit stripping, though there has been a reluctance to take on some of the most powerful corporations in the world. One of the surprises of 2020 was finally seeing support for public country-by-country reporting being voiced by leaders of the 'Big Four' accountancy firms of PwC, KPMG, Deloitte and EY.[22] They represent exactly the sector who've been involved in obscuring tax transparency. If we know where global firms actually generate their income, that's a meaningful step towards requiring them to pay tax where it's earned, not if or wherever they'd like.

There's a lot of jargon involved – those accountants and lawyers are earning their fees by keeping this deliberately, confoundingly boring – but basically we're talking here about putting this information out in the open, then applying a formula that makes the books a company keeps match with the activities they conduct in the real world. You create that formula (formulary apportionment, in the lingo) based on factors like sales, payroll or physical assets.[23]

The Tax Justice Network explains it like this:

> Imagine a company with 10,000 employees in Sweden, 10,000 employees in Tanzania, and two

tanned accountants throwing paper aeroplanes in an office in Bermuda. Under current rules, the profits are all shifted to Bermuda, which doesn't tax them. So it gets taxed nowhere. But under unitary tax, you would take the company's global profits then allocate nearly 50 percent to Sweden, nearly 50 percent to Tanzania, and almost none to Bermuda. Each country can tax its portion of the global profits at whatever rate it likes.[24]

Countries can then use this real-world info to override the 'transfer pricing' that companies do to profit shift, and say, 'You earned it here, so you pay the tax here. We're not buying that Apple Inc 1 and Apple Inc 2 are two separate companies that have nothing to do with each other.'

This, of course, is easier said than done, but the signs are positive that we will at last plug the leaks draining tax revenue from our societies. The Organization for Economic Co-operation and Development (OECD), a group of 36 higher wealth countries who negotiate together on standards and shared policy positions, have increasingly turned their focus towards tax-base erosion and profit shifting. The ICRICT warn that we shouldn't let the OECD set the terms of a fair new tax for the world – they tend to preference their wealthy members (often home to the most powerful firms) at the expense of the developing nations, who are also squeezed by multinational tax dodgers.[25] Instead the ICRICT recommend that tax treaties should be managed at the level of the United Nations and that developing countries be given equal voting rights and equal rights to amend the action plan on tax. They also think the OECD is setting the bar way too high in regards to the revenue of corporations covered. They want it lower, in order to achieve greater consistency and applicability in the developing world as well.

It's not perfect, but we're pointing in the right direction. I take this progress to be evidence that the social licence for this kind of free-riding is coming to an end. Google's parent company, Alphabet, announced in early 2020 that they're going to stop using the Double Irish Dutch Sandwich profit-shifting arrangement that has allowed them to stash about US$24.5 billion each year (AU$37 billion) in Bermuda: though some have surmised that this change of heart might just mean these multinationals have found new ways to hide profits that monitors haven't picked up on yet.[26]

I know much of this stuff is dry and hard to get excited about, but remember that currently we're unwittingly giving the richest companies (and people) in the world access to all the benefits of society with no obligation to reciprocate. The more of us who know this and demand change, the more likely we are to get it. Part of the solution has to be finding ways to explain what's not working, expose the companies that are profiteering from the loopholes and show that there are functional alternatives. As citizens, it's helpful to be able to name the alternatives we're asking for – like unitary taxation and transparent country-by-country reporting – so we know what to demand from our governments. As consumers, we can use our collective power to avoid or call out those businesses who aren't paying their fair share.

One way we can do that is by finding out who's playing by the rules and who isn't. A not-for-profit community benefit society in the UK decided to make this happen and in 2014 launched the Fair Tax Mark. It's a tick of approval for stockmarketlisted companies, private enterprises and social enterprises who've signed a Fair Tax Declaration – a pledge to pay the right amount of corporation tax at the right time and in the right place – and make their prosocial tax behaviour a selling point. We really need this at a global level too. Fair Tax Mark research in late 2019 found a US$155 billion dollar gap between what the 'Silicon Six' platform giants – Facebook, Google, Amazon, Apple, Microsoft and Netflix – actually paid in tax since 2010, and the US corporate tax rate.[27]

To address tax dodging by platform giants in particular, many countries – from the UK to France, India and even Australia – are floating the idea of a 'digital services tax', such as 2 per cent on income rather than profits. Yes, this could be another step in the right direction, and it puts the issue of tax injustice on the agenda, but does it go far enough? Tech companies are simply the most visible face of the bigger issue of profit shifting. Let's name the problem and push for a change across the board. Imagine the caring services and regenerative society we could pay for with that $500 billion that is dodged every year? It's time for big business to pay its share.

Tax pollution, not people

Almost everywhere you look, today's tax system is unfair and illogical in so many ways. I don't resent paying tax, as it goes to fund the public goods we need as a society, but when huge multinational corporations and wealthy individuals avoid paying their fair share, and when tax breaks encourage bad behaviour and planetary devastation, you can start to see why people hate taxes.

Tax systems around the world have failed to adapt to 21-stcentury reality.

We've inherited a model designed for the industrial, pre-globablised age and it's spluttering in the digital era, now that money knows no borders. It was designed for endless production and greedy consumption, but now we know our planet's resources are limited. Outdated tax policy is at the foundation of the unquestioned status quo that's warping society and destroying the planet. But it doesn't have to be that way.

'The fact that we emit carbon when we step in our car doesn't hurt us: it hurts the system and the world. It's outside of our little personal space, and that makes climate change such a difficult issue to communicate,' Femke Groothuis explains.

So, what we [at Ex'Tax, short for Value Extracted Tax] try to do is expand that narrative to all the externalities that are being created. And about how governments can shift their tax systems to put a price on those externalities, having the polluter pay. And then reduce the tax burden on labour. So, ordinary people who work for their money can actually have more money in their pocket and employers can more easily hire people as well.

It's a more sustainable type of economic growth that is based on human capacities and talents of people, rather than what we extract from the earth, what we use in terms of resources and how we interact with nature.

In our system today, taxes on labour (like payroll and income tax) inflate the cost of human time and ingenuity, making human time and skill more expensive to employ, while pollution is made artificially cheap by subsidies and accounting that fails to factor in costs to the planet and human health. In the European Union (EU), for example, 51 per cent of tax revenues come from taxing labour, while taxes on natural resources and consumption account for only 6 per cent of taxation. This means the political system is skewed to maintain a status quo that can't and won't last. Instead, can you imagine a tax system that rewards and funds a more caring, creative and sustainable world?

The good news is that there's a solution ready to roll – The Ex'Tax Project – which is one of the most thoughtful, comprehensive fixes I've encountered. Femke Groothuis is their 'wavemaker' and advocate in chief. We chat on the phone one evening and she talks me through the conventional approach to taxation, which has us frozen into making the poorest possible choices for people and planet, fooled into thinking this is as good as it gets.

Over the years, the heavy tax burden on labour has made labour so expensive that there's been a constant pressure on employers to reduce those costs by putting more pressure on fewer employees, to have as few employees as possible and have them do as much work as possible. In health care, that means fewer nurses and having only 10 minutes of time with your doctor, even if there's maybe a big decision to be taken or big news to be received. The same happened in business: we moved from customised or handmade products to more standardised and mass-produced goods. This is where IKEA comes in with a Billy bookcase rather than having a carpenter create a bookcase just for you.

We shift to mass consumption, mass production; we shift towards lower service levels; we shift to outsourcing labour to low-income countries; we shift to automation and robotisation – just in order to do more in less time, in terms of human labour. This whole process over the decades has got us in a situation where we actually have started to believe that labour efficiency is a good thing. We've become completely used to the fact that there is no personal care, and we have forgotten about resource efficiency.

So, what we're saying with Ex'Tax is, 'Look, without losing what we may have gained in some smart ways to do things, we should re-learn that personal attention is really what makes us happy.' And that we can have that, if we change the financial incentives. We can have more personal care, we can have more doctors and nurses and we can have more teachers. I'm not sure how it is in Australia, but here my kids are in classes of 30 kids with one teacher who is overworked, who doesn't know everything, who can't really take time to take care of kids that might need some extra help or have extra interests.

Femke stops to look up the English translation of the word she's searching for.

'It's *meagre.* It's not quality of life. We can do better. To have a teacher with 30 kids versus having one teacher with a support system around that teacher to help the kids with their interests and to help them flourish ... we could organise for that. We're just not doing it.'

The day I speak to Femke in late 2019, her home country of the Netherlands is wracked by a very unusual crisis – known as the Nitrogen Crisis. Farmers had jumped on their tractors and blockaded the country's capital of The Hague, joined by construction workers with heavy machinery. These workers had been blindsided by a legal decision of the highest court in the land, which ruled that the Dutch government had given out more permits to emit nitrogen than could be used while still meeting the Netherlands' EU commitments on protecting nature reserves and waterways. Because nitrogen pollution – in the form of nitrous oxide and ammonia – is emitted in construction, industrial agriculture and in car exhausts, that meant the country had to implement dramatic change, and they had to do it overnight. Construction permits were slashed almost in half, meaning only 47,000 of 75,000 planned houses could be built in 2020. The speed limit on motorways was cut from 130 to 100 kilometres per hour as apparently cars emit more nitrogen when driving faster. As emissions from agriculture account for 46 per cent of nitrogen pollution, some politicians suggested halving the number of livestock in the country.

The Nitrogen Crisis is a taste of what the future looks like when we crash into our planetary realities without having a plan B in place.

'It's about running into a boundary set by international regulation on health and nature protection, and it's about neglecting the external costs that come with our consumption and production system,' Femke says in the course of explaining the Nitrogen Crisis to me. 'And just postponing, really, dealing with that type of issue. And then running into this boundary where actually judges say, "You can't go any further because you're damaging both health and the natural environment."'

The disruption created by the Nitrogen Crisis demonstrates how society and the economy have been made more unstable by governments living beyond their environmental means. Some politicians refuse to take action on climate change because they say it'll be too expensive to transition to a new kind of economy, and they won't risk the jobs or economic output we have today. But when you see a crisis like this rock a country, it becomes crystal clear that maintaining today's system, which doesn't account for impacts on ecosystems, isn't stable economic stewardship at all. Actually, that devaluing of the environment makes the whole system incredibly fragile. The moment one resource starts being properly measured, or becomes scarce, the whole house of cards falls apart.

That's the kind of risk Femke is working to eliminate with Ex'Tax. It's a systems-level redesign of taxation to make it a force for good, a new approach that incentivises investment in care and human capital and reduces exploitation of our environment. Ex'Tax would prevent sudden breakdowns like this by more transparently and accurately accounting for the costs that get left off the books. What if using finite natural resources, and polluting waterways, land and the air, was more expensive than doing the right thing? But Ex'Tax isn't just a stick, imposing costs to change behaviour. It's also a carrot, spurring a positive shift towards hiring more people to apply their minds, hearts and hands to build the solutions we need.

Ex'Tax would make it cheaper to engage human creativity to design better products, improve efficiencies or deliver more high-touch services (ones that rely on human interaction and effort, like those in the care economy, education, healthcare and eldercare, for instance). It would also remove the perverse incentives whereby workers are currently subsidising their robotic replacements, as we all do when companies get to deduct spending on tech from their accounts. Unlike today's tax system – which emerged before work could be moved to find the lowest paid people, and before we knew the environmental impacts of a linear (take-make-waste) consumption model, Ex'Tax proposes to shift taxes from labour to natural resource use. So, not only would it be cheaper to employ more people to be more hands-on, and more engaged in solving problems, we'd finally have a taxation system that put a real price on using the precious resources of our natural world.

I've learned a lot writing this book, but one of the things that has stunned me the most was learning about the obscene scale of environmentally harmful subsidies: I knew we were paying polluters, but I had no idea how much.

The International Energy Agency estimates that, globally, we spend about US$400 billion a year (that's almost AU$600 billion) to make fossil-fuel use cheaper.[28] That means significant amounts of the tax we pay are actually used to give wasteful industries an unfair advantage over energy-efficient industries. Our taxes help fossil fuels to be kept artificially cheaper than generating new, cleaner forms of energy. And we pay a lot: these subsidies are over four times the value of subsidies to renewable energy. I'm even more astonished when I learn this is the most conservative estimate of the scale of global fossil fuel subsidies: the (hardly very radical) International Monetary Fund (IMF) go further. By their estimates, we paid polluters subsidies as high as US$4.7 trillion in 2015 and US$5.2 trillion in 2017. The reason their calculations run so high is that they're trying to take into account some of the costs society bears as result of these polluters, such as poor air quality affecting health and cutting lives short. The researchers find that if fuel prices had been actually at 'efficient levels' in 2015 – that is, not subsidised – then 'estimated global CO_2 emissions would have been 28 per cent lower, fossil fuel air pollution deaths 46 per cent lower, tax revenues higher by 3.8 per cent of global GDP, and net economic benefits (environmental benefits less economic costs) would have amounted to 1.7 per cent of global GDP.'[29]

The picture is just as bad for other scarce resources: the IMF estimated that in 2012, water subsidies totalled about US$456 billion.[30]

The argument in favour of these subsidies is always that they're helping the poorest people afford fuel and water, which may have some truth to it, but doesn't take into account the benefits heavy industry gains by being able to operate wastefully without implementing resource efficiencies. Plus it isn't the most efficient way of making water or energy affordable for households and carries a heavy opportunity cost for the poorest people they're supposedly helping. By spending four times the amount on destructive fossil fuels rather than investing in the energy sources of the future, we're doing nothing to protect and prepare the populations who are most vulnerable to the impacts of climate change and resource disruption.

Not only are the environmental impacts often rendered invisible or abstracted by today's accounting and tax practices, but so are the spill-over effects on human lives. Ex'Tax is one of the first models to seriously attempt to measure some of these impacts and demand that the true social and environmental costs are taken into account.

'Basically, these sectors are poisoning us,' Femke says. 'Every Dutch person loses about a year of life because of air pollution. But nobody's talking about it – we think it's totally normal that we live in a hotspot of air pollution.'

While we're blind to the invisible subsidies and ill-effects of the status quo, we're also oblivious to what we could gain by flipping the script on tax, but the upside would be transformative in the lives of millions. In 2016, Ex'Tax worked with accounting giants Deloitte, EY, KPMG Meijburg and PwC to chart the potential impact of a tax shift on the 27 countries of the EU, and found that an Ex'Tax transition over five years would result in 6.6 million more people in employment in the European Union and a 2 per cent increase in GDP. That's because this model reduces the cost of hiring people, as well as reducing the amount people pay in income tax, while maintaining the same tax receipts for governments. In the EU, that means moving a staggering €1716 billion (that's AU$2818 billion) in tax revenues from labour to taxes on natural resources and consumption. It means people pay less tax and polluters pay more. It's a great tool to decouple GDP growth from the use of natural resources, resulting in a 6 per cent reduction in CO_2 emissions, as well as reductions in water use and energy imports.

Initially, Ex'Tax focused on the wealthy countries of the global north, like Femke's home country of the Netherlands, as well as Finland and a broader plan for the EU. Just recently, they jumped in to assess the potential impact of an Ex'Tax shift for a developing country, and they started with Bangladesh, a country very much on the front line of climate impacts.

'There's 165 million people there and it's a growing population, with two million young people entering the labour market every year, which means that there's a huge need for decent jobs,' Femke explains. 'At the same time, they're extremely prone to the climate crisis. They're already paying the price of the emissions done by other countries.'

Bangladesh is tiny geographically – it's about the size of New York state in the USA – and incredibly densely populated. It's a delta, a low-lying country vulnerable to floods, cyclones and landslides, with sea-level rise a real and urgent danger: two-thirds of the country is less than 5 metres above sea level. Climate refugees are already part of daily reality: it's estimated that

700,000 Bangladeshis are displaced every year due to natural disasters.[31]

If you check the tags on your clothes, it's likely more than a few of them say 'Made in Bangladesh'. Their economy is reliant on the highly polluting and energy-intensive garment industry. The Bangladeshi garment industry also takes a huge toll on people: we should never forget the horrific Rana Plaza disaster in 2013, when a garment factory in Dhaka collapsed, killing 1134 people in what has been labelled 'mass industrial homicide'.

If Ex'Tax could have an impact here and redesign a tax system for social and environmental justice, Bangladesh could leap ahead in energy and resource efficiency, shifting their industries and environment to sustainability, while improving people's incomes and quality of life. This could be an example to the world that climate action and caring for people go hand-in-hand.

Femke explains:

> The technicalities of the tax reform will look different in every country or region, but the ultimate

goal behind it is to align fiscal policy and financial incentives with the goals of achieving economic growth based on human capacity, rather than the extraction of natural resources. That's a global perspective that doesn't have to do with whether you're a low- or high- or medium-income country, so we took our tools and focused on Bangladesh. We learned a lot about the country, had a lot of conversations and figured out the number of tools in terms of revenue-raising measures is fairly limited. [That's] because of the tax structure not being as strong as [in] many other countries. But still there are options. There is an option to put a price on carbon emissions by focusing on bulk emitters – industry and the power sector – and there's a large amount of money going into fossil-fuel subsidies.

If you can reduce those, you raise a lot of domestic resources that you can use to support both infrastructure – for example, trains, roads, houses and defence against the climate-crisis impacts – or you can use those revenues to invest in social spending. So, you can help the poor section of the population to have a higher disposable income, which in itself supports the regional and local economy, because people can actually spend more money and can feed their kids better, they can start businesses, they become more self-sufficient.

Bangladesh (and many other developing nations) are improving the lives of their people by focusing on meeting the United Nations' Sustainable Development Goals, but the goals aren't achievable without a plan for paying for them. The revenue shift that Ex'Tax offers could fund that world we want.

'Developing countries face an annual financing gap of US$2 trillion: international co-operation is not bringing that amount of money at all. So, there is a need for aligning policy and raising revenues sustainably in developing countries in order to achieve the SDGs,' Femke says.

Some countries and regions have implemented elements of the Ex'Tax approach: in 2008, the province of British Columbia in Canada introduced a price on carbon that was used to lower other taxes, which has proven the case as the economy has grown while carbon emissions have gone down, more than in Canada's other regions. There are now 28 emission trading systems and 29 carbon taxes around the world – mostly focusing on taxing carbon or other resources – but these stickled approaches have been easy prey for the cashed-up fossil fuel barons to take down.

There's a terrible example from Australia's recent history: a major review of taxation was commissioned in 2008, known as the Henry Review, which recommended a host of major changes to the tax code to help make things fairer, particularly for women (who are disincentivised from returning to work after kids by clumsy tax and transfer policies) and to help the country as a whole benefit from the mining boom that was then in full swing. For years, Australia has allowed corporations to dig up its mineral wealth – something which, I believe, should belong to the nation – and make extraordinary profits, on which they pay a royalty to the state and very little federal tax. At the time of the Henry Review, mining companies were making profits of close to 50 per cent on their investments – an astronomical amount for any business – while paying less than 10 per cent on taxes and royalties.

The Labor government at the time picked up one of Henry's recommendations, a Resource Super Profits Tax (RSPT), which proposed taxing these profits at a 40 per cent rate for returns above the rate of capital. That's a bit confusing, but basically, it means for profits (after expenses) over about 6 per cent (which was the standard return on investments at the time), they'd have to pay 40 per cent tax, while they'd also benefit from a tax cut across the board on those initial, standard profits – a tax cut that would have been paid for by the huge boon the RSPT would bring in. It was estimated that in its first year, the RSPT would have brought in AU$9 billion:[32]

imagine the social benefit this money could have provided, the jobs it would have created, the projects it could have powered, helping to transition Australia from its chronic reliance on exactly these kinds of extractive fossil fuel industries.

Sadly, all we can do is imagine.

The forces that profit from fossil fuel destruction rose up with an almighty howl of entitlement and indignation. Flush with cash, big miners like BHP and industry lobbyists the Minerals Council of Australia threw $17 million dollars at undermining the RSPT. They commissioned a media campaign saying this tax shift threatened Australian prosperity and jobs, and flooded the airwaves with their message – at the height of the campaign, their ads were playing 33 times a day on average on the television networks, alongside massive print and radio buys. The government tried to fight back with their own media campaign: prominent economists wrote an open letter and opinion pieces in support, and even the International Monetary Fund backed it.

But the forces of fossil fuels had deep pockets: aided by the fact that as well as being the forces hastening planetary peril, these companies are also shameless tax avoiders. Richard Heede at the Climate Accountability Institute analysed emissions since the 1960s and listed the companies with the biggest climate footprints, naming four companies – Chevron, Exxon, BP and Shell – as responsible for 10 per cent of global carbon emissions since 1965. And yet, despite their massive environmental impacts and huge profits, they contribute almost nothing to the countries they base their mines and wells in. Journalist Michael West dived into their books and found some astonishingly creative accounting. For example, despite revenue of AU$7.8 billion over three years from their Australian operations, Chevron has paid zero tax.[33] Exxon is even worse, generating AU$24.8 billion over three years in their gas extraction operations, and paying zero tax.[34]

Their cheerleaders might claim these extraction economy companies benefit the country through employment and contribute through payroll tax. Not so much. Across the entire country, mining employs approximately 238,000 people, according to the Australian Labour Market Information Portal.[35] That's less than 2 per cent of the workforce, a number which is steadily falling as this industry contracts and pours much of their ill-gotten gains into automation.

By leveraging their financial might, the extraction sector managed to confuse the issue of the RSPT in the public sphere, destabilise the government to the point that the governing Labor Party had a 'spill' (that's Australian for an 'internal party coup') and the Prime Minister was replaced. Cowed, the government watered down the RSPT and created the Minerals Resource Rent Tax instead, a much less onerous tax on resource wealth that generated a tiny fraction of what the RSPT would have. Possibly even worse, all the other Henry Tax Review recommendations were shelved and Australia's tax system was left as dysfunctional and perverse as ever.

The lesson from that terrible episode is this: to make a shift like this stick, you've got to lead with the human benefit, the return to the community in infrastructure and to individuals in lower income tax and greater employment opportunities. You've also got to find a way to take the fossil-fuel money out of the picture, because the massive wealth of that sector enables them to buy the airwaves and dominate the conversation to tip the balance in their favour.

As author and activist Naomi Klein points out in her book *On Fire,* you've got to de-fang the coal, oil and gas beast by undermining its own fragile dependence on future profitability: making it clear they'll never be able to build another mine or drill another well without facing a tsunami of public opposition. Cutting that influence out of politics is crucial before a transition like this is possible. As we saw earlier in our story, one of the greatest achievements of the young leaders in the Sunrise Movement has been to get a significant number of political candidates to commit to refuse to take donations from the fossil-fuel companies, while in Australia, USA and the UK, another important move will be reducing the influence of the climate-change-denying Murdoch/Fox media.

Klein writes: 'With less misinformation skewing debates, and a clear separation between oil and state, the path would be far clearer for the kinds of robust regulations that would quickly reign in this rogue sector, because all extractive companies function within a non-negotiable "grow-or-die" framework: they need to constantly reassure investors that their product will be in high demand not just today but well into the future.'[36]

***

If the toxic fallout from the mildly ambitious RSPT is any indication, in Australia at least, it's unlikely that governments are going to be brave enough to lead on the tax shift we need to build the future we want. The good news is that some of the business world is out in front: the CDP (formerly known as Carbon Disclosure Project) is a UK organisation which holds big business to account, using the influencer power of investors and consumers to put pressure on companies to report on their impact on climate change, water security and forests. So far, they represent 525 investors with US$96 trillion in assets and 120 major buyers with a combined purchasing power of US$3 trillion. More than 8400 companies worldwide have made disclosures to CDP, and a number of those are going further by adding a resource tax to their accounting, which they take into account when they're making decisions about their supply chains, even if their governments are too timid to take action. Femke explains:

> There's 1300 companies applying an internal carbon price in their books – or in the process of implementing one. They actually work with a fictitious carbon tax that they process in their books to improve their long-term decision-making ... For example, Unilever has put a price on carbon internally, [the revenue] has been put in a fund and they invest in low-carbon technologies. Apple is doing that too. It's a

super-interesting dynamic where actually businesses are ahead of government. And they say to government, 'We think there should be a price on carbon, we think there will be a price on carbon. And you're not arranging for this quick enough, so we'll take our responsibility and implement that pricing system even if you don't.'

One of the reasons I'm so excited about Ex'Tax – despite the big challenges I can see in convincing recalcitrant governments like ours to take the leap – is that it's the accounting method that underpins a transition to a circular economy. That's a way of describing a manufacturing and consumption ecosystem in which nothing is wasted and resources are recovered and reused at the end of the life of a product. It's the opposite to the outdated, linear make-take-dispose approach of today, which our tax system reinforces through what it subsidises.

In the business-as-usual approach, companies doing the right thing aren't competing on a level playing field with those who waste materials, use toxic and finite resources or pollute. Bad operators benefit from invisible incentives on the resource side and those who are trying to make a positive difference are weighed down with taxes on workers who could make better products or deliver human-centric services. Femke says the circular economy is gaining traction in the business community, but as companies adopt the approach, they hit a wall when they discover how the market is distorted by policies that encourage wasteful products and processes. Femke says:

[The circular economy] is a total redesign of products and supply-chain services, and every company that steps into that field – like IKEA, who's aiming to be circular in 2030 – they soon find out that to change your business model, with the financial incentives that are in place currently, is really hard to do.

If there's no price on externalities, you compete with a product that can pollute for free.

To create a product that doesn't pollute takes you a lot of time and effort as it's so labour intensive and knowledge intensive. [Currently], there is no level playing field for circular activities, but the more companies move into that direction, the more they will encourage governments to change the rules of the game in favour of circular business models.

We're quite a way through our journey in this book, shining a light on the creative solutions and transformative mindset shifts that can help us build a more caring and sustaining world.

All the movements we've been exploring seek to embed structural change at the foundations of the systems we have – or to rethink them completely – so that we can turn our ship in a new direction. We need to address the disconnect between what our society says it values and what it pays for. We need to elevate work that enhances human life and restores our planet, by rewarding the human capacity to care and create. It's all eminently possible, but we have to actively name these values, talk about alternatives and choose a new path.

To bring these possibilities into reality, we need to make sure our money – whether through tax or in our financial system – is working for the benefit of society, and not against continued life on our one and only planet. Let's stick with the money and find out how it can be spent on the stuff that really matters.

7

Reform finance

As I was starting this chapter in 2019, banks and bankers were the villains-in-chief in the Australian news narrative. Every radio broadcast, current affairs show and newspaper was filled with stories about the Royal Commission into Misconduct in Banking, a hearing process into bad banking practices exploiting people and ruining lives. Royal Commissions are one of the ways governments in this country launch probing investigations into systemic issues or major mishandlings; from the impact of British nuclear testing to Aboriginal deaths in custody, from cross-border corruption to responses to the abuse of children in care. But there's a catch: since it's the government of the day that sets the terms and scope of investigations, if they're not really out for change, quite often the tiger is sent out without any teeth.

Most Australians are understandably sceptical that anything will change the practices of our 'big four' banking oligarchy, organisations that were exposed for charging dead people fees for life insurance and pushing exploitative products on vulnerable people, among other outrages.

These dominant commercial banks have been doing nicely out of Australia's addiction to the property bubble: in 2016, The Australia Institute found that our banks are the most profitable in the world. Their earnings accounted for 2.9 per cent of our entire country's GDP, which means that for every dollar earned in Australia in a year, approximately 3 cents of it was a bank profit.[1] While that has started slowing down thanks to falling interest rates and the outcomes of the Royal Commission – and it's likely the COVID19 crisis will have an impact on their bottom line – at the time of writing, they're still making billions in profit every year.

Australian banks have also been cynical players in the shift from fossil fuels to a renewable energy future: they trumpet their environmental responsibility while continuing to fund climate destruction by bankrolling the fossil fuel industry. In early 2019, the environmental activist group Market Forces found that Westpac had 'increased exposure' (that's banking lingo for 'lending') to coal mining by 140 per cent on 2017 levels, and over the same period ANZ had increased funding to coal mining by 27 per cent.[2] Across the board, in 2019 the big four had $29 billion of Australia's savings sunk in fossil fuels, while only $11.5 billion was invested in funding renewable energy.

Having said all that, it seems counterintuitive to now tell you that there are bankers and finance renegades helping us fund the future we need. They're reforming the financial services sector to be a force for creation, not just extraction, by building new banks with public benefit at their foundation and establishing whole new currencies that reimagine money as a tool for supporting the local, the human and the real economy. They're building goals of positive environmental and social impacts into their foundations, and finding ways of using money to do good while generating returns. I don't hold out much hope that the dominant banks of today will suddenly reform their ways, or that the solutions lie in cryptocurrency or digital payments wizardry, but I do have hope that here in the real economy, solutions are being tested that could blossom into a wholly new, generous and prosocial (as opposed to antisocial) financial system that works to serve our messy reality.

That distinction – between the realm of finance and the 'real economy' – is a necessary one for us to explore for a moment, and Giuseppe Littera has an excellent (if disturbing) analogy to explain it to me. Giuseppe is one of the five co-founders of Sardex. For the last ten years, Sardex has been rewriting the role of money on the Italian island of Sardinia by creating a system that keeps money circulating locally, rather than being used in hedges and gambles or stockpiled offshore.

More on them later. For now, it's Saturday night in Sydney, Saturday morning on the island of Sardinia, and Giuseppe is on the phone excitedly talking me through a paper from the Bank of International Settlements.

Claudio Barrio is the head of monetary policy at the central bank of central banks [the Bank for International Settlements]. When he talks about the monetary system, he says it is joined at the hip. On the one side you have the real economy and the balance of trade between countries, and on the other hand you have the financial side of the monetary system. That's where you have the 'too big to fail', you've got derivatives, you've got all sorts of things.

Now, one thing that's crazy is: if it were a body, the real economy leg would be 1 metre long. The other side would be 2.5 kilometres.

It takes a few seconds for the image to form in my head, and then I can't help but laugh. A more appropriate response would be to cry. I've read all kinds of stats, but Giuseppe's picture of the size of the financialised economy versus the 'real economy' most of us operate in captures how distorted the world of money from money has become. That 2.5 kilometre leg represents the money that washes around stock markets: it includes investments and a lot of retirement savings, sure, but it also includes bets being wagered against future upturns and downturns, liabilities grouped together and gambled on. There are some socially useful benefits to some of this swirling cash: the argument has always been that the flow of capital that the finance sector provides helps fund the loans and purchases that people and businesses need more money to make. But increasingly, the connection to the tangible world has become more tangential, and the cash splash more self-serving. That comically long leg throws our real world off balance, with devastating, long-term impacts.

Dutch economist Servaas Storm writes that the size of the asset pool for 'money from money' transactions (like overnight securities lending, derivatives, etc) is over US$500 trillion – that's eight times the value of global GDP.[3] It's hard to imagine the vastness of it, but let's pause here for a moment for that to sink in. Every shopping trip, every tenancy, every crop harvested or herd sold, every load transported, every public transit trip, every bit of product traded or made in every country on Earth – all of that – times eight, every year. That's how big the financial bubble has inflated and floated off beyond the real economy.

At its most elemental, money is a tool and a fuel, intended to help people trade goods and services. Originally, the finance sector emerged to help makers and traders in real goods and services insure against crop losses, disasters or lean times. In the past few decades, the operations of the financial sector have become much more removed from the physical world of goods and services, and many businesses have felt their access to credit contract even as the world is awash in liquidity. In the UK, where the financial sector is hugely dominant in the national economy and politics, less than 10 per cent of bank lending goes outside the FIRE (finance, insurance and real estate) sector.[4]

Even from within the industry, there are critics of the way the scales have been titled too far in the direction of financialisation: they say the money market is driving the economy, rather than serving it, to all our detriment.[5]

Back to those wonky legs.

'That's my reading and putting [Claudio Barrio's] words into an image,' Giuseppe explains. 'He doesn't see it as problematic that much, but it recognises and highlights that in the past 20 years, all of the recessions and depressions that happened around the world were ultimately initiated by the financial side of the monster. And that is where it doesn't get funny anymore.'

Sardex is a currency and a system that resets the equation and restores money to its original purpose as a tool of trade. Sardex keeps money circulating in businesses around the island of Sardinia, rather than being hoarded, gambled or sent offshore. Every unit of Sardex circulates around the island an average of 12 times a year, used solely for transactions creating value in the real economy. They're used for dentist visits and dinners, for furniture and fruit, even for cars. This is money that works for people, to fuel small businesses and provide liquidity when cash flow is tight, harnessing and augmenting the activity that was waiting to happen if only people could get the credit or cash to spend.

'The whole point,' explains Giuseppe, 'was, "Can the private sector that is active in the real economy join forces, pool their productive capacity together, and on the back of that productive capacity extend credit to one another and trade without interest?"'

For the past ten years, Sardex has allowed businesses to trade in goods and services when they don't have cash. The organisation sets a credit limit that caps their spending depending on their size, and they can use that limit to buy goods or services from other Sardex members. When others trade with them in turn, their 'debt' is repaid and the system is in balance. You don't generate interest by stockpiling Sardex in your account: this is a currency designed for circulation, not accumulation. Giuseppe says the terms and conditions every Sardex user agrees to even allow Sardex organisers to charge negative interest if hoarding behaviours should arise.

Sardex serves to formalise and extend the barter and trust relationships that would have existed long ago in the villages that dot the island, beyond immediate networks and across this semi-autonomous Italian region, with its 1.5 million people.

It sounds simple enough, but there was nothing easy about the last ten years, Giuseppe assures me. After the 2008 global financial crisis, money had trickled all the way up and was nowhere to be found for businesses on his home island, or in many other places besides. Public funds went to bail out the excesses of bankers and financiers, to counterbalance the instability generated by the risky financial games they'd been playing. That left the people in the real economy with austerity measures and cuts to government budgets, as well as a contraction in access to credit. In Sardinia, there was 50 per cent youth unemployment, negative wage growth and GDP per capita was on the slide. Things were looking bleak for the island, and you'd think that people might put up their defences and stop taking risks. But that's exactly when Sardex's five founders came forward with their idea. Even though it seemed like giving away goods for free, on good faith, businesses were persuaded to take that leap of faith. How did the Sardex founders do it?

'Coming back to the beginning, it was telling them that they could be part of something that would help them overcome the crisis together. So, the message was more 50:50. [The first half was] "Stick together because you're in the same boat", sort of a wake-up call. And the other was more business-oriented and it was the typical pitch that you do when you bootstrap a community currency, and that is: "Can you imagine selling a little bit more of what you produce?"'

The other secret? 'We never never ever overpromise shit to no one,' Giuseppe says. 'We tried everything but bullshit. And I think that is also a reason why we got more trust and the community also trusted itself more.'

Interviewing Giuseppe is unlike speaking to any other start-up founder, and not simply because of his conviction that success relies in part on underpromising and then overdelivering. He insists on explaining how deeply unqualified he and his cofounders are to be doing this, how many missteps and mistakes they've made along the way and how little profit they're making now ('I often say a well-managed sandwich shop in Milan makes way more money than we do,' he quips).

'There is still lots of frictions because of our initial lack of experience – none of us had managed any company before – so it's been a miracle we survived all this learning and failures. We've made tons of mistakes.'

Giuseppe and his co-founders – Gabriele Littera, Piero Sanna, Carlo Mancuso and Franco Contu – all grew up together in Serramanna on Sardinia and felt something had to be done to help lift their home out of the crisis. None of the team had experience in economics or finance, but what they did have were deep connections to communities on the island and a determination to try something new. While studying in the UK in the mid-2000s, Giuseppe had come across the story of WIR, a currency invented in Switzerland in the 1930s that is an 'economic circle', a network for trade within a community – and when he shared it with the four others, they saw a way forward. The world of finance seemed to have forgotten Sardinia, so by launching Sardex, Giuseppe and his friends created a platform for their community to help themselves.

There are growing numbers of 21st-century complementary currencies out there, many of them inspired by WIR, but in my opinion, none match the scale and ambition of Sardex. I was excited to see Brixton Pounds being accepted in shops around the South London suburb, and several pilot projects are underway in Europe, including the SoNantes digital currency being trialled around Nantes in France and TradeQoin and Makkie in Amsterdam, the Netherlands. But while these and other complementary currencies aim to connect and support businesses in a suburb, town or city, Sardex extends across the entire island.

'We didn't do a "city thing", if I can call it that, because we are from the countryside,' Giuseppe says. 'If we did a city thing, it would have been a 10,000-person currency. We chose to do an island-wide one – and that's 1.5 million people – to increase our hope of being heard and having business owners first, employees and consumers later, join this community effort.'

Even if there have been trials and tribulations along the way, it is working. In ten years, Sardex has facilitated 400 million euros of activity between 4000 companies, 3000 workers and, more recently, 5000 consumer members. Giuseppe says that so far they're 'stuck at goodwill' with the regional government, who could play a transformative role by supporting a local currency like Sardex. The regional government spends seven billion euros a year; if they prioritised local procurement in their tenders or if some of their spend was paid out in Sardex, that would be a big boost to keeping money circulating in the real economy, close to home.

As to whether technology does have a role to play, Giuseppe is adamant that Sardex wouldn't function if it was just an app: 'You really need people on the ground; you need committed participants. As much as I like the cryptocurrency world – I'm very fascinated by it as a technologist and as a curious person – we needed something that has social adoptability built in, and that's hard. We're talking about institutions, not just code. That's why we have a very cautious approach to the new technologies that we could employ and could probably make everything more replicable,' he says.

'You can copy–paste tokens, you can copy–paste code, but you cannot copy–paste trust.'

Bank the unbanked

Local liquidity is an important place to begin to redesign money to work for people. Another is remittances, that transnational flow of worker pay we talked about in relation to care work. It's probably not front-of-mind for those of us with banking apps on our phones or bank branches on our high streets, but making remittances less exploitative and more transparent would take millions of people closer to financial security and empowerment.

People leave their home countries for lots of reasons, and economic opportunity is right up near the top of the list. It's an enormous personal sacrifice to leave your family to work far from home, often for years or even decades, but many people find themselves making the difficult choice to leave and work in countries where they can make more income. The money they send back, or remit, forms a large proportion of the income of some developing countries: the World Bank estimated global remittance flows to be $613 billion in 2017. In countries like Liberia and Gambia, remittances account for between a third and 20 per cent of GDP.[6]

But for many the costs of sending money home are steep – for people sending money to Sub-Saharan Africa, it can cost up to 10 per cent of the amount being transferred – and matters are complicated when transferring to regions where there are no banks.

While in some parts of the world we're struggling to contain the influence and correct the behaviour of our banking institutions, in other parts of the world, the very lack of financial infrastructure holds people back. Around 1.7 billion people are 'unbanked'[7] – that is, lacking access to a bank account – which means they have limited ability to save, access credit, transfer funds or insure themselves against risks.

'How different the meaning of the word "bank" is in developed markets versus the rest of the world,' Claudio Lisco muses over coffee. 'For me, a bank might be my mobile app, because I never go into a branch, or an investment bank like JP Morgan, who may not always do the right thing. For others, going to the bank can be like a social activity.'

Claudio is telling me about his experience working in remote islands of the Philippines, where what are known as 'rural banks' – which more or less operate off-grid – provide most people with access to the savings and credit they need to run their businesses or plan for the future.

A technologist and former banker, Claudio now leads a team at ConsenSys, a company founded by one of the creators of Ethereum, a platform for financial transactions that – like cryptocurrency poster child Bitcoin – operates digitally outside the banking system. Ethereum is a bit different to Bitcoin and other cryptocurrencies: from the outset, Ethereum has positioned itself as the foundation for a new ecology of technologies enabled by the public distributed ledger called a blockchain. These are things like smart contracts, identity assurance, tracking of provenance and supply chains and much more.

In his role at ConsenSys, Ethereum's research lab, Claudio is working on projects around the planet – and all from his new home base in Sydney. One of the first he tackled at ConsenSys was remittances to the Philippines. It could, he says, be replicated in many contexts globally to help more of the unbanked world gain financial security and more control over the money they earn and send home.

The Philippines is a great place to start solving this problem. It's the third largest recipient of remittances in the world, after India and China. Some 10 million Filipinos work overseas and the money they send home accounts for up to 10 per cent of their homeland's GDP.[8] The Philippines is an archipelago of thousands of islands with varying levels of technology and infrastructure and, perhaps arising from that, the country has one of the lowest levels of banking in South-east Asia – in 2017, only 12 per cent of the adult population held savings at a formal financial institution leaving 70 million Filipinos unbanked.[9] This presents a daunting challenge for communities that are reliant on money being transferred from abroad.

Outside the major cities, the Philippines is served by 454 rural banks. These can help people with their everyday money needs but they aren't connected to each other, to national banks or to international networks like SWIFT (those codes that allow you to transfer money overseas). All this means that Filipinos rely heavily on networks like Western Union, which can be very expensive, or informal networks like moneylenders or pawn shops, which offer very little in the way of security.

Claudio and his colleagues at ConsenSys were invited to help design something better. In collaboration with Unionbank, the largest bank in the Philippines, they created an Ethereum-based payment network for remittances, then ran a six-month pilot to flush out and address any problems. The ConsenSys tool is a fascinating combination of the very high tech and the extremely low-fi. The system was built on a closed cryptocurrency ledger to manage the transfers and track transactions across the Philippines, but its public faces are the same trusted rural banks that are at the heart of many communities.

'One of the banks we worked with had set up an ATM at their main branch, but people just used the security guard as a bank teller, handing him their card and PIN, because they didn't trust the machine. When we understood that they trusted human interaction, we left that as a core part of the user experience,' Claudio says.

He explains that although many people have smart phones, an app just wouldn't cut it in this context. Because the trusted human element has been built in, this tool could spread even to more remote parts of the Philippines, where even the rural banks don't reach. 'The service could be provided by a rural bank but also by anywhere that had good cash flow, for liquidity, and credibility in the community.'

The pilot went so well that Project i2i launched in early 2019, with clearance and support from the Central Bank of the Philippines, 130 rural banks already on board, and a plan to add the remaining 346 rural banks to the platform by the end of 2019. If it can work in the Philippines, this may be a positive step towards financial inclusion for hundreds of millions of people.

Build public banks for public good

For some, the problem is not enough access to financial services, while in the developed world we are often wary of a financial sector that seemingly operates with little environmental or social responsibility.

To build a fairer world, the benefits banks receive from our governments have got to spark a mutual obligation – a responsibility to act in the interests of local communities or future generations – one that's consistent throughout their operations and which is at the core of their business.

'We pool our idle cash, our deposits, in the banking system and we protect them with insurance, allow [banks] to leverage equity capital, and then allow them to renew or recycle,' radical banker Kat Taylor explains. 'For every one dollar of equity banks have, they can join at least nine dollars of deposits to make a ten dollar loan. At ten times, that's exponential leverage and very powerful.'

Deposits from people like you and me form about 60 per cent of the basis for the loans the banks offer, and on which they earn phenomenal profits, as we've already seen.[10] To protect the deposits we keep in the bank in the form of our account balances, governments provide banks with a publicly funded safety net: in Australia, that's called the Australian government guarantee on deposits and it covers anything you have in the bank up to $250,000. Kat's point is that instead of insisting on impeccable behaviour in return for this ability to turn our bank balances into profitable loans and to issue debt, governments have enabled the anti-social behaviour in the financial sector, without demanding they maintain their lending to the real economy.

As we've already seen in our story, banking can be a tool for inclusion and is essential for a functioning economy, but to get better outcomes we have to set boundaries and non-negotiable obligations to society, and prescribe a healthier future for a sector that is backed by taxpayers around the world.

There are few signs that the dominant players today are making genuine change: instead, do we need to support and grow new kinds of banks that can serve as more socially minded solutions to the need for credit and finance?

There are movements, coalitions and leaders taking action to make banking better. Some of them, like Ellen Brown, founder of the Public Banking Institute, an American think tank, want to run banks as a public utility, to handle the deposits, loans and business of the state, saving taxpayers and ratepayers a fortune in interest and finance costs that could be directed instead to fund public works and social programs. Others, like radical banker Kat Taylor, are founding private banks that have benefit at the foundation, a sustainable development agenda and focus on green energy. A banking system that puts social benefit first is possible, and they're showing us how.

'What we mean by a public bank is a bank that takes government deposits and makes loans to government entities at a lower rate, to use our own [public] money more efficiently,' Ellen Brown explains. 'You've got so much liquidity rolling around in the state that you could consolidate.'

One of the world's most exciting new economic movements is building on foundations that are a century old. In 1919, a political movement called the Nonpartisan League arose on the plains of North Dakota in the United States. It was made up of small farmers who were furious that the power to fund their operations and the logistics chains to process their grain all rested in the hands of out-of-state corporations who could squeeze them at harvest time when their cash flow was weakest, then control the channels to market, holding their industry over a barrel.

But in unity, the farmers discovered power. 'When it was set up, the Bank of North Dakota (BND) was a farmers' rebellion,' Ellen Brown tells me. 'They were losing their farms to out-of-state banks and they wanted to keep their money in the state and use it for their own purposes. And that's what they did: they set up their own bank and they set up their own granaries.'

The farmers harnessed political power – they briefly won control of both houses of parliament in the state and got their own governor elected to enact their goals, establishing the Bank of North Dakota, a state-owned railroad company and a state-owned grain elevator and mill. They also brought about changes to tax policy in the state (including a highly progressive distinction between earned and unearned income – something we could use now). Their political moment of dominance was very short-lived, but the BND dodged attacks and survived the 20th century, helping North Dakota to thrive relative to its neighbouring states, particularly after the GFC.

'After the 2008 crisis, North Dakota was the only state that escaped the credit crisis: it had the lowest unemployment rate in the country, the lowest default rate, the lowest foreclosure rate. So, it's doing really well compared to the other states,' Ellen Brown says.

The BND isn't a retail bank, meaning it doesn't have branches on main streets. What it does is take deposits from state taxes and the funds that different government departments and municipalities hold, then leverages that, lending against those deposits to back community banks, who then build relationships with and lend to small businesses, farmers and individuals.

An author, lawyer and community organiser, Ellen Brown has played a significant role in promoting the cause of public banking and also in highlighting the unique case of America's unlikely socialist bank, deep in the red states of the Midwest. She's a self-made expert, one of those people who comes across a topic, devours everything she can find on it, and writes and organises tirelessly to ignite other people's curiosity and desire for an alternative. Her organising post-GFC helped sow the seeds of the not-for-profit Public Banking Institute, which formed in 2011. Its purpose is to support public bank initiatives in multiple US states and foster the provision of affordable credit with public purpose. Following the BND model, a state bank could use money that's sitting in the bank accounts of every government department or municipality to make low-interest loans back to governments. These loans could fund investments in public infrastructure or be offered to local community banks, who could then lend out to the small businesses being left behind or ignored by the commercial banking sector.

Says Ellen:

> If you are a Wall Street bank, you are required to make the most money for your shareholders that you can make. So even though you might have a lot of small businesses that are perfectly viable and would not be investments that would lose you money, still if you've got a big hedge fund that's going to pay you double that, you've got to go for the hedge fund – that's your business model. So, they just don't wind up catering to local business. That's one of our arguments for why this is really a win–win: 'We're not even treading on your [big banks'] turf because you don't want this turf. You're not servicing the local community, and that's what we want to do.'

Surfing this wave of change, the California Public Banking Alliance brought together movements in LA, San Francisco, San Diego, Oakland and beyond. They convinced legislators of the potential of public banking to save governments millions in bank fees, to fund investment in affordable housing and renewable energy and to help small businesses secure credit at low interest rates.

There was a big step forward in October 2019: after many hurdles, California Governor Gavin Newsom signed the state's Public Banking Act, opening the door for city and county officials to sponsor public banks, and LA City Council have voted to begin the process of scoping their own Public Bank. It's going to be a slow process, but the ship of state has turned.

In 2017 alone, the City of Los Angeles paid US$170 million in banking fees and US$1.1 billion in interest to Wall Street banks: Public Bank LA could save the city millions and open up investment in community assets like low-income housing, provide funds for community banks to lend to small businesses and co-ops, and fund a transition to a green economy. As well, they're ideally placed to provide financial inclusion for the staggeringly high 30 per cent of Angelenos who are unbanked. There's another recent driver: in California, since the legalisation of cannabis, these newly legal providers aren't able to use federally backed banks for their deposits. Public Bank LA could meet the needs of this burgeoning industry being excluded from the security of banking. Watch this space.

There are two lessons to draw from the experience of the public banking movement. Sometimes, the solution doesn't come from the future but from understanding the past. And persistence. If at first you don't succeed, regroup and try again. Eventually, the times will catch up with a great idea.

Ellen is surprised I'm so interested in the history of her country's banks yet I don't know how Australia fits into the story.

'You guys started this in Australia,' she tells me. Sure enough, it's all there in her book, *The Public Banking Solution.* To my astonishment, she has chapters in there recounting the rise and fall of public banking in Australia, and its enduring influence. This is the story behind the bank most of us grew up seeing as the default bank: when the ads asked 'Which Bank?' all Australians knew the answer. But not many of my generation or younger would know the story of its creation or its alienation from public purpose.

The world had been thrown into turmoil at the end of the 19th century by a banking crisis in America (sound familiar?) that reached as far as Australia. In response, in 1913 the Commonwealth Bank of Australia (CBA) was created at the stroke of a pen, backed not by a capital endowment (aka a big deposit to draw on) but 'by the entire wealth and credit of the whole of Australia', a statement the CBA's first governor, Dennison Miller, apparently repeated often. When all too soon there was the threat of a run on the banks at the outset of the First World War, the CBA calmed everyone and averted panic by guaranteeing the nations' deposits at every bank. The CBA financed the war effort, with barely any interest applied, and then financed the purchase of ships that established Australia's export economy. Through the CBA, £350 million was spent to aid the war effort, and in the years that followed the CBA financed home building and the infrastructure efforts of local government. On top of it all, they then handed any profits over to the Commonwealth government.

This went on swimmingly until Dennison Miller died in 1923, by which time the British establishment had realised their former empire, the Commonwealth countries, were gaining economic independence and slipping out of their control. Watching this all unfold from the motherland, the Bank of England asserted that Australia was living beyond its means by creating its own liquidity, and instead demanded that all future credit was to be extended to Australia from the Bank of England, to be then just managed by the CBA. Australia kept up the public works. But now we were borrowing from the Bank of England to do so, paying interest to them rather than drawing on our own credit. When the Great Depression hit and international bankers were no longer lending, the social impact was devastating. Through it all, the Bank of England demanded their loan interest be paid. Imagine the human suffering that might have been avoided if Australia had been able to continue employing people and financing its own recovery through public works – maybe even delivering an Australian New Deal – instead of experiencing 32 per cent unemployment and austerity measures to pay British bankers?

When I was a kid in the 1980s, even though it hadn't regained its original glory, the CBA was still in public hands. Every kid was encouraged to set up a Dollarmite account at school, saving in money boxes shaped in the image of the CBA's main branch in Sydney's Martin Place. Then, in the 1990s, I remember a debate about privatising the bank. The big claim was that, suddenly, mums and dads across the country would become shareholders, with all the financial empowerment that would follow. I doubt that many people knew what we lost as the first true public bank slipped further away from public benefit, or the story of how Australia had flourished thanks to the Commonwealth Bank being designed for the common good.

And now we see history repeating. Roughly a hundred years on from the Bank of England's swifty, the world is still recovering from one crisis triggered by the irresponsibility and unchecked greed of financiers, while reeling with the impact of a second hit in the form of a global pandemic and economic shutdown. Once again, people around the world are realising that public banking could be a means to fund the transition we need to a sustainable, inclusive economy for the 21st century. Can we learn from history and see the mines ahead, the ones that sunk this crucial piece of financial infrastructure the first time round? Our task now is learning from the stumbles of the past as we organise for the future.

Know where your money sleeps at night

'At a minimum, we have to stop banks from causing so much damage and migrate them toward producing benefit to all and harm to none. Otherwise, there isn't enough charitable or governmental resources in the world to clean up after their excesses,' Kat Taylor says. 'Those tails won't wag that dog.'

Kat Taylor is the founder and CEO of Beneficial State Bank (BSB), a bank she has brought into being through the mergers of a number of smaller community banks, with a clear focus and a foundation driving its activities. Today, BSB serves people in California, Oregon, and Washington on the US West Coast, with $1 billion in assets, 17 branches and 250 workers. To me, the numbers are impressive, but Kat assures me that BSB is 'mighty but tiny', at banking-industry scale.

'But even that evolution gives us but some pretty petty cash to lose in the car carpet of the largest banks, whose assets are measured in the trillions.'

As well as drawing on the networks and principles of the four originator banks, Kat and her team studied the approaches of South Shore Bank in Chicago, Self-Help Credit Union in North

Carolina and New York, and microfinance pioneers the Grameen Bank in Bangladesh.

'We sought to stand up on their foundation the best next-generation version of all three. We've done our best to structure the bank in a way that makes it a tool to better the lives of the people in our community while enhancing our natural resource base,' Kat says. 'But the banking system at large continues to punish those most vulnerable, endow those already too powerful now, and crash the planet. Something more must be done.'

We can only build the kind of future we need if we bend the banking system to be a part of the solution: banks can no longer fund environmental destruction and the industries that accelerate climate change. Banks can no longer be parties to speculative property bubbles or enable predatory business practices while relying on the public purse as a safety net for their risky and damaging behaviour. Instead, banks must be compelled to focus on providing the fuel for the green, inclusive economy that we need to have a sustainable and fair future. If they won't change their stripes, maybe we need to create a new generation of ethical banks designed with public good at their core, ones with their own finance sector version of the Hippocratic oath: first, do no harm.

'At BSB, we insist that 75 per cent of our loan dollars are in the hands of borrowers producing that new economy,' Kat says. She continues:

We judge that true if those loans are producing something we desperately need, like affordable housing or renewable energy. Or if the borrowers themselves are also governed in the public interest, like BCorporations or worker co-ops. We prioritise lending to individuals and organisations – including businesses in low-resource communities, communities of colour and immigrants – because their voices have simply been left out of the economy for too long, and that is why that economy is not serving us in any way now.

Most importantly, we do not allow the other 25 per cent of our lending to work against our bottom lines for social justice or environmental wellbeing. And we never separate those two goals as they are flip sides of the same coin – divide them and they conquer each other.

It's not enough for financial institutions to have a corporate social responsibility program and a few renewable energy projects on their website when they're still funding activities that hasten climate destruction. The US example Kat cites is that 'in a mere month, $100 million of deposits flew out of the banks that financed the Dakota Access Pipeline at the expense of First Nation rights: a critical local resource called water, and accelerating global climate change.'

Kat describes the critical insight to be gleaned:

It's more important that banks refrain from lending to and investing in pernicious activities than that they engage in prosocial or pro-environmental behaviours. In the last ten years, the biggest banks in the [US] system lent $250 billion just to coal, when the industry has largely declared bankruptcy and already shifted their pension liabilities onto the American taxpayer, not to mention accelerating climate disaster. We should have insisted that the biggest banks first stop their devastating support of fossil fuels before they parade around their meagre commitments to what is already a profitable activity called renewable energy finance. Even billions of dollars of renewable energy finance cannot overcome the banks' continued complicity in climate disaster. First no harm; then some benefit.

What kind of projects does BSB fund? In their first ten years of operation, they provided US$84 million to affordable housing projects and US$76 million to environmental sustainability projects, US$26 million to education and US$23 million to healthy food projects, as well as over US$75 million to economic development and manufacturing projects. They're also supporting the kinds of business structure that increase equality, like BCorps, co-ops and worker-owned enterprises, to the tune of about US$15 million over that time. They won't fund fossil fuels, private prisons, pay-day lenders or other business models they deem exploitative.

Kat Taylor's bank shows us how this can be done in practice, while still making a profit. She says they aim for 'resilient profit-taking, only taking enough to fund modest internal growth and survive any shocks in the economy' rather than profit maximisation. She says beyond resilient profit-taking, usually profits either come from over-charging customers or underpaying workers. BSB pay their workers 150 per cent of the living wage (as calculated by MIT) rather than the minimum wage. Kat Taylor says mainstream US banks have an 'obscene but common practice' of under-employing and underpaying bank tellers, to the extent that one-third of tellers – people who are actually employed full-time working in a bank, likely one raking in billions in profits – rely on public welfare. BSB extends this to the difference between CEO and median salary ratio. In most US banks, the CEO is paid over 200 times more than the median worker, whereas at BSB, it's 6:1.

Even with this heightened level of social responsibility and a focus on ethical investment, Kat says BSB has to be 'reliably profitable', both to meet the conditions of the Federal Insurance Deposit Corporation insurance (which uses public funds to guarantee individual deposits up to $250,000 – that's the US version of the public safety net I mentioned earlier), and to continue the bank and foundation's social justice mission. Rather than aiming for constantly growing profits, Kat explains that the BSB set a target for their profit goal: 'We bracket 6 per cent at the low end to make sure we remain sustainable and 10 per cent on the high end to protect against overcharging our customers or underpaying our colleagues.'

It's important to the broader mission of BSB that the bank be profitable. A bank with positive social values has to be seen to perform financially so it can be an exemplar to the sector that another way forward is possible, and that it will help them be resilient and also attract new generations who value values.

Says Kat:

We can't just be a good bank that's resiliently profitable and pats itself on the back for making some positive impact. If we did that, the banking system would never improve. So, even our theory of change includes that we do what we do so well that we attract the attention of the large regional banks. And they see through our currency – our impact metrics – that if they act more like this bank and produce those impact metrics in some form, they will be successful. Especially with the younger generations, who are the largest cohort ever to travel through US markets and elections. We've worked really hard to develop impact metrics of output, outcome and shift at the systems-change level, because we want our loans and banking practice literally to produce a new economy.

Millennials and Gen-Zers have wised up from the Boomers and see that only an integrated life makes sense. You cannot clean up on Saturdays or in retirement what damage you and your firm caused from Monday through Friday. If banks want new-generation business, they must measure and report transparently all corporate practices and engage in self-assessment. And the results had better comport with what next generations want in their one wild and precious life.

Not everyone is in a position to start a new bank: Kat and her partner, Tom Steyer, are billionaires themselves, Tom having made a fortune in the hedge-fund game. (I was surprised to see his name come up recently when he joined the crowded race to be the Democratic nominee for President). Twenty years ago, they decided to turn their resources and energy towards 'good energy, good food and good money', and the BSB is one of their key plays towards supporting renewables and making money work for more people. Kat says:

Our job is to change the banking system for good so that all banks hew to those standards. And that change will only come when we fully awaken all bank customers' agency in and accountability for their banking. Money, the invisible part of our personal supply chain, is powerful – and we have to get the power back. We all have choices about where to bank and we all have responsibility to bank in alignment with our values. In society, not attending to where your money is put to work is not a neutral position. In fact, if you don't know where your money sleeps at night, it is almost certainly working against your values with more power than you will ever have individually.

***

There are signs that change is in the air. Beneficial State Bank is a member of the Global Alliance for Banking on Values (GABV), a global network of banks that want to be part of the solution to the challenges the world is facing. Members call themselves Values-Based Banks to differentiate themselves from the business-as-usual banking model.

I first learned about GABV when I met Sonia Reinhardt from Germany's GLS Bank in mid-2019. Sonia was running an education program on the role banks can play in building the sustainable housing sector we need and invited me to explain the work I'd been doing on housing affordability. Sonia was on secondment in Sydney at two member-owned Australian banks, Bank Australia and the Teachers Mutual Bank Limited. As part of the GABV network, these Aussie banks had been able to invite Sonia to train their staff in impact leadership, giving them the ability to 'lead from the future, not from the past', challenging them to explore the role banking can play in providing affordable housing, closing the gap on Indigenous disadvantage, and taking action on climate change. I ask her what 'leading from the future' means in the context of banking. Sonia explains:

We are having challenges in the present that don't have equivalents in the past. When we face a problem we are so used to saying, 'Oh, how did I handle this challenge a year ago?' but we can't do that anymore because there are no such experiences.

People ask, 'How do I know what's in the future?', but innovations usually happen in the margins, right? So, if you go out to the margin and look for the innovation, you can say the future is already there, just have to push it into the mainstream.

Over the last ten years, the GABV has brought together 62 financial institutions: between them, they serve more than 70 million customers and manage over US$210 billion. They work together to share knowledge, resources and conduct research, and while they operate in a range of different regulatory and social contexts, they share a common set of principles. Sonia explains:

My home bank GLS Bank is a founding member of the GABV. Our

CEO got together with the other founding members right after the GFC and they said, 'We really want to show the world that there is a way of doing business that's not harming people or planet, but it's actually supporting them.' They're all relatively small and mid-sized banks, so it was also this idea of getting together and having a stronger voice together. When you are CEO of a values-based bank, you can just go to the neighbour bank and discuss challenges because it's a completely different mindset. So, I think it was really important to have like-minded people in a knowledge exchange network.

When I read the principles that unite these banks,[11] I felt a surge of optimism. Every one of them echoed the points I was hearing from the financial sector change-makers I'd spoken to and addressed the ways today's business-as-usual approach to banking is failing to add value.

First of all, GABV banks have to meet triple bottom-line objectives –

benefit for people, planet and profit – but they can't simply minimise harm. They have to perform to a higher standard by using all of their money and activities to do good in the world, not just a bit they set aside for their feel-good charity programs or green deposit programs. Their second principle is about being grounded in the real world of local economies and of being supportive of those new or unconventional business models we talked about in an earlier chapter. I was excited to observe that a lot of the activity of these principled banks was focused on supporting the 'real economy' Giuseppe and I talked about. The GABV defines this as 'economic activities that generate goods and services as opposed to a financial economy that is concerned exclusively with activities in the financial markets'.[12] About 75 per cent of the activity of Values-Based Banks is lending in the real economy, compared to about 40 per cent for 'Global Systemically Important Banks', the major banks that dominate the economy.[13]

Values-Based Banks also commit to avoiding financial constructions that mitigate risk by bundling debts together (the kind of practices that brought on the GFC). Instead, in order to reduce risks, they develop real relationships with each customer and try to understand their banking needs. They're also focused on improving their resilience to shocks and increasing their accountability. Sonia tells me the incredible fact that her home bank, GLS, actually publishes the details of every commercial loan it makes in its quarterly newsletter as a way of being utterly transparent that they are being consistent with their mission with every agreement they enter into. Most importantly, these principles have to be embedded in every part of their operations. For instance, their sales teams can't be out taking risks and making plays that their other teams might later have to atone for.

This approach is paying off. Values-Based Banks are growing at a significant rate. Admittedly, they're relatively smaller and they have a long way to go to compete with the dominant players in global banking but they've had higher growth in loans, deposits, assets, equity and total revenue compared to the big banks over the last ten years since the GFC; they're demonstrating greater stability; and have a better record of retaining clients too. Values-Based Banks have proven they have a higher return on assets, showing that focusing on positive impact makes more dollars and cents than the profit-at-all-costs approach.

Values-Based Banks aren't just changing their own operations but are pushing their whole sector to have a more positive environmental impact, and they're doing this using the language that the banking world understands. In late 2019, GABV released research with the European investment bank KKS Advisors and Deloitte showing that even for the conventional banks, 'a genuine ESG [environmental, social and governance] focus increases firm value'.[14] Basically, they're proving that if banks prioritise people and planet in their investment approach, it's actually better for their bottom line.

At a moment when once again the global economy is on a precipice, we need to move our money to those institutions that are demonstrating they're more stable, more resilient in the face of crisis, and more likely to be contributors to the inclusive and sustainable future we need.

Return money to its proper purpose

As we've seen a few times in this story, sometimes the best new ideas aren't very new at all. I've found, for instance, that one of the oldest financial traditions is also one of the most exciting sources of inspiration and innovation.

Islamic finance is one of the most enduring forms of ethical financial practice. Islamic law, or *Shari'ah,* is a set of principles that seek to balance the tension between the spiritual and material that devout Muslim people experience when trying to adhere to their faith. This requires a proactive sense of social responsibility in a world that prioritises profit above all else. To address that, Islamic finance (also known as 'Shari'ah-compliant' financial services) has strict rules that require money to be used to fuel the productive, real economy – so there's a philosophical connection with those Values-Based Banks we explored earlier. There's a strenuous prohibition on financial speculation, or any of those 'money from money' plays, to the extent that charging or paying interest is forbidden. This throws up a lot of challenges when interacting with the mainstream banking world. In Islamic finance, you can't just put your money in an investment fund and plead ignorance of what you're investing in to get returns: it requires a high level of accountability as to what kind of world your money is funding.

It's a complex area. There are a range of approaches: from those who design loopholes to get around prohibitions, to people who are using these constraints as a driver to build a better path for investment that can meet the biggest goals society has set for our future. To begin to get my head around the concept of Islamic finance,

I turned to my friend Mahir to take me through the basics.

Mahir Momand is a man who has helped millions of people and lived many lives, and they're all fascinating. He spent years as a microfinance pioneer in his home country of Afghanistan, first at the Microfinance Investment and Support Facility for Afghanistan for the World Bank and later as the CEO of Islamic Investment and Finance Cooperatives Group, using finance to help people move away from crops like poppies, one of the economic foundations of the Taliban, and towards food and saffron production. Microfinance is a brilliant tool for providing small-scale unsecured loans, a 'bank for the poor' made famous by Muhammad Yunus and the Grameen Bank in Bangladesh, which has had a monumental impact in the economic empowerment of women in particular. I'd recommend Yunus's book, *Banker to the Poor,* or if you want to be part of a positive microfinance chain yourself, check out Kiva, an online microfinance model which has lent out US$1.4 billion since 2005, to people and groups who need help to fund their farms or businesses, introduce green energy or improve their prospects with education. But that's a whole other story, for another time.

That empowerment that Mahir was helping people in Afghanistan achieve through microfinance was a serious threat to the business model of the Taliban, making Mahir and his colleagues a target for their violence. A shadow of pain passes over his warm, enthusiastic face when his story touches on this point. To avoid their fury, Mahir shifted to a Shari'ah-compliant business model, thinking that would appease them, which is how he became an expert in the field. Sadly, the attacks continued, and he eventually had no choice but to flee the country. Mahir has now directed his talents to building networks for migrants beyond large cities through Regional Opportunities Australia. But on arriving in Australia, Mahir first turned his expertise towards trying to get our banks to embrace the opportunity that Islamic finance represents.

'The Australian financial sector, financial services are not as diverse as the Australian community,' Mahir says when we meet in my office in the heart of Sydney:

So, if we look outside this window down the street, look at the type of people that you see. Very diverse right here in Sydney. But if you look inside a financial institution, namely, ADIs – Australian deposit taking institutions, which are banks and credit unions – the products, the financial services that they provide are very non-diversified, very conventional. Just kind of like focused on the biggest segment of the community.

But there are other people in Australia – Muslims are the second fastest growing community in Australia, I believe, more than a million people. We are a country of 25 million people, and we have more than a million people of Islamic belief, and these people are financially excluded: I know people in the community who have been living in Australia for 40 years, not seven or eight years like me, of Muslim background. They're very financially stable but they have not bought houses so far, and the reason why they haven't done that is because they don't want to get a loan, pay interest on it because they see it with a clear contradiction to their religious beliefs. These people are missing out on opportunities, and Australia is missing out on opportunities.

As Mahir points out, banks could unlock a significant customer base through establishing Shari'ah-compliant financial products like home loans, investment and bank accounts, but at the moment, no mainstream Australian financial institutions provide this kind of service, leaving it to non-ADI institutions like Melbourne's MCCA Islamic Finance & Investments, an Islamic finance co-operative.

Increasing access to and understanding of Islamic finance is important for financial inclusion, but also a potential source of funding for exactly the kind of positive, real-world social impact we need but that often lacks access to capital. That's because in addition to needing to avoid those abstract 'money-from-money' instruments, money invested through Islamic finance is required to do good in the world. Mahir explains:

In a country like the United Kingdom, it's highly active: they're mostly labelled under 'ethical banking' because the five principles of Islamic finance prevent investment in certain sectors that are socially harmful to the community. For example, if they are deposited into a financial institution, as the financial institution, you can't put that money into anything that will be socially harmful to the community. For example, whether that is gambling, armaments, pornography, even gossip media is classified as socially harmful.

There's also a shift in the relationship from customer to partner. Author and Islamic finance lawyer Umar Moghul points out that one of the major strengths of the Islamic finance approach is that it demands that financiers have skin in the game, creating a spirit of partnership rather than speculation.[15] This reduces the exploitation that the mainstream banking system has built in, making banking a tool to more evenly spread benefit from investment. Rather than being the bank that profits from your mortgage payments, whether or not the value of the property rises or falls, or whether or not you can afford to make your loan repayments, in a sharia-compliant loan the banker is your partner in profit as well as loss. Moghul writes:

> Islamic finance challenges impact investors to consider legal and financial mechanisms as an expression of purpose, as well as a defining factor in outcomes. Though on its face a restriction, the prohibition of *riba* [interest] engenders creativity, calling on markets and communities to design mechanisms built on risk sharing – as opposed to the risk shifting that has become a hallmark of financialization, and that helped produce a financial system that disproportionately benefits very few.

What such structures might lead to, in terms of de-concentrating ownership, reducing concentrations and gaps in wealth, and constructing participatory economies merits further study.[16]

Too often, if Islamic finance is discussed at all, it's only in terms of what is forbidden, and what people can't do because of the constraints it imposes. But Shari'ah isn't just about preventing harm (*mafsada*), it's about enhancing welfare (*maslaha*) too. There's a powerful positive flipside: Islamic finance is all about money being used for its proper purpose, turning money back into a tool to help people and protect the planet, rather than just making profits.

We're not talking about a tiny niche: 22 per cent of the world's population are Muslim, and there's over US$2.5 trillion in Islamic finance funds under management today.[17] The Islamic finance sector is growing at a much faster rate than the traditional sector, expanding at a rate of about 10 to 12 per cent a year.[18] But that's not all. There's also an estimated further US$1 trillion per year accumulated across the Muslim world in the form of Zakat, a percentage of personal wealth that is required to be given to charity every year.[19] This money-with-a-conscience presents an enormous opportunity to improve lives and protect the environment through the Sustainable Development Goals (SDGs). There's a gap of about this size – about $3 trillion – that needs to be invested every year to help developing countries achieve the SDGs.

There are already projects underway showing how this could be done: in Indonesia, the world's most populous Muslim-majority country, the United Nations Development Programme (UNDP) are working with the national Zakat collections agency Badan Amil Zakat Nasional (Baznas) on targeted poverty alleviation programs that are designed to help Indonesia meet the SDGs. In a joint report, they note that 'striking commonalities exist between zakat and other forms of Islamic finance, and the SDGs, with their common focus on alleviating poverty and hunger and reducing inequality by redistributing wealth',[20] and they connect the aspirations of the SDGs with the five principles of Islamic finance, but they go further. The traditional approach to Zakat is more like almsgiving, helping the very poor get by and meet their short-term needs. Baznas are doing the cultural and political work in Indonesia to shift the focus of Zakat to be empowerment and poverty alleviation for the long-term. They give the example of more focused giving in North Sumatra to develop the productive capacity of five villages of fisherfolk, making capital investments in their equipment and boats, but also investing in health clinics, scholarships and early childhood education for these communities.[21] In Jambi Province in Central Sumatra, Zakat has been directed to build four micro hydroelectric plants to provide renewable energy for about 4500 people, schools, businesses and mosques in communities that didn't have electricity before.[22]

There are many more ways the SDG and Islamic finance connection is being developed: in 2017 Malaysia established the world's first Green Islamic Bonds, or Sukuk, which uses a partnership approach (kind of like a public–private partnership investment) to fund infrastructure for sustainability.[23] Being Shari'ah-compliant means investors own a percentage of the assets funded, rather than a debt instrument like a mainstream bond, and then the funds they've contributed are used to pay for construction of solar power, biogas or wind farms, renewable energy transmission networks, public transport or even energy efficiency programs.

I've barely scratched the surface of the potential that Islamic finance and ethical instruments offer: for example, on my last visit to Singapore my friend (and amazing city-maker) Stella Gwee introduced me to the concept of *waqf,* the dedication of property or other assets in perpetuity for a positive social purpose, by showing me some of the buildings it has preserved and social infrastructure provided in her neighbourhood.

There's much more to explore in Islamic and ethical finance, and I am so excited to keep learning about it, and about other global traditions that could reconnect capital with conscience. This is an opportunity to be grasped and it presents a solution at a significant global scale, one of the answers when people ask how we can pay for the change we need. We have to look beyond the standard models and the dominant cultures – and sometimes, to some of the oldest systems – to find next-century solutions. It's possible that Islamic finance and ethical banking could provide some of the patient, principled capital that we need to fund a wholesale global shift to renewable energy or to finance affordable and efficient housing, just for starters. Let's help money serve its proper purpose in delivering a more just and resilient world.

8

Restore the commons

There's something we're missing. It's a gap in our language that's leading to a failure in imagination: a conceptual narrowing that's forcing us to choose between black and white, rather than being able to paint with the whole spectrum of colour.

When we think about the policy possibilities and tools at our disposal with these blinkers on, we can only think about services, resources or efforts as either coming from the public sector or the private sector. But those aren't the only options, and we don't just have to choose between government or business as a source of solutions, a custodian of assets, or a partner to work with. There's another deep well we can draw from: the commons.

These are the things we share, that we jointly contribute to, which we collectively maintain and steward for our common good. Usually when people talk about the commons, they're referring to physical things, like pastures that shepherds use on hillsides, fishing grounds or community gardens, that only a small number of people use. These physical commons aren't owned by any one person or company; they sit outside government or market control and are cared for by the people who use them, who set rules to allow everyone to benefit. Sometimes, the commons are more vast and elemental, and they touch us all. Clean air, waterways, beaches and public space are all part of the commons.

There are people exploring whether renewable energy could be established as a commons. Imagine the potential if neighbours could create distributed energy commons together (say by each of us having solar panels on our rooftops) and then work collectively to share the use of it (say across a networked street). There's a strong precedent for co-operative, bottom-up leadership in the history of community wind energy in Denmark, for example.[1]

Other commons are more abstract, like language and knowledge, domains that are enriched by multiple contributions, cared for and developed by no single set of caretakers but used by us all. Online spaces and protocols like Wikipedia or the open-source software community are great examples of 21-stcentury commons, as is the internet itself, a resource that's greater than the sum of all its individual contributions.

Here's the thing that trips a lot of people up when talking about the commons: because it's easiest to use agricultural, old-world examples to explain the idea of the commons, it can often make people think that the commons isn't merely an old concept, but an outdated one: I believe the mindset and language of the commons is essential for the 21st century. It's an alternative to the private and public: it reminds me of the beautiful phrase I learned from Rojava's story, 'society leading itself'. The language of the commons needs to be rediscovered as we try to put purpose and participation at the foundations of the solutions for our century. Because here's the thing that connects with me the most: while we might think of the commons as resources and spaces, the most important thing is that *commoning* is a verb – it's something you do, that we do together – it's a set of principles and a process for giving citizens control over the things that matter to us. Commoning requires trust in our neighbours and belief in ourselves, and it empowers us to make decisions that will serve the common good, for those who benefit now and those we are responsible to in the future.

In this chapter, we'll explore projects and meet people who are using commons thinking to harness a resource we're letting slip through our fingers: the data we generate in our digital lives. They're finding ways to restructure our relationship with the tech giants to ensure data – sometimes called the 'oil of the 21st century' – delivers value to the many, not just the few. One of these is New Zealand data scientist, James Mansell.

Treat data as a public good

'What's the new social contract for the new millennium?' James asks.

Right now, we have these two models: it's free-market rape and pillage, the Facebook business model, or you overregulate like the EU and lock everything down. Really, it goes back to John Locke and the original social contract. There's a personal good in me keeping my information private. And there's also a personal good for me in the public good of making that all available too: it's good for me if health researchers can look at my data. I just don't want them to abuse it.

What's the relationship between citizen and state, the public and private good, when it comes to data? I'm going to keep working on that, but in the meanwhile, we need to set up some of these data commons as a way of working through the minefield of all that.

James is leading a movement that applies that concept of commons to our data. He believes the solution to the issues of data protection is reclaiming the data commons for public good: particularly to support the more effective provision of public services, and to give individual citizens the opportunity to be treated as unique people, not siloed strands of interactions. This could be our chance to reset the power imbalance between each of us as individual technology users and the platform giants who hoover up and sell on enormous amounts of information about our preferences, habits and interactions.

We're right to be cautious about what data is gathered on us, by whom, and how decisions about our lives and opportunities might be skewed by flawed data sets and artificial intelligence.

Political scientist Virginia Eubanks has written powerfully about the 'automated inequality' that occurs when we let machines make decisions about people's lives, relying on data sets that have structural biases embedded in them.[2] In Australia, we've seen it play out in the form of so-called RoboDebt, automated debt notices sent to welfare recipients, many of them wildly inaccurate. There are suggestions that the notices contributed to a number of suicides.[3] We've also seen the lack of trust in the digital stewardship of our personal information play out vividly in the reluctance by many to download the COVIDSafe app during the pandemic: mishandling data can have serious real-world consequences.

But it's not just governments we have to worry about. The worst offenders in the exploitation of data over the past decade have been the corporate tech giants. Platform monopolists like Google and Facebook have built the most powerful and profitable media empires in history through their access to – and monetising of – the data we all create moving through our hyper-connected lives. What happens to that captured information? Do you know whether it is sold on – to market research companies for example – and are you comfortable with that? Do you know how the data is to be used? The Cambridge Analytica/Facebook scandal is a dramatic and well-known example of data being captured and used without consent. In the run-up to the 2016 US Presidential election, Donald Trump's campaign team contracted the services of Cambridge Analytica (CA). Among the services CA offered was 'influence operations'. Later, it was found that they had accessed data from an estimated 87 million Facebook users to extract behavioural insights, some of which the Trump campaign was able to use to influence voter behaviour.

Understandably, such cases have driven governments to regulate around data use. Europe's strict General Data Protection Regulations (GDPR)[4] set the benchmark and countries such as Japan, Brazil, South Korea and India have followed their lead, as has the US state of California. As James and other critics in the tech space have pointed out, while well intentioned, creating new bureaucratic hoops for tech companies to jump through actually preferences the incumbents, making it even harder for challengers to emerge, and it can lead to a more fragmented and less socially useful data commons.

It doesn't have to be this way. Data could be used to create opportunities, not limit them, and to add value for people, not just punitive governments or voracious corporations. That's the promise of the data commons, and that's what James Mansell is working on in New Zealand.

After studying philosophy, James eventually found himself director of innovation at the Ministry of Social Development, where he saw first-hand how access to information could have positive or negative effects on people's lives. He found that siloed, domain-specific lenses on the delivery of services could have damaging impacts when delivering sensitive public services like child protection and health, and he brought this experience to his appointment to the New Zealand Data Futures Forum, an independent group of experts tasked by government with recommending a model for data sharing between public and private sectors.

'The principles we came up with are that people need to be in control of their own data, and it needs to be of value to them. Then you've got to convince people to pool their own data to get shared insights. The real value comes when you can start to integrate different kinds of data, when you link, say, health data to financial data. That's when you can achieve economies of scope.'

A data commons requires two key steps. First, each of us has to have individual control over the use of our data, and we have to have trust that it will be kept secure and not used against our interests. Then our collective data points have to be pooled within a 'social data exchange' for a de-identified, bird's-eye view of the interactions of society as a whole.

Of course at that point, marketers are prepared to pay big dollars for the sort of insights that data scientists can mine.

'One piece of data on its own is not that valuable. It's really when you pool it together that it becomes valuable, which is where a commons notion comes in,' James says. 'How do you redistribute the value to the community? That community needs to figure out how they're going to manage their shared data asset, their shared commons, and set the rules of the road. Do you have the "right to be forgotten", or get off the commons, if you stop trusting people?'

I think commoning is a process and mindset that we can adapt for the digital age, but first, we have to address a persistent, destructive myth – 'the tragedy of the commons' – which has served to undermine commoning. It was triggered by one flawed piece of research by academic and bioethicist Garrett Hardin which suggested that people could not be trusted to share a field, a stock of fish, a forest or any other store of assets without exploiting it. That research has been used ever since to make the claim that private ownership, or enclosure, is the only way to protect resources.

This damaging myth needs to be busted in order for us to build a future that puts people and community ahead of private gain.

Political scientist Elinor Ostrom proved Hardin wrong, and won the Nobel Prize for Economics in 2009 by showing how the commons are instruments of co-operation that do work: but they require discussion, rules and management to be effective. The commons won't manage itself: it needs us to be stewards of it. This isn't about delegating control to governments, over markets: to make the commons work for us, we all have a role to play as engaged citizens in setting the rules that allow us to share resources – including data – and we all have to have a say in deciding the fairest way to distribute the rewards these common pool resources generate.

Elinor wrote about how, in the usual approach, we only have a set of binary options to choose between when managing the resources of our world:

'The market was seen as the optimal institution for the production and exchange of private goods. For nonprivate goods, on the other hand, one needed "the" government to impose rules and taxes to force self-interested individuals to contribute necessary resources and refrain from self-seeking activities.'[5]

Commoning creates a path that is community-led, based on active citizenry, consensus and bottom-up decision-making and focused on outcomes for a range of players, rather than the self-interested mindset of markets or the top-down approach of governments. This is the thinking we need to design outcomes that generate public good as their first priority.

Ostrom designed eight principles for guiding the commons, explaining that 'organised commons require strong collective-action and self-governing mechanisms, as well as a high degree of social capital on the part of the stakeholders.'[6]

More urgently than ever, in our privatised digital age, we need to reclaim the language of the commons to expand our civic imagination and generate more options for what is possible with the resources shared and those we create together: like our data. A data commons approach repositions it as a public good and a shared resource, one that can be managed for a collective public benefit, rather than roped off behind the proprietary walls of different apps or internet platforms, banks or government departments.

Francesca Bria, Barcelona's Chief Technology Officer, is a leader in designing a new social pact to enable the best use of data for public good, while guaranteeing digital sovereignty – our right to privacy and information self-determination. Francesca has championed the positioning of data as a public infrastructure and a common good, particularly the data captured via the sensors that more and more cities are installing to gather information on environmental and logistical factors, such as air quality, noise, water use, pedestrian movements, transport, waste and resource recovery, and so on. This forward-thinking practice has prompted a call for open cities, rather than smart cities. With transparency, findings from the data can show ways we could all benefit, and cities could derive efficiencies and revenue. It reaffirms James Mansell's key point: information has to be gathered and used in a way that gives citizens a feeling of confidence that we're being served, not exploited.

The UK's Open Data Institute (ODI) are approaching the idea of making data a shared community asset by establishing data trusts, legal mechanisms to safeguard what data is gathered, how it is stored and how it is used.

ODI also want us to see data being treated as infrastructure, and they compare it to transport networks in a city: it can be used to enhance how we get around, build connections and generate value, but the questions of who owns it, who has access and what it costs matter too. If we can have confidence that the data we generate together is being managed ethically and for our shared benefit, we're more likely to update it or allow it to draw on our activity or information, which makes it more valuable. The community could then have an informed conversation about when and how they might allow private companies or researchers to have a license to access the data. That's a world away from a Silicon Valley company simply taking ownership of it, finding ways to monetise it and then locking it away. Plus it means we as citizens – the people who contributed to the commons – might benefit from it, in the form of more informed public services or license fees from those users.

Move beyond governments and markets

At the foundation of a functioning commons is trust: and it's also an essential prerequisite for a more functional and less corrosive data ecosystem.

For those who contribute their data, it would be ideal to have confidence that our digital rights will be respected: that we have transparency and control over what is known about us and how that information is used. For those who might access the data for research or marketing reasons, they need to be able to trust that they're getting accurate and up to date information. No one is really getting that experience today.

A major strength of the commons approach to data is that it provides a path that is beyond the market or government: the goal is empowering citizens so we ourselves develop ways of increasing trust, developing norms of reciprocity or crafting new rules to manage our shared assets.

That's why James Mansell has turned down New Zealand government funding for the data commons. Starting with government funding would 'erode trust from day one,' James reasons. 'It needs to be bottom up, or as a collective impact initiative ... if it's a genuine commons, we all have to have a stake in it and what the rules are of the commons.'

This is really important. We can't expect a bottom-up world to emerge from a top-down approach: we can't delegate all our responsibilities to our elected representatives and then expect trust to flourish. We need to have a bigger discussion as citizens about the data we create, the terms under which it is gathered and stored, and how we share the risks and rewards. A commons approach to shared data requires creating an equal playing field for all the players – individuals, community groups, businesses and government – to come together and negotiate the shared rules from the outset. Because data is most useful when it's more complete and connected up, managing it as a shared public resource creates an opportunity for a data dividend to be paid out: through the efficiencies created, but also by charging businesses and researchers for access. If we had a data commons, with rules set by users, we could implement controls and oversight that would prevent abuses like the Cambridge Analytica scandal and we'd have the opportunity to derive revenue and social benefit from our shared pool of data.

James says a complete data commons is still far from being achieved in New Zealand, though they're further along the road in this area than most countries, and he's starting to put the framework and platform into practice for a rather unlikely project: ridding the country of introduced fauna that have become pests.

Predator Free NZ is a project to eliminate all rats, stoats and possums from New Zealand by 2050. Mansell's company, Toha, is providing the tech platform to bring together the many civil society and scientific organisations (including students and volunteers), businesses and government agencies who are needed to undertake this mission. By starting with a clear goal and less sensitive data to share – possum data, not your medical records – Mansell hopes Predator Free NZ can be a test case for the data commons before moving on to health, financial, educational and other rightly guarded information.

The data commons movement is growing. In Barcelona and Amsterdam, the DECODE project (it stands for DEcentralised Citizen-owned Data Ecosystems) has run pilots which show what the data commons looks like in action, as the shared data set that enables non-exploitative models for sharing resources and participatory democracy.

A data commons entails gathering the data in one safe place, identifying and prioritising problems that can be solved via analysis of that data, and then devising methods that are socially useful to address them. It's the opposite of the usual start-up approach, which is to first design a solution that can best dominate a market, scraping up all the relevant data ('scraping' means programmatically extracting data from a third-party website; a common example is establishing a feed for live stockmarket data) and then hoarding the value it generates.

For example, in Barcelona DECODE worked on giving citizens control over what information they needed to share in order to use that city's Decidim participatory governance platform. The objective was for people to have their say and be verified as legitimate contributors without having to reveal too much to strangers or government departments they might not trust. Another pilot asked citizens to collect air- and noise-pollution readings, which were then encrypted and shared anonymously: like Predator Free New Zealand, this was a lower stakes way of working with citizens to determine where the boundaries should be, and how they feel about contributing to a common pool resource of data. From this, they developed a Data Commons Manifesto, which sets out the state of play today and the future that is possible when we're empowered, not exploited, by the data we create, and when we can harness it as a shared resource for broad benefit.

The Manifesto reads, in part:

Although we produce data, we do not control it. Data controls us. More precisely: who controls data and technologies, controls us. Data has value, but it is extracted and exploited without our awareness, and concentrated in a few hands. The most valued companies base their business model on it, and the trend is pervading the rest. States rebuild themselves around data, as well. The quest for profit and power fuels today the datification of the world...

A fairer data economy implies advancement towards a robust model of data commons, one that goes beyond open data by attending not only to the potential of open access to data but also to the conditions of its production, to the power over and the protection from it, to its governance as well as to the social responsibility for its impacts. It implies avoidance of datacentric visions by looking not only to data but also to the technological, legal, economical, social and other structures that define it. Strong data commons also go beyond regulations and initiatives centred on individual control over personal data by pointing towards the centrality of the collective dimension.[7]

This moment we're in is the beginning of the transformation of data from a private to a public good. How does that sit in the evolution of the digital era? It's barely 30 years since the birth of the world wide web and from that standing start, the growth of data has been exponential, the reach of technology in our lives absolutely dizzying. The first years of any technology are pretty wacky: when I think about the stage we're at right now, the image of auto polo keeps coming to my mind.

Auto polo was a game that was all the rage in the 1910s, when the automobile was at the cutting edge of innovation. Cars were a novelty, and the public first saw them at fairs and show days. The sport of auto polo was just as ridiculous and terrifying as the name suggests. It was a twist on regular polo but people drove cars instead of horses and attempted to whack a basketball around a field with mallets. They stripped the cars of doors, windshields and roofs; there were two men to a car and two cars to a team. Four cars would race around the field at up to 65 kilometres an hour punting the basketball towards goal posts. Unsurprisingly, it was a very dangerous and expensive sport, and after a few years enthusiasm waned. (As for driving cars in general: eventually, rules came in and motoring became more regulated and somewhat safer.)

Today, we're basically at the auto polo stage of our data ecosystem. That's a roundabout way of saying that it's early days yet. We can't get complacent or waste any time, but the way things are at the moment isn't the way the digital world has to work forever. No one has set any rules yet and so we're bumping into things, finding the edges as the private sector tests where society will draw the line.

By applying time-tested principles and processes like commoning in this new context, we can move from this lawless, winner-takes-all mindset to one in which we take back the power and set some rules that allow us all to benefit from this digital age. It doesn't have to be disruption at all costs. Let's upgrade to include social accountability and a broader vision of the kind of data-enabled economy and society we want to live in.

9

Rebuild for equity

All these ideas – these utopian impulses – that we've seen so far have the potential to transform how we work, how we make decisions and set priorities as a society, how we incentivise the positive and eliminate the destructive when it comes to business, the natural environment, and how we care for each other.

If we manage to gather these glimpses of utopia and make them a reality in one place, we'll see the physical results in our cities, the place where our priorities take physical form.

Winston Churchill famously said, 'We shape our buildings, and afterwards our buildings shape us.' The uses and groups that are prioritised in our streets, built environment and shared spaces, and the choices we make about ownership, design, construction, transport and public assets go on to determine the options open to us in our everyday lives and the experiences of the generations that follow us.

When thinking about the places we live and how we'll live together as we prepare for the century ahead, before we can start to compare one project with another, we have to take ourselves back to first principles and ask: what's the purpose of a city? Who's the city for? And why should we focus on the city as the dominant form the future will take?

The city should be for every one of us, a place where we can find opportunity and connect with each other, a place to be ourselves and find a way to contribute to our shared future. We have to meet the challenge of improving city life, because cities are the future: around the world, every single day more than 200,000 people move permanently into cities. That's an unstoppable flow of around 1.5 million new urban dwellers making cities home every week. More than 50 per cent of the planet's population live in cities today; by the end of the century it's estimated that 85 per cent of us will live in cities.

People move to cities for a multitude of reasons, but broadly speaking, we're drawn to the city's role as an engine of opportunity. The human need for connection and collaboration is what drives the success of the city as a form of social organisation: economist Edward Glaeser puts it even clearer than that: 'We are a social species that gets smarter by being around other smart people, and that's why cities thrive.'[1]

The purpose of a city is to bring people closer together so that human flourishing is more likely to happen. There are more options for self-expression and new ideas, trade and communication. You can find yourself, be yourself and find your people, all of which may be harder to achieve in places with smaller populations. People tend to earn higher wages in cities: there are more jobs to be had. There's also more likely to be improved access to education and healthcare.

A city isn't a scheme or a property play: it's for, by and about people.

Obviously, I'm a city-lover and am unashamedly biased but I'm incredibly optimistic about the role cities can play in building the future we want. Pop culture might be full of dystopian images of smoggy, crowded *Bladerunner*-esque megacities, plastered with neon advertising, steamy with the heat and smells of millions of people jostling for scarce space and resources, but cities are our best bet when it comes to minimising our carbon footprint and making the most effective use of resources, at the same time giving more people the ability to improve their prospects and quality of life.

Cities can be hungry beasts, consuming energy and water, drawing food in from miles around or concreting over the productive food-bowl land that initially drew people to that particular part of the world. But studies of the 'urban metabolism'[2] – the city's appetite and capacity to consume – show us that cities tend to become more energy efficient as they become denser. The larger the population, the easier it is to support extensive and efficient public transport systems; apartment buildings use less energy to heat and cool than stand-alone suburban houses; and projects like water recycling or distributed energy generation become more viable at scale. It's not something we can take for granted, though – left to business-as-usual thinking, cities can also be congested, polluted disasters – which is why we so desperately need to knit together some of the thinking we'll explore in this chapter to make sure cities are delivering on their potential to be part of the solution.

Often when we're discussing the solutions we need for future cities, people talk about driverless cars, green walls, micro apartments, sensors and robots. Sure, a lot of that stuff is useful, and it has a part to play in a positive, fair future too. But let's start with the world as it actually is for most people. The citymakers we'll meet in this chapter are learning from the way people build cities for themselves, empowering communities to enhance what already connects them and adapting the imperfect and impermanent into safer and more sustainable communities. They're thinking about the obstacles to spatial equality – from the social and cultural to the way 'form follows finance' in how and what we build – and testing out ways of constructing cities that bust through those barriers.

Their approaches could potentially transform the way billions of people live. Exploring the work of radical change agents in cities across the poor and rich world, I've found clear similarities in the solutions, even though the contexts could not be more different.

We need to look beneath the surface and the spin to determine what really makes a city work for the people who live there and to find the principles that enable urban flourishing everywhere. The visionaries we'll meet are each contributing a small slice of the solution we need to build sustainable, liveable and inclusive cities for tomorrow, building not on perfection but from the realities we're faced with today.

Map the margins

Some of the most densely populated places in the world aren't even on the map.

'If you go to the government records, you find some of these areas in the informal settlements are designated as swamps. And some of them – you're laughing, because it's designated as a forest,' Kenyan community organiser Joseph Muturi tells me.

A classic example is Kibera – a name which means 'forest' in Nubian – one of the world's biggest slums. Located on the outskirts of Kenya's capital city, Nairobi, it's home to up to one million people.

As cities grow, people claim space where they can, turning river banks, railway embankments and parks into shops and streets jammed with houses, without an urban plan or infrastructure to serve them. Often the inhabitants are crowded together at incredibly high densities. In Nairobi, 63 per cent of the four million residents live in unplanned settlements, occupying just 5 per cent of the land area while the wealthy minority stretch out and make themselves comfortable.

When you live in the blank spots on the map, you can fall between the gaps.

Joseph has been fighting for the people left off the map for years, as national leader with Muungano wa Wanavijiji, a social movement connecting these officially invisible settlements into the urban fabric of cities. While GPS mapping a district might not seem like a pressing priority for a community with more urgent needs for survival, this work is essential to make the invisible visible.

'For us, this mapping is to put a face to the faceless: it's to make sure that they are mapped and in the county's plans, for the county to pay attention to these areas which provide the bulk of the workforce in the city,' Joseph says.

Visibility isn't simply an academic or theoretical issue: being left off the map means governments don't officially recognise these communities, and as a consequence, slum dwellers get no access to essentials like water, sewerage, transport, schools and hospitals. They lack the security that comes with a lease or mortgage and the consistency and health benefits that come with power lines and water mains, so their vulnerability to disease – and pandemic – is disproportionately high.

All of this feeds into what Joseph calls the 'poverty penalty'. For instance, providing waste collection, power, water, toilets, you name it, becomes a business opportunity for 'informal service providers', who can hike up the price.

'It's very very expensive to live in an informal settlement,' Joseph tells me. 'Poor people pay more [for] basic things we take for granted. For example, they pay for each use of a toilet. For electricity, which is very poor quality, residents pay three to four times more. [But] if all of us decide to switch on our TVs at once, it will trip. The water supply is very unhygienic and dangerous, which is why there are sometimes cholera outbreaks. Housing is very expensive too.'

Joseph Muturi and the organisation Muungano wa Wanavijiji are using mapping for material impact in Mukuru, Nairobi, a settlement under threat of demolition. If you're not officially on the map, and don't have the protection of land titles or formal leases, what's to stop the bulldozers making reality match the theory?

Mukuru is a settlement that has been growing for over 50 years and is now home to approximately 138,000 households, somewhere around 400,000 to half a million residents. To put that in an Australian context, imagine the entire population of Tasmania living together in an area under 650 hectares, which is about the size of Sydney's Marrickville or Melbourne's Northcote. Mukuru is a place where people live, work and study, so every decision about this place has multiple impacts on thousands of lives.

'We have collected all the information: so what? We have numbered all the structures: so what?' Joseph says. 'Then what you answer is the "then what?"'

In this case, the 'then what?' meant taking legal action to stall evictions, taking to the streets in protest and lobbying the government to claim a window of time for the residents of Mukuru to plan the future of their so-called unplanned settlement. Muungano wa Wanavijiji convinced the county to declare Mukuru a Special Planning Area, and then corralled and focused the activity of non-government organisations pursuing their own projects in the area – there were 42 of them. The NGOs were invited to work together instead, and with the community, on one ambitious plan.

'We don't want one NGO building a toilet in one corner and another building a bio toilet in another corner. We want to consolidate all that knowledge and resources to one very holistic approach to development,' Joseph says. 'Bring all of them. Let's do something big together.'

Muungano designed an organising structure for distributed decision-making and public participation that directs the County Integrated Development Plan from the bottom up. The smallest unit of decision-making is a cell of ten houses: neighbours discuss and contribute to setting the brief, with their feedback and direction scaling up across the settlement. Focusing the work of NGOs and academics, Muungano created seven sector briefs – covering land rights, health, education, energy, water, transport and sanitation – aligned with the existing county departments. Those briefs were written, tested and tested again with the most important people in this conversation – the people who live in Mukuru today.

Says Joseph:

The rationale is to help the county develop a plan, but we want the plan to be owned by the poor people in Mukuru. We want the residents of Mukuru to tell the consortiums, 'This is where we want the hospital, this is where we want the roads to pass, this is how we want the housing to be done and this is what we can afford, this is what we want you to do to address education.'

Most plans are formulated in a boardroom somewhere, but this one was formulated on the ground. We don't want it to be an NGO or academic plan, we want it to be owned by the residents of Mukuru.

This will be a long process – the seven sector briefs are still being tested with the community – and there are many challenges to come. The issue of security of tenure and land ownership is also one we'll return to, as it's a tension felt in cities around the world, and sometimes the most well-meaning processes accelerate processes of gentrification and result in poorer residents getting pushed out. But Muungano wa Wanavijiji's resident-led approach is a world-leading model for inclusive upgrading that improves quality of life without displacing communities, seeks to make the voices of the marginalised majority heard, improves conditions and removes these 'unfreedoms' of access.

***

Mapping matters: it's a first step towards claiming justice in the delivery of infrastructure and services to the marginalised. This is why it's at the core of a global campaign called Know Your City. Drawing on local knowledge, Know Your City asks residents to map the streets and places they know, and then links together community efforts like Muungano wa Wanavijiji's for knowledge-sharing through Slum – or sometimes Shack – Dwellers International (SDI).

A network connecting organisations driven by urban poor across Africa, Asia and Latin America, SDI amplifies the leadership of people who live in informal settlements and connects good ideas and communities across the globe.

'There is so much knowledge, experience, exposure within the network: they mobilise resources for people who cannot access them. It is comparing someone who is alone with someone in a much larger family,' Joseph Muturi says when I ask him what it means to be part of SDI.

'One of the biggest projects that we have ever pulled through is the railway relocation action plan. Much of it we learnt from India. We took the Kenyan Railways officials and showed them [their relocation plan] was not the only way to do it, and now we have 10,000 people who were facing eviction who now have houses next to the railway lines. Also, we have smaller countries which learn from us.'

Talking to some of the visionaries and advocates I've met in writing this book, it's clear that we have to address the challenges of city-making not just in the comfortable surroundings of the developed world, but by working with people creating their own solutions. Lorena Zárate, President of Habitat International Coalition, says we should call these places 'habitats made by people'[3] rather than slums, to reflect the ingenuity and resilience of the people who make their own cities, with very little help – sometimes with outright opposition – from governments. Worse than failing to provide power lines, sewers or garbage trucks, many governments actively work to remove these places made by people through forced evictions and slum-clearance programs like the ones Joseph is fighting against.

We need to embrace these bottom-up solutions and see the utopian glimpses in them because the fastest growing places in the world are shantytowns and slums, refugee camps, *favelas* and *barrios.* It's estimated that more than one billion people will live in informal settlements like Kibera or Mukuru by the year 2030.

***

In many cases, people aren't drawn to urban life chasing opportunity but are pushed into it fleeing conflict.

Right now, there are 60 million displaced people in the world and 20 million of them live in refugee settlements like Zaatari, Shatila, Dadaab and Domiz. These names are not as famous as London, Paris or New York, but these 'refucities' may be the archetypal cities of the next century. While most were initially built as temporary solutions, some of these camps have lasted for generations: Shatila in Lebanon has housed Palestinians since the 1940s and now shelters tens of thousands displaced by other conflicts across the region.

Refugee Republic is another mapping project that makes the invisible visible. It's an artist-led project mapping Domiz, a refucity in northern Iraq.

Domiz is 60 kilometres from the Syrian border and is home to 32,000 people – though at times its population has swelled to over 55,000 – mostly Kurds fleeing the Syrian conflict.

Originally designed to house 1000 people when it opened in 2012, it has grown into a small city and doesn't show signs of slowing: 100 children are born in the camp every month.

Camp life is a reality for millions of people who are displaced today, pushed from their homes by conflict or climate change. For those of us who are lucky enough to be oblivious, there's little understanding of the ingenious and resilient ways people create their own cities wherever they have to.

To harness the power of film to build understanding of daily life in a camp, Refugee Republic charts key sites (money exchange, baker, mechanic), then overlays footage of activity along main streets at different times of day and graphics explaining how residents build up their homes from standard-issue tents to solid houses. The soundtrack includes interviews with the people who've built businesses and a community in the desert. They're making the best of their circumstances but still long for the homes and neighbourhoods they were forced to leave behind.

Of course, our goal should be to prevent or resolve the conflicts that cause such displacement, and to communicate to our leaders that wars are more likely when, like in Syria, persistent drought has pushed people off farms, away from work and into crowded cities. The next best outcome is to ensure that people can find welcome where they flee, but a lack of visibility of camp life can also alienate people seeking refuge, and turn them into 'other', or 'not like us'. Projects like Refugee Republic are important because they invite the world in to understand that these refugees are exactly like us: inventive and resourceful, ready to contribute and share. If we can't walk in their shoes, storytelling projects like this one at least allow us to see the streets they walk on and the community they've created from the rubble.

More than most places in the world, Dhaka in Bangladesh is already feeling the effects of waves of climate-change refugees moving into informal settlements in the city – we'll learn more about that soon – which is why I'm excited about a Bangladeshi project that works to improve life in informal settlements by adding a digital layer of information to the physical layer of life off-the-map.

Dhaka is a city of 15 million people in which 35 to 40 per cent of people live in informal settlements. Kolorob is a mobile app and digital mapping platform that offers the kind of crowd-sourced ratings and feedback mechanisms most of us have come to expect and applies them to unplanned communities in Dhaka.[4] The first iteration of the app mapped over 2000 businesses and services that previously had no digital footprint. This made deliveries and search possible, as well as reviews and ratings, which in turn helped good businesses to expand their customer base. The second phase, Kolorob Jobs, adds a job market function – think Seek, Monster or Indeed for the residents of informal settlements – to connect the 40 per cent of young Bangladeshis who are unemployed with job opportunities.

Honour local knowledge

'A slum is not always a place of sorrows and grievances: it's a place of hope as well,' observes researcher Razia Sultana. Her point is that it's hard not to judge a book by its cover and only see what's missing or what doesn't work in informal settlements, but the formal and informal are always interconnected.

'Without incorporating slum dwellers, the city cannot be sustainable,' Razia says.

Born and raised in Dhaka, Razia is acutely aware of a stigma dividing the city. Slum dwellers are looked down upon and seen as a problem to be dealt with rather than as a hard-working, useful part of the community. By contrast, Razia sees slum dwellers as part of the solution to the challenges that Dhaka faces.

For starters, she laughs, she'd never be able to find her way around her own hometown without the local knowledge (and driving skills) of the slum dwellers who form a significant part of the city's workforce. But in her work, she probes much more deeply into their skills and experiences as she analyses Dhaka's assets.

Dhaka needs all the help it can muster. One UN Habitat report opens like this:

Take one of the most unplanned urban centres in the world, wedge it between four flood-prone rivers in the most densely packed nation in Asia, then squeeze it between the Himalaya mountain range and a body of water that not only generates violent cyclones and the occasional tsunami, but also creeps further inland every year, washing away farmland, tainting drinking water, submerging fertile deltas, and displacing villagers as it approaches – and there you have it: Dhaka, the capital of Bangladesh and one of the world's largest megacities. Add the expected impact of climate change to this cauldron and it's a recipe for disaster.[5]

Razia Sultana has been working with this unforgiving set of facts throughout her working life. She began her career in the Ministry of Foreign Affairs in Bangladesh, focusing on migration, climate change and urbanisation: all issues that impact Dhaka's informal settlements, which swell to welcome climate migrants.

'Climate change is really a visible issue in Bangladesh, especially in coastal areas, because it is a low-lying country surrounded by a great delta. Every year, we face cyclones, flash floods, river erosion; so, every year, hundreds of thousands of people migrate to Dhaka,' Razia says. All the people pushed to the city need shelter, and many of them move onto riverbanks and green spaces, where they end up removing the trees that could help the city deal with its chronic air pollution problem. Five of the top ten causes of death in Bangladesh are linked to air pollution, and Dhaka is consistently ranked as having some of the worst air quality in the world.

'Bangladesh has been labelled the second-least liveable country in the world: the air pollution is so acute you cannot even take a breath,' Razia says. 'I started thinking about urban greening as an important element in improving air pollution.' Noting how this and all the other issues she works on come together in informal settlements, Razia shifted her focus to urban greening within them. Her subsequent PhD research focuses on the way individuals in Dhaka's slums are cooling and cleaning their own environment by growing plants, vines and even trees in the congested alleys of informal settlements.

'They're also facing tremendous heat in slums: within 5- to 6-foot [~1.5–2 metre] shacks, five or six people live. Can you imagine when it's over 40 degrees, without bathrooms, ventilation? Scarcity makes people frugal, which is why slum dwellers are using their self-generated knowledge, using whatever they have to hand. Governments and NGOs should support this kind of innovation. If they work in collaboration, the city could be turned into a liveable environment.'

Right now, very few aid organisations are focusing on how natural systems could play a role in dealing with Dhaka's health and heat challenges. With more urgent pressures like pandemics and great migrations dominating the agenda, it might be hard to understand how greening could be a key element in designing solutions for sustainability and liveability in slums. What Razia's work shows us is how much untapped potential there is, hidden in plain sight, but invisible to the powers that be.

In slums there are lots of problems – food, water, energy, shelter. They say urban greening is an ornamental issue, a secondary issue. There is no scope for community garden initiatives, because of land scarcity in Dhaka. Slum dwellers don't have space, but they do have the intention for greening and gardening, because most of them have come from the rural areas. They have shifted their livelihoods, but many people are not satisfied. In the back of their minds, they want to practise what they know ... people try to nurture this individually. Governments see [slum dwellers] as a burden, but they are also resources in themselves as they have latent competencies – indigenous knowledge being passed down generation to generation. I try to highlight this hidden knowledge.

In Razia's research, she documents examples of how farmers-turned-city-dwellers are ingeniously carving out spaces for trees and plants wherever they can: in cans turned into planters, with vines planted in narrow alleyways.

When we understand and honour the skills of the people left out of the conversation, we find creative solutions and deep knowledge. We're going to need everyone's contribution to solve the complex problems of our time.

Maybe we've been looking for innovation in the wrong places. We've been looking for Silicon Valley tech gurus to make our cities 'smart' and provide digital infrastructure, but I'm most inspired by seeing people in the places left off the map documenting their knowledge for tangible benefit. Maybe NGOs don't need to import solutions as much as they need to resource and elevate bottom-up creativity. And maybe to achieve change at scale we don't need global monoliths as much as we need local, distributed organisations developing their own solutions, networked globally to share their ideas and learn from each other.

Develop skills and relationships, not just property

To build the world we want, we're going to need social sustainability, not just the environmental kind. Another way to describe it is resilience – the capacity of people to bounce back at times of crisis or adapt for change. In this regard, one of the key factors is having people you can turn to and learn from in good times or bad.

Resilience arises when there are strong human bonds in a place. These connections can disintegrate when there aren't enough accessible, welcoming civic spaces – shared places that aren't about shopping, gambling, work or worship. We need places that belong to everybody so we can encounter difference, appreciate the range of experiences our neighbours have, and learn to embrace perspectives that are unlike our own. We need places to bump into each other, for the wonderful, accidental, serendipitous moments that help us feel like we belong in a place, that we're seen and we matter.

I feel like I get this from my role as a councillor. I always say I have a small-town experience in the heart of Australia's biggest city because, apart from during the pandemic-related shutdown, I attend a different community event most nights of the week (during lockdown many turned into Zoom calls and even one memorable 'Friday Quarantini' online drinks with a community group). In my usual day-to-day, I spend a good deal of time meeting people in libraries, parks and centres or at festivals and markets, and run into people I know in each of the villages that make up the City of Sydney. While sometimes it means issues leap out of my inbox and meet me in the street, the upside is significant: I feel incredibly connected to this place I live in. On my street, the houses back onto a small park and neighbourhood kids feel welcome to open the gate and pop into our yard. We adults share a compost bin, as well as kitchen appliances or tools when needed. Picnic lunches take place out there every couple of months and there are lots of chats in the street. It's wonderfully warm. Having that shared communal space of the park as a 'bump-space' means we all begin with a level of comfort and ease with each other that's unlike any other place I've lived. During the COVID-19 lockdown, the park became the icon for a new neighbourhood WhatsApp group, as all these physical contacts shifted online and helped us put names to faces. We found ourselves sharing dorky memes, tips on grocery supplies and offers of plant cuttings, and most importantly, a sense of connection when each of us felt more cut-off from the world than ever before.

Shared social spaces and moments like these need to happen in far more places than my lucky street. And it's about more than the feelgood factor, as important as that is too. We need more places where we can have the essential conversations about the world we're passing on, what alternatives are possible and how we can make the shifts that are so urgently needed.

Architects have a crucial role to play in designing the physical infrastructure that brings people together, but they're not the only key players. Artists, community organisers and researchers are making interventions in their streets, towns and cities to build social infrastructure – places that give people a reason to talk to their neighbours, somewhere to gather and a way to value each other's knowledge and ideas.

So far, we've explored what happens when your cities are bursting at the seams, attracting the ambitious and vulnerable alike. But some places are emptying out instead. When a sizeable population contracts, this presents its own challenges to resilience and can accelerate the process of polarisation – pushing the experiences of city and country or thriving and struggling even further apart.

Regional centres in the UK, USA, Europe and Australia that relied on industrial production in the past have suffered with globalisation and economic shifts away from manufacturing and mining. As they lose their ability to attract and retain people, they see their social fabric disintegrate. In China, rural villages are sometimes called 'hollow villages' if the working-age people have moved to the cities for education and jobs, and only the elderly remain.

Xu Tiantian, one of China's most exciting new architects, sounds a bit disappointed when I tell her I've never had acupuncture.

'It's soothing, and not as scary as it looks,' she tells me. 'With needles, you look for the minimal intervention to activate the spot and promote circulation.'

Tiantian is telling me about acupuncture so she can explain her approach to reviving the 'hollow villages' that now dot China's rural landscape.

Most villages have a history of hundreds of years and a community of families living there for many generations. You have to be very careful to make only the most minimal intervention, not only with the buildings but also with the community, and their history and context.

But acupuncture is also to activate. In ancient times, the villages were connected by their traditions: 'You have the best fried tofu and we have the best brown sugar, so we trade'; these used to be economic and cultural connections. By activating this new program based on traditions and skills to promote the circulation between these villages, this is also a key to restore the rural identity of each village. It's like the alternative medicine of looking into this situation.

Tiantian's work, through her architecture studio DnA, is both aesthetically striking and remarkable for its sustainable and imaginative interplay with nature. She uses 21st-century design to champion ancient, locally distinctive traditions and rebuild communities by inserting delightful social spaces into places that have begun to suffer from neglect, thanks to the creative brain drain.

When I first encountered her work, at the Venice Architecture Biennale, it was so completely absorbing that I didn't want to walk away: a rare achievement in what is an overwhelming showcase of the best of the best in the world of design. Her installation was a topographical landscape of seven villages in Songyang County, five hours south-west of Shanghai, featuring a collection of fascinating buildings. Walking across the landscape of the installation, you were struck by the sensitivity with which Tiantian had slipped these moments across villages in the county. She had drawn on the array of specialities the villages offered – from tea to theatre, soap to tofu – and conveyed a sense of the relationships of trade between these ancient places. I stood absorbed by a model of a stunning green-domed theatre on a hillside, woven out of living, growing bamboo. In the accompanying video, a proud construction worker stood inside the finished product explaining that they'd borrowed techniques from local basket weavers to make it, and in doing so had created one of the region's most popular tourist attractions. Another chapter in her 'Songyang story' is a long covered bridge spanning the reservoir and river that winds through the hilly Songyang County. The structure expands at the centre to form a unique town square connecting two villages. The architecture is beautiful, but Xu Tiantian doesn't want me to get distracted by that.

'The building is not the purpose, it is the beginning,' she says. 'It's a means to an end.'

For Tiantian, architecture is a medium to integrate history and new possibilities into a social program. This isn't about imposing the shiny and new on these villages but using a contemporary aesthetic to honour their traditions in such a way that 21st-century people can begin to appreciate them again. This may even draw some of them back from the cities that have lured them away. Tiantian tells me about two young people who returned to the village from Hangzhou to set up a fabric-dyeing workshop, using local teas and plants to dye fabrics, selling their wares online and collaborating with fashion designers. She warms to the topic:

It's inspiring to see young people setting up start-ups in the ancient village. This is the most positive effect going on in Songyang at the moment: these young people have had their experience in the big cities, and once they return home, they can bring new ideas and new concepts and businesses.

We have designed the Damushan Valley Teahouse in a tea plantation. This young lady is 30 years old. She used the space not only for a cafe but for hosting a tea educational program, so she could recruit students coming from Shanghai and Hangzhou to come to Songyang for a week to learn the tea ceremony. In the first year, she was able to attract over a thousand young people from cities to learn and explore the countryside. She started to think about innovative tea products and set up a new production line. And now, in her second year, she has sold over two million euros of products.

These young people are creating a new magnetism in this region. With this tea production, she'll go into the mountains to work with local farmers; she'll work with ginger and brown sugar, also from the region.

Architecture has a role not just in constructing but in caring for place by respecting the communities and traditions that have tied people to it and to each other. Tiantian's philosophy is that new ideas and technology shouldn't erase what has come before but draw on a depth of knowledge to develop solutions that enhance human connections and creativity.

'History, culture, craft and new technology can be integrated with architecture and landscape too,' Tiantian says. The challenge prompts her to work a bit harder and to leave her professional comfort zone in order to really understand the people she works with.

If you work in such a situation, you are a professional, but you are not only a professional. You can engage more and develop your knowledge as well: that's how I feel about the past five years working in Songyang. I learned a lot about local agriculture and landscape too. This is essential content when you work with the buildings too: you have to learn how to cook the brown sugar, the fried tofu, tea oil, the rice wine. You have to learn and understand the process and local life, instead of just being an architect and talking about structure, material, program. You have to expand your world scope.

***

City-makers are blurring the boundaries between architecture and art – and between an aesthetic intervention and a social mission – in the old industrial world as well. It's not the kind of art we're used to seeing in galleries, but 'social sculpture' is a tool artists are using to intervene in the power dynamics of our cities through the built environment.

In the UK, Liverpool was a success of the industrial age. The shipping port where Britain's industrial exports were sent out into the world, with a thriving working class providing labour in the docks and warehouses. From the early 1980s, the shift to container shipping and the exodus of manufacturing jobs to developing nations hit the working class hard. Margaret Thatcher's Conservative government allowed Liverpool to fall into 'managed decline', and the subsequent New Labour government cleared out blocks for big projects which failed to eventuate, scarring the urban fabric of Liverpool with empty houses boarded up with tin.

After years of activism, a local community group claimed ownership of Liverpool's Granby Four Streets area in 2011, establishing a Community Land Trust. Essentially, that's a way to take property out of the market and hold it in perpetuity for community benefit: more on this shortly. They worked with Assemble Studio, a UK collective of artists, architects and designers, to turn derelict terrace houses into affordable housing and community space while training a new generation of local craftspeople to do the refurbishment. Generous, community-driven and beautifully designed, the project is a model for urban regeneration and skills development in post-industrial cities, and demonstrates what's possible when empowered and engaged communities take control and are supported to develop new opportunities.

Similarly, American artist Theaster Gates has applied the cash and cachet of the art world to the project of remodelling the South Side of Chicago. When the area hit hard times, Gates was dismayed at the way the formerly grand buildings were allowed to decay. Some were even bulldozed to deter squatters and drug dens. After the GFC, buildings were being sold at bargain-basement prices, so he started using the money generated through his art practice (selling pieces from the buildings themselves, and staging social actions) to buy up as many properties as he could.

His shift to artist-as-property-developer began slowly. After Theaster acquired some important local record and book collections, he bought the house next door to his to display them. Then he decided his art practice would be bringing cultural institutions and community infrastructure back to a place in danger of being erased by poverty and the racist history underlying urban-planning choices.

Theaster worked with locals to build a library, gallery and community space (Stony Island Arts Bank), record library (Listening House), mixed-income housing (Dorcester Art + Housing Collaborative) and training program (The Ash Project and Dorcester Industries) to give young people from the South Side access to job opportunities.

He's taken the model to cities from Bristol in the UK to Kassel, Germany, presenting a hands-on model of artists sculpting society. I walked into a Theaster Gates artwork, *Twelve Ballads for Huguenot House,* at the documenta art exhibition in Kassel back in 2012, and suddenly found myself in the most creative share house I'd ever experienced.

As I wandered through the building, walls, staircases, bedframes and tables were being built by the residents out of the stripped remains of a beautiful building from Chicago that had been slated for demolition before Theaster acquired it and repurposed it. For the 100-day duration of documenta 13, a band called the Black Monks of Mississippi lived in the house with Theaster and some local craftspeople, hosting performances and community events, inviting visitors in as they created the building and nurtured an ongoing dialogue about displaced peoples. Among them were the persecuted Protestant Huguenots that the house was originally named for and the migrant people who'd built both grand buildings in the now-faded heydays of Chicago and Kassel alike.

Theaster Gates trained as an urban planner and practised art as a ceramicist and sculptor before he decided to mould neighbourhoods. This is something much harder to work than clay: using buildings, entire blocks and suburbs as the materials of an art practice that refuses to accept that some places are deemed too damaged for cultural infrastructure or beautiful spaces. He uses the power of companionship, music and creativity to heal and to show what's possible when generous civic spaces are given back to communities who've had them torn away.

Build spaces for sharing

The kitchen is the heart of a home. So, what happens when you don't have one? Beyond the family home, what could a kitchen be for a community living on the edge? How can it be a place that heals and unites, not just a place that feeds us?

I'm talking to Tiago Mota Saraiva, an architect and member of Portugese collective Ateliermob, about the much-celebrated communal kitchen they built in a barrio 15 minutes from Lisbon. Terras da Costa is located just behind a beach town of weekenders for city dwellers and yet is a world away. This barrio is home to five hundred residents, most of whom are undocumented immigrants. They're living in this shantytown without security of tenure, electricity or water: the closest water source is 1 kilometre away. Even though so much needs to be done in this place, when the residents had the opportunity to lead the process and set their own priorities, a shared social space – a kitchen – was at the top of the list. Tiago and his team were on hand to make it happen:

One of the oldest people from the neighbourhood had the idea of the communitarian kitchen because she organised a lot of communitarian lunches. Every [project participant] was symbiotic in a way: the municipality provided the water to arrive there, also the electricity, and we [said we'd] manage the kitchen.

For a certain period, it was used as a kitchen but right now it's mostly a community centre; kids now do their homework together there. It's their public building. When they have something that they have to discuss, they announce all over the neighbourhood saying, 'We will have a meeting this time, this day', but they never say that it is at the kitchen because for them it's obvious now.

The kitchen is a J-shaped wooden building (made from wood donated by another architectural team), open in the middle. The long edge of the J houses a large communal table. There's a kitchen, laundry and jerrycan-filling station along the bottom and short edge.

During the planning stages, the community united around the idea of a shared social space and counterintuitively decided to place it in exactly the most troubled and dangerous part of the barrio, the drug-dealing hotspot.

'It was the spot where the cars could come – the drug drive-in,' Tiago says. 'And they wanted to occupy that area. The municipality understood that they have to support it because this was a thing that came from the neighbourhood to change the idea that people have of the neighbourhood. It was very funny [after the kitchen was finished], all the awards and media that was around it. It decreased almost totally drug-dealing because from one day to another, the neighbourhood was too visible. You can have the TV news coming in live from there – your boss is gonna see you drive past!'

Ateliermob is a co-operative – not your usual architectural practice. They invite their clients to join their co-op, so the clients stop being clients and start being long-term collaborators.

They commit long stretches of time to any community they work in. For example, for this project they started working in Barrio Terras da Costa in 2012, built the Cozinha Comunitária (Communal Kitchen) in 2014, and to this day are still helping the community through major hurdles, like finding a new site where they can establish themselves with more secure tenure and better services. As the Terras da Costa site is an ecological and agricultural reserve, it won't be possible for this community to settle here permanently, but Ateliermob see the residents' right to place as not restricted to rebuilding in the same location. Tiago explains:

'It's the right to stay in one area so that you can keep the kids in the same school, you can keep the same relationship with the bus line that you normally use to go to your job. We've discussed with them four places in the one-kilometre area that are to be urbanised that could be the placement for them.'

To build lasting change, Ateliermob have begun aiming for prevention rather than cure. They don't just design buildings: now they intervene in the political systems that are the cause of exclusion. They help to design laws that work for the people who don't usually get to set the brief, ensuring they're written with input from the experts who are usually called in to triage the symptoms of inequality, not address the root cause. This is the next evolution of socially engaged practice: actively leaping into the fraught space of politics to shape policy from the bottom up.

'We also started to be a social movement. When we started to understand the proportion of things, we also started to say, "Okay, now we have to become even more political." So, we approached the political parties that were doing, for example, the law of housing and say, "We can do the basics of it, and then you can discuss it."

'We get our lawyers and engineers and designers and people that work in the neighbourhoods, and then get together so that we can produce something to give to them,' Tiago says. 'I always use the expression, "Use the other guys' tools to try to do good stuff."'

Design smart policy, not just smart cities

Right now, the most popular future-city discussions in the world revolve around the so-called 'smart city'. I get invited to a dozen smart-city conferences a year. Their focus is slightly different every time, but for the best part it's a way for Business X or Sector Y to sell stuff: a smart city is seen as a city packed with sensors and Internet of Things devices, gathering data and automating decision-making for seamless public services and responsive urban systems.

Toronto Waterfront was a smart-city precinct proposed in Canada by Sidewalk

Labs, part of Alphabet, Google's parent company. Features like underground rubbish-collecting robots, heated footpaths and free wifi were heavily marketed. But there was a protracted public battle as citizens bristled at the idea of handing over 12 acres (4.8 ha) of precious public land and exposing their personal data to the biggest company in the world. Alphabet pulled out in May 2020, blaming the pandemic, but in my books, local activists really won this round against a global Goliath. Waterfront was typical of the smart-city projects we tend to see in the news: tech-coated land and data grabs couched in sensors and gadgetry.

Like Bellamy's urban utopia or William Morris's crafters' paradise, Toronto Waterfront and many of today's smart-city plans are totally removed from the reality of cities as the chaotic, bottom-up collaborative human creations that they are. Often they're starting from scratch and imposing an abstract ideal on the world, rather than starting from reality and trying to make it work for people. Increasing efficiency though technology is a useful goal for a smart-city, but more often than not, smart-city visions are really rich-city visions, offering marginal improvements to the comfort and convenience of the wealthy, rather than helping more people live more sustainable, connected lives.

'The smart city is not a technological issue, it is a political issue,' Professor Mat Santamouris says. 'You get the governance right and the technology follows.'

Like Xu Tiantian in China or Ateliermob in Portugal, Mat is making cities fairer by starting with those who don't usually get to set the brief. An energy physicist and expert in high-performance architecture, Mat Santamouris is improving life for the energy-poor and constructing energy-positive settlements that will help cities be part of the solution in a warming world.

'Energy poverty is really, in my opinion, one of the major issues actually in the world. Just in Europe, we have 150 million energy-poor officially accepted by the European Parliament. 150 million,' Mat says emphatically. 'Just understand: 70 per cent of the Portuguese cannot afford to heat their houses.'

Mat has worked for decades on energy and housing projects in Europe, Japan and Singapore, and recently relocated from Athens to Sydney. As it turns out, we really need him here. In all his years of research, Mat says there's only one country he couldn't find data on energy poverty for – Australia. His observation is that Australia refuses to acknowledge the reality of energy poverty and, as a result, is well behind in addressing the issue.

In a recent project in Western Sydney, Mat's team installed 150 sensors in low-income homes, compiling data on energy use, indoor temperature, comfort levels, ventilation, CO_2 – total environmental quality. He was shocked to find that during winter, the indoor temperatures were as low as 10°C, and in the early days of summer, as high as 38°C – an astonishing set of extremes that suggest these homes are poorly designed to the point of being dangerous.

'The first victims of climate change and local overheating is the low-income population,' Mat says. 'So, in my opinion, the very first priority is to protect low-income households.'

Heatwaves are becoming more common – and extreme – as temperatures rise with climate change. In the UK summer of 2018, during a 15-day heatwave there were almost seven hundred more deaths than the average for that time of year.[6] Older people and people with heart conditions are more likely to be affected. Higher temperatures can also exacerbate the impact of air pollution, which can be deadly for people with respiratory illnesses. Mat says there's a 'huge penalty' paid by people in the west of Sydney: during heat waves, they experience a mortality rate that's three times higher than those living in the east.

In this city, the places with the highest ground-temperatures are often in areas where local governments lack the resources to invest in urban greening, shady parks, cooled community centres or pools. They're usually places with newer building stock, sprawl and McMansions: cul-de-sacs of single-family dwellings baking in the sun on treeless streets, built without breezeways and reliant on air-conditioning, which becomes unaffordable as energy prices soar. Poor urban design isolates people and compounds disadvantage: often, these buildings are found in the very places where the vulnerable are pushed by rising property prices or as social housing is moved out of the city centre.

Redesigning the way we build our houses, buildings and cities would have an enormous social benefit and significant environmental impact: building and construction are responsible for 39 per cent of global carbon emissions. Of that 39 per cent, the lion's share (28%) is spent heating, cooling and lighting buildings, while the rest comes from the materials themselves. It's a way we could make quick gains to help reduce our impact on the planet and improve people's health and quality of life in the process.

In Mat's view, Australians have the most expensive, poorly built housing in the world: bad news for anyone who owes the bank a million dollars on a mortgage or who's paying 30 or more per cent of their income in rent. But what he means is that our housing is poorly insulated for the heat and the cold, with little to no air flow – for cooling breezes and to remove harmful gases – and we're reliant on expensive energy for light and temperature control.

There's a better way, and Mat has helped design it. ZERO-PLUS settlements are whole precincts or suburbs that are energy-positive. They're powered by community-integrated renewables – that is, power generation and storage at the neighbourhood level, rather than the building-by-building solar panel and battery approach we usually see – and advanced tech is built in. In the settlements already constructed, Mat says they've found it's 16 per cent cheaper to build this kind of sustainable, networked community than the traditional approach of stand-alone, one house at a time development.

ZERO-PLUS settlements in Cyprus, Italy, France and the UK feature some extraordinary technology. SBskin glass bricks do more than let light into buildings: they're embedded with solar cells so they can also collect energy. WindRail adds wind power to the renewables mix, but not in the form of turbines or windmills: instead, a curved unit on top of a building, covered in solar panels, also converts wind into energy. Photovoltaic pavements gather energy. Photocatalytic paint and panels on the surface of buildings actually remove pollutants, like volatile organic compounds, from the air. These settlements use every possible bit of wall, roof or street to generate power and restore the quality of the essential commons like air and water: they're the physical embodiment of the 'regenerative city' that Sydneysiders challenged us to create through the citizens' jury process that we discussed in chapter 3.

It's thrilling to research the different technologies Mat shows me, but I worry I'm straying into techno-utopianism again. Yes, there are so many incredible, so-good-they're-almost-sci-fi design advances out there, and the palette of technological innovation available to draw from grows daily, but what's really brilliant here aren't the specific tech solutions. What we need in order to catalyse change is way more boring: we need more demanding planning and building codes so that every house upgrade and every new building being designed has to go beyond business-as-usual. Regulation pushes industries like the construction sector to build to a higher standard, and in doing so, creates the market that turns today's cool prototype into tomorrow's Bunnings supplies. We need to go beyond approving each building on its own and instead plan whole suburbs that do this, remove the counter-productive limitations that conflicting agencies impose (I could go on about this: more in a moment) and require every building to do more than passively reduce its harm: they should actively produce energy, clean air and recycle water.

'We have to bring everything together in integrated design and integrated policy: we need to decrease temperature and energy consumption and increase comfort, in every action and in every project, this has to be implemented and taken into account,' Mat says.

People fall in love with a building like One Central Park in Sydney: with its luscious living vertical garden walls, it's a splendid symbol of what our cities could be if they lived up to their green potential. But smart and green city innovation truly starts to make an impact when it's not exceptional, and when we demand that it becomes the norm. While it's cheaper and easier to do this when you're starting from scratch, these techniques can also be used to adapt and retrofit our buildings, streets and suburbs now.

The reality is, our cities today are pre-existing conditions: we don't often get huge swathes of space to redevelop using new tech. It follows that we need to build in higher standards for retrofitting, and we need to embrace networked approaches like community water and energy as we see urban infill (the rededication of land to new purposes) become more common.

Occasionally, there are opportunities to make impact at scale, for example, in Sydney's Green Square – as long as there's political leadership and the ability to require developers to do more, which is a rare combination. The City of Sydney had that when we led the renewal of this 278-hectare former industrial area, only four kilometres from the city centre. As I write, it's halfway through its transformation into a space with homes for 60,000 residents and workplaces for 20,000. The City worked with developers to secure 40 new pocket parks and contributions that have provided an aquatic centre, stunning underground library, creative centre, school and child care – and the centrepiece: a water recycling system and treatment plant housed in a building that could also be home to locally generated power, with the right settings in place.

The water recycling system is working across 14 hectares, but it's small-scale compared to what could have been – what could be, if the state government agency responsible for water didn't make water recycling totally uncompetitive by sticking extra charges on it. This is the opposite of those subsidies I uncovered in researching Ex'Tax. If you can believe it, we have government agencies here imposing extra costs to make water recycling totally cost-prohibitive.

We had the leadership, we had the influence and the moment, but what we didn't have was the ability to control the levels of government above us, whose policies are actually working against establishing a market for recycled water or local energy. Recently, the City of Sydney also laid water-recycling pipes under the city's main thoroughfare: George Street. The hardware is all set, waiting for a day when a state government shows the leadership to make simple amendments to policy that will change everything. Until then, we'll flush clean drinking water down toilets on the driest continent on earth, and we'll let new energy futures flounder as they try to compete against those heavily subsidised fossil fuels discussed in chapter 6.

It's one small example of how the problem today is not technology, it's policy, and that's what we see in Mat Santamouris's work too. In Europe, the requirement for net-zero development has spurred industries on to brilliant innovation. Slowly, the challenges of energy poverty and environmental impact from the built environment are being met. But to get there, we need to rebuild the policies that are blocking the future we need.

Invent new old models

While it might seem comparatively minor in comparison to the stresses experienced by those facing extreme housing instability or the physical dangers of energy poverty, affordability is an escalating issue in global cities everywhere. One of the ways that city-makers around the world are dealing with a lack of affordable, quality housing is by banding together into housing co-ops, pooling their energy and resources, and building it themselves.

Housing co-operatives aren't a new idea. Pioneered in New York City in the 1860s, they were exclusively for members of the wealthy set who wanted a country house and a city residence. The idea caught on elsewhere, and co-op apartment buildings were all the rage until the Great Depression saw many of these well-heeled residents fall behind on their payments. The housing co-op model then declined in the USA and became relatively uncommon in the UK and Australia in the 20th century.

But they didn't fade away everywhere. Despite being very different contexts, Latin America, Switzerland, Austria and Germany kept the co-op dream alive and are now at the forefront of housing solutions for a new century.

In Sweden, about 16 per cent of people live in co-op housing, and it's also commonplace in Zurich in Switzerland, which has a long tradition of co-op housing and secure long-term rental. Vienna, a city which frequently tops those 'most liveable cities in the world' lists, has an astonishingly high level of beautifully designed and generously appointed public and co-op housing. A third of all the housing is city-owned, a third are co-ops and a third are privately owned.

In Latin America, they've been using the co-op housing model for people with lower incomes since the 1960s. Uruguay is one of the world's leaders, with over 600 co-ops around the country connected to the Uruguayan Federation of Housing Cooperatives for Mutual Assistance, housing 22,000 households – that's about 2 per cent of the country.[7]

Typically, Uruguyan co-ops are made up of between 10 and 50 households, with one vote per household in regular assemblies, which is how all major decisions are made. Assemblies and community gatherings are all held in a common room, or *salon,* which is always the first room to be built in a co-op. And here's the extraordinary part: everyone who lives in the co-op contributes to its construction. Each family is required to give 21 hours of labour a week to the building of the co-op, in whatever way they can best contribute, as a way to keep costs down and to build relationships between future neighbours. The co-op owns the land

and building, but if people want to move out, they're paid out for their time contributed and also for their part of the value of the co-op, which is set in a special unit of value established in housing law. This is to prevent speculation and to help keep housing affordable.

Since 2004, the Uruguayan model has been exported to seven other Latin American countries – Guatemala, Honduras, Nicaragua, El Salvador, Costa Rica, Bolivia and Paraguay – with the help of the NGO We Effect. Interestingly, that NGO is funded by 60 Swedish co-operative and employee-owned companies as a way of extending their social impact, which is a beautiful illustration of how democratic business models keep doing good well beyond the interests of their owners or shareholders.

New models for co-ops and non-speculative housing are emerging elsewhere too. Since the fall of the Wall in 1989, Berlin has experienced the best and worst of a creative-led resurgence. With affordable space and a relatively low cost of living, a progressive, vital culture and a location at the centre of Europe, Berlin attracted generations of artists, technologists and makers, drawn in by the opportunity for experimentation and exchange. I lived there for a short time in 2012, and I found the biggest obstacles to my productivity were having too much fun and too many fantastic things to see and do, too many great occasions and places to dance and learn and spend time exploring creativity, which is a pretty good set of problems to have. (Berlin, I still blame you for that book I didn't finish writing but I can't stay angry at you.)

The downside of being the coolest city in the world has been the steady rise in the cost of housing, which has forced original residents out as new arrivals stream in. In reaction to this, a new model of co-op, the Baugruppen (it means, literally, 'building group') has emerged, through which groups of families and individuals come together to jointly purchase land and finance medium-density development.

By cutting property developers out of the process, Baugruppen can be 20 to 35 per cent cheaper per square metre than comparative developments. But the crucial difference goes beyond cost: Baugruppen are developed by and for the people who will live in them. In the traditional build-it-sell-it model, property developers have no real reason to build for high environmental performance, especially as it requires higher up-front investment but only offers savings in the long-term. Being focused on long-term usefulness for their owner–builders, not short-term sales profits, Baugruppen also tend to deliver smaller individual homes and more communal spaces like gardens, guest rooms, workshops and roof terraces, which encourage community and social connections, as well as being a more efficient use of valuable urban space.

As the model has matured and gained acceptance, financial institutions and local governments across Germany have seen the benefits of Baugruppen in building communities for people, rather than for the financial return. Many offer facilitators to support prospective Baugruppers in securing sites and financing, while some cities offer lower land tax or council rates to incentivise this development type. Some even offer council-owned land at a discount.

This shift, from limited cases to accepted model, reduces risk and offers systemic protections, which allows the model to expand and scale up.

The Baugruppen model is being enthusiastically adopted in Australia, reborn as the Nightingale model, and architect Jeremy McLeod and his studio, Breathe Architecture, are their primary champions. Baugruppen and Nightingale offer a way for people to band together to cut out the middleman and build the kind of generous, liveable and sustainable communities everyone should be able to live in: places that use less energy and provide more shared space; places that provide for bike parking and are close to transport, but that cut out the expensive and inefficient additions most people don't realise are eating into affordability, like car spaces and second bathrooms.

So, why doesn't everyone get to live like this?

In the business-as-usual property model, developers need large amounts of capital (usually, equity from other properties or funds from big investors) to be able to buy land and obtain the finance and insurance needed to design and build. They usually sell their housing off the plan, before it's built, to reduce their risks in the project. Once they secure buyers, developers are pretty much free to squeeze as many savings as possible out of the project, in the materials, care or time taken. Often that's not the intention from the outset, but it's easy for costs to blow out as every extra day adds more interest to the massive loans most have had to take out for the project. Their investors require a 20 per cent profit return on property development as a market standard. Also, there are big loans on offer for customers (thanks to all that money floating round the financialised world for mortgages on real estate) and every possible incentive pushing people towards buying rather than renting. The upshot is that there are always more customers looking to buy real estate, even if it's poorly built, energy-guzzling housing that's designed for short-term profit, not long-term quality or liveability.

That's what Nightingale is designed to overcome. Investor finance is structured in such a way that any investment that doesn't deliver a 20 per cent return isn't worth the risk. So, even though the world of FIRE (finance, insurance and real estate, as we discovered earlier) is awash in liquidity, it's hard to direct it to be useful in the bricks and mortar world, where people might want to build a building to last.

To overcome that, Jeremy has pulled together capital from networks of supporters and people who want to be part of a positive new model for housing. Mind you, it takes an incredible number of discussions and outreach to make it work.

'For Nightingale One we needed $3 million in equity, and the idea was we would really democratise the capital. We take all the big money out of it. We had 27 individual shareholders putting in $100,000 each. It was really hard to kind of bring all that together: most of them were mums and dads, friends of mine, other architects. We did the same thing with Nightingale Two, Three, Four: lots of small-scale investors. And by the time we get to Nightingale Village, you know, there's seven projects all running simultaneously. And when each of them need to raise about $3 million in equity – I need $21 million in equity – it's a lot of people to talk to. It means you've got to get, like, 210 investors.'

Against the odds and the obstacles the status quo presents, Nightingale are making an impact: in 2019 alone, they sold 283 apartments. About two hundred of those were part of the Nightingale Village in Brunswick, one of Melbourne's most sought-after suburbs. There, seven leading architecture firms created a precinct of beautifully designed apartment buildings that adhere to the Nightingale principles. These are 100 per cent fossil-fuel-free building operations (through an embedded energy network), deliberative design that includes the input of future residents, transparency in costs and a contribution back to the community through more generous interactions with the street and the provision of workspace and social spaces.

Across Nightingale Village, 20 per cent of the housing is affordable – run by a community housing provider – and another 20 per cent will be reserved for 'community contributors', using a definition Nightingale have developed themselves. They found that the usual description of 'key workers' used to designate people eligible for some community housing projects is very limited and doesn't include the contributions that creative producers, artists or First Nations people make.

Oh, and did I mention that they sell these apartments well below market rates, and there's an affordability covenant built in for posterity? That means that if you sell your apartment in the future, you're contractually obligated to accept a capped price and required to pass the original discount on in the future sale price. You'll get an increase in value, sure, but this is about providing affordable homes in well-served locations from now into the future, not just adding more fuel to the property price bonfire. As you can imagine, people are lined up around the block to be part of it.

'We typically tend to sell at about 15 and 20 per cent under market,' Jeremy says. 'We're selling superior design, superior construction and at a lower rate, and we're selling carbon-neutral housing. We do all this stuff with transparency and so when we ballot an apartment, generally in the right area, it ballots incredibly well in whatever the market. So, the last project we balloted, we had a 300 per cent subscription rate.'

None of this is easy to design or manage, and listening to Jeremy describe the work that goes on behind the scenes – before the first sketch is drawn or shovel of soil turned – you understand that it takes more than the skills of an architect to achieve these kinds of outcome. Jeremy often says that he didn't set out to build more housing but to build a new housing model, and from my conversations with him, it's very clear that being in the vanguard of that revolution is all-consuming and exhausting work. The Nightingale Model educates other architects to replicate and deliver this process in different contexts, but the unique set of skills required makes this tough to scale. It takes a sophisticated understanding of the financial system; the patience to push and wend around outdated planning regulations (ones that require car parking for every unit, even when you're next to a train line, for example) and litigious objectors who can add to the time or cost of projects; a network of engaged, principled investors; and the ability to negotiate with governments and NGOs to help them see that they need to adapt too, in order to achieve outcomes that are usually in all their lists of goals and best-practice case studies.

The next big leap forward Jeremy is undertaking is unlocking Australia's collective wealth – our superannuation, or pension fund schemes – the white whale of impact investing. Thanks to our compulsory super schemes, Australians have $2.9 trillion under management. If even a small proportion of that was used for prosocial goals, it would make a huge dent in the problem of needing 'patient capital': money that can be used to generate a slightly lower, but secure, rate of return. Funding housing to be people's homes, as opposed to simply assets for property speculation, would provide an excellent long-term investment, yet the current giddy rates of return from the build–sell market of churn and the abstract world of finance make it hard for real-world good value with values to compete. As always, being way out in front means Jeremy is the one who has to navigate past all the icebergs, and he's met more than his share of sharks along the way.

'The problem with the superannuation companies was that, for them, it was all about deal size: we're asking – for them – not much money,' Jeremy explains. 'And we're also asking for a concessional rate of return [that is, less than the 20 per cent they'd get from a standard property play]. And so they're seeing Nightingale still as a development investment, and we've been trying to explain to them that it's not a development, it's actually a housing or a construction project.'

Despite the difficulties, Nightingale have had success in partnering with one superannuation fund so far: on Nightingale Village, they've secured $20 million in capital from not-for-profit Social Ventures Australia and HESTA, the industry fund for the health and community services sector. It makes a lot of sense, considering HESTA members are from those essential, key contributor sectors – 80 per cent of them are women working in the care sector – and, as we've already explored in our story, while the work they provide is crucial, they're some of the lowest paid people in our society. A project like this helps ensure essential workers can afford to live sustainably and beautifully: it's absolutely something that I think more super funds should see as part of their core business.

Rather than make every architect a guru of the Nightingale Model, as brilliant as it is, I think we need to find the potholes Jeremy has uncovered through his persistence, and fill them in to smooth the path for the ones who follow. He's built a model that offers a new way to deliver the kind of housing we want to live in, so let's figure out how we adapt today's flawed system and the crooked, archaic incentives to allow more of that to thrive.

Question highest and best use

There's a bit of wit attributed to Mark Twain: he was asked his advice on a good investment and he apparently replied, 'Buy land, they're not making it anymore.' It's a gag but there's a lot of truth in it. Land just gets more and more expensive, seemingly all on its own. No one's creative energy or hard work increases the value of their own land. It's an asset that grows in value thanks to the stuff that goes on around it (like public infrastructure or transport being put in) or due to demand – because no matter how networked and digital our lives get, or how long we spend on Zoom calls, we're physical beings that haven't yet figured out how to upload ourselves into the cloud.

Where I live, you don't have to do anything at all for the value of your land to go up by about 5 per cent every year, which is great if you own it and terrible if you want to do anything interesting with it. Jeremy from Nightingale says it's near impossible to make one of his projects work in Sydney because the cost of the land makes up about two thirds the cost of a project. According to one school of thought, this is socially created wealth being transferred to private pockets, and the biggest cost is that it doesn't generate socially useful land uses.

Associate Professor Louise Crabtree is an expert in permanent affordability and sustainability in housing, and she's my go-to guru when it comes to understanding how land value works. And how it works against the ways humans use it for things like food and shelter, as she explains:

Very strange things happen when land is treated as a commodity, because it's so fundamentally tied to shelter and to systems of provision, such as growing food or what have you. When the land itself is ascribed a dollar value and then treated as something that can be speculated on, we get stockpiling. Basically, we get people looking at how to maximise the financial return that they can get on that land, rather than looking at how it can best perform those functions with regards to shelter and provision and livelihoods.

You get this stifling of innovation as well in land markets. It's one of these sectors where the ostensible market logic of capitalisation translating into a desire for innovation just doesn't happen, other than innovation in terms of 'How can we get more money out of this land?'. You don't actually get excellence other than in the form of profit-seeking.

I've worked on projects with property developers, and I've seen a lot of big property developments come across my desk as a decision-maker. For example, I'm a member of the Central Sydney Planning Committee, which is the authority that has to sign off on all projects over $50 million in the City of Sydney. There's a phrase that's used all the time in this world, when we talk about the kinds of thing that might happen on a piece of land: highest and best use.

It sounds noble, right? I wish I lived every day applying myself to my highest and best use. But what it means in practice is maximum financial return, and in the overheated property market of most big cities, that's residential development over all else. And in my city, it means a very specific type of residential development: apartment blocks full of two-bedroom, two-bathroom apartments, the kind you can rent out to young professional couples or two singles sharing. That's the highest and best use right now, because it's also the kind of property unit that's easiest to get a bank to lend you money for. So, we have blocks full of buildings full of this same type of unit. But it doesn't cater to the actual needs of the community (good luck if you have a family, want to live alone or are downsizing), purely because the market is designed to extract the maximum return from this one specific housing type. There's nothing highest and best (for humans) about it.

Louise Crabtree says that in the jargon of property speculating, the phrase 'highest and best use' of property is interchangeable with 'highest flippable return'.

Anything outside the narrow bank-approved product category is rare or an exception that needs to be incentivised or regulated for. We need planning regulations to require a housing mix in buildings, which requires developers build one-bedroom dwellings for singles or couples, or accommodation with more than two bedrooms so families have somewhere to live; or for housing to be provided that's inclusive (such as universal design, so people of different needs and mobilities can live there); or sustainable, such as carbon neutral or net positive design. Highest and best use doesn't provide for that, so society has to intervene in the form of regulations.

There is a way we can make land work for people to live on it and use it, as nonsensical and unnecessary as that statement should be. One of the best things we can do is to remove land from the equation altogether.

There's a lot more to Louise's work, but she's well-known in city-maker circles as a global expert in community land trusts and other mechanisms to help redesign the way we provide shelter for people: tools that separate the use of the land from its market value as a speculative asset.

Here's how it works: you take the land, which might be owned by a government or community entity, like a church for example, or a private owner, and you put it into a trust, which manages the land to be used for a community benefit, such as affordable housing. The developer can then take out a long-term lease on the land, build on it and pay a set rent to the owner of the land – one that's fair and stable for the long term; not one that goes up as fast as land prices. The people who actually live in the building on that land own shares in the building – not ownership of individual chunks of land. Or they are tenants, and everyone is now only paying for the cost of using the housing, not for the staggering, always-increasing cost of the land as an asset. Louise explains:

There are ways of unpacking the ways in which property has traditionally been bundled up as a financial package. And a lot of these are more collaborative and community-oriented models, so it's not you as an individual property holder with your parcel that you hold title to against all others, and look to speculate on. It's looking at your right to that property as something that's bound up in social relations, so it's more 'I am a member of this entity' – whether it's a co-operative or community land trust – 'and together we are making decisions about what we think highest and best use means here.'

According to Louise, that's one of the social benefits of these non-speculative models: people aren't atomised individuals out to use their home or investment property as a retirement plan. Yes, it's an asset and you can get a return on it, but the primary purpose of that house is as a home, a place that will be affordable for someone to live in forever. You have security of tenure – certainty that you can continue to live in one place rather than having to pack up and move every couple of years – and you can put down roots. Because you own shares in the whole rather than title that stops at your front door, you're more likely to feel a sense of ownership over the common spaces too. You might have more useful ones – workrooms and playrooms, or a shared guest room, for example – and you're definitely more likely to know your neighbours. As joint decision-makers in the future of that place, Louise tells me, residents have more opportunities – and the shared motivation – to make decisions about the place that take in the bigger picture. The flow-on effect, in her experience, is that it's common to see thoughtful, community-minded responses to other development in the area.

Louise continues:

> In the US, community land trusts often talk about themselves as 'the developers who don't go away', in contrast to a for-profit entity that comes in, maxes out the units they can fit on a site, possibly

builds stuff that's not great, and then leaves. Whereas because these community land trusts are organisations that are there in perpetuity, they tend to build things that are going to last – that have high environmental performance, that will have high water performance, are thermally efficient, well designed. You know, because if it falls apart, they've got to clean up the mess. So, it sort of changes the logic and changes the relationship. It's more about an ethic of stewardship and common purpose rather than, 'Well, let's just build this quickly and get out.' So, you definitely see a more proactive stance [from neighbours], because people are like, 'Well, yeah, we want to see more of this in our community. We want to see more of this in our city, because it is good quality, it's housing people. It's building the stuff that we know we need. And we know it's not going to be detracting from the quality of our place.'

Community land trusts are not a new phenomenon – they started in the USA in the 1970s, inspired by village land holdings in India that go back centuries. Right now, they're having a moment in the spotlight as people all over the world look for alternatives to a property market that's failing people everywhere. Big cities with major affordability problems are realising that this model could help counteract the rampant property speculation that's pushing many residents and important social uses out.

Housing affordability and sustainability specialist Louise Crabtree again:

We're seeing cities like London and New York that are realising we need policies for actually putting land into a non-profit vehicle and keeping it there in perpetuity so that we can get these better outcomes. Historically, where these may have tended to have been smaller scale projects – you know, a community of a few dozen or a few households coming together – we're now starting to see municipalities realise this is something that's got to be bigger scale. We've got to have structural interventions and models for holding things in perpetuity and for having that discussion around what highest and best use means.

Sydney is one of those cities: it's one of the most expensive places in the world to live, and property prices play a big part in that. One of my key goals for my time on council is to use our city as a laboratory to model the kinds of solution we need to see in the world. I want us to address the lack of affordable space for living and for working, for experimenting to launch new businesses or services, as well as creating art or presenting culture. The City of Sydney has already made impact within the constraints of the system we have, providing subsidised community and creative spaces and funding hundreds of affordable housing units, but what I'm most interested in is figuring out how we might generate and incubate new models for making housing and space affordable at scale. This isn't about subsidy: it's about shifting the whole market towards prosocial ends, helping to prototype or kickstart new ways of providing things that mainstream market business-as-usual has failed to.

To do that, my colleague Philip Thalis and I asked the City of Sydney to run a new kind of competition in 2019: the Alternative Housing Ideas Challenge. We asked the world to send us their best ideas for ways to redesign housing models, making changes at either planning, design, construction, financing or management stages of the process. The response was brilliant: we received over 230 entries from all over the world, from architects, students, developers, researchers and more. Seven entries were selected as finalists and funded to develop their ideas further. Working collaboratively with each other and with City staff, they had the goal of testing their models and getting feedback from financiers and other contributors. Hopefully, we'll be seeing some of these models being built in Sydney soon.

I was thrilled to see Louise and her colleague Jason Twill, another socially minded disruptive property renegade, selected as finalists. Their proposal was to develop the institutional infrastructure that's needed to enable community land trusts – in combination with other innovative approaches to development – to take off here too.

It's easy to get fixated on property ownership as the only pathway towards housing security, and perfectly understandable when every possible incentive in Australia is pushing us in that direction. But owning a patch of soil isn't the only solution, and it shouldn't be the only way our society strives to meet people's housing needs or give us a feeling of ownership and stability in a community. Incentives that push people to derive their income from being a landlord – particularly in retirement – are now teetering on the verge of policy failure. We saw the downside of our national obsession with property thrown into stark relief as the pandemic hit in 2020. The economic consequences of the COVID-19 pandemic, which saw whole industries shut down overnight and a million people out of work in a week, resulted in a lot of people being unable to pay their rent: if a tenant can't pay, and evictions are put on hold, which is the moral thing to do at a time like this, what happens to their landlord's debts or income stream? How can there be peace of mind for tenants when their future is decided by the individual financial circumstances of their landlords, rather than there being a fair and uniform approach to housing security?

It is possible to design an investment asset that funds housing, provides income for investors and minimises the risk: we just need to move from a one-to-one model of property investing – the 'mum and dad investors' as landlords are revered in the Australian political discourse – towards an institutional form of housing investment that spreads risk more evenly and provides the capital that could fund a revolution in housing provision. That means that rather than buying an investment property, you'd be investing in a property fund. The fund might invest in a block of units – even affordable housing, for example –

so your risks and return would be spread across the whole project, or everything that fund owns. That cuts the risk of ending up with no income if your individual tenant can't make rent. This sort of institutional funding for housing would likely result in a better mix of housing types (not everyone would be wanting to take the safest option by buying and renting out those two-bed-two-bath units for a start); there'd be more funds for more innovative developments like Nightingale or for affordable housing, which provide secure but slightly lower returns. Louise says all the elements are coming together to make this shift possible.

It's changing the mentality around what it means to be investing in property: rather than it being this really hot and unstable thing – which, sure, may deliver some really awesome windfalls but also comes with a lot of risk – to a far more risk-intelligent strategy.

We're starting to see the creation of infrastructure that can enable it. We've got the National Housing Finance Investment

Corporation, which is a channel for institutional funding into the non-profit housing space, so we've got a vehicle there. Currently, it's mainly the super funds that are looking at putting their funds into that. That's really how we generate a parallel market that is channelling those funds that would otherwise go into investment properties, into this more structural, longer term and more stable investment vehicle, rather than those mums and dads thinking, 'Well I'm going to go buy that flat and rent it out.'

The advantage [of this alternative approach] for the mum and dad is they don't have to deal with being landlords. Someone else is doing that, somebody who does this for a living: it's their business, and you don't have to think about that anymore. The hot water system blew up? Who cares? It's not your problem! You don't even need to know about that stuff. Your money is in there, doing what it does, and you can get it back whenever you need it.

What you see where we've got these big, stable institutional rental markets, is you get better outcomes for tenants, because everyone wants stability. Last thing you want is to be flipping tenants every six or 12 months and dealing with all of the mayhem that creates and all of the noise around securing and releasing bonds and dealing with repairs and maintenance and all of that churn. You just smooth all of that stuff out of the system. People can have two-, five- or ten-year leases; they can hang pictures, you know, all that sort of stuff. If you look at the European examples where these sectors are running, they just deliver. You get a much calmer market that's got far more stable and steady returns.

Redesigning the housing market in Australia is a particularly sticky problem because there are so many sectors, from construction to finance, that have a stake in the status quo. It would require visionary and brave political leadership to take on the tax deductions of one million landlords, but at a moment when 'safe as houses' investments have been shown to have as much risk as anything else, this could be the opening that leads to a better housing system. It is thrilling to see viable alternatives take root that have a lot to offer us, in terms of sustainability and quality of life, a sense of community and housing standards.

It's time for us all to really question what would be the 'highest and best use' for our precious land and for the money we spend on our housing, and to interrogate the models we have today, starting from the ground up.

Make land contribute value

Scaling up from the level of the home or apartment building, how could we make every city block work for the citizen, rather than prioritise the investor above all else?

Whenever there's a big property redevelopment, and a two- or three-storey building or block is knocked down to make way for a sky-high new building, there's 'value uplift' taking place. That's planner and property developer lingo for money – lots of it. We know that land forms an enormous part of the cost of any home or building, and when a landowner is permitted to dramatically increase the amount of housing or commercial units on a piece of land, its value goes through the roof.

So, what would happen if society, and the community around that land, actually took a slice of those profits too?

After all, the streets and services, the buses, parks and schools around that development would have to work harder to accommodate more residents or workers. Usually, developers are required to mitigate this impact by making a financial contribution in the form of an open space levy, a public realm contribution or by doing works on adjoining footpaths or public spaces themselves. All of that is important and necessary, and it shouldn't change, but it doesn't address the core fact. So much of the financial value that's created when buildings are allowed to go up in the air in our cities only exists because of the activities of citizens like you and me, making connections, and providing art and industry in the streets around them.

As explored earlier in this chapter, it's not the land itself creating the value, it's the people all around it, but land has become the store of wealth that goes up and up in value, sucking out the hard-to-monetise human activity all around, and stockpiling it in the form of land value.

Indy Johar from European think-tank Dark Matter Labs explains the concept using the example of a house in the middle of Sydney:

> If I was to ... move that physical same house and put it in the middle of the outback, how much is that house worth? Next to nothing? So, where's the value of that house coming from?
>
> The value of that house is coming not from the house itself. Here's the key words: the value of the house is coming from the *monopolistic access to public goods.* It's coming from the right to labour markets, transportation infrastructure, schools, other life

amenities, environmental assets – all these other things that sit around it.

So, what we have is a thesis of land, which is saying, you know, 'My land is my castle', versus the reality of the property market, which is not about land but its monopolistic access. That is what you're trading. If you've seen the house price inflation in our houses, it's actually not your house that's going up in value. It's those public goods that have gone up in value relative to everywhere else in the world. So, Sydney's public goods become more valuable, and thereby landowners have basically extracted that value to themselves, as opposed to the public good and all citizens that live in Sydney.

Indy has been thinking about this in the context of cities as generators of innovation. The start-up boom ignited a buzz around the intangible knowledge economy – the world of value being created from data, digital content and audience engagement, as discussed earlier in our story – which in turn has sparked a frenzy of venture-capital investment. To grow those businesses, start-up incubators have sprung up all over the world – places where people with ideas work together in close proximity to share talent and ideas, to build networks and find new customers and suppliers. That kind of sounds like the reason we move to cities: so what better incubator to invest in than the city itself?

Indy explains the connection between the intangible, or innovation and knowledge economy, and the skyrocketing price of land.

If you look over the last 30 years at where has wealth actually grown in the UK, what you figure out very quickly is net wealth has predominantly grown in land. Everything else has been nominal – it's grown by one and a half times – but land has grown five times. And so, you realise, for all the talk of innovation and start-ups and all that, the best investment in the UK was land.

Our thesis is this is actually a structural shift in our economy, where we move from a tangible-assets economy – you know, products, services and things like that – to an intangible-asset economy. They are non-tradable soft goods, highly synergistic; they are interwoven with each other; they have very powerful cluster effects ... So, what you end up having is a situation when land becomes the mechanism of actually taxing intangible goods ... our economy has gone from tangible goods to intangible goods and land.

An architect by training and a provocateur in practice, Indy Johar is part of a community of brilliant thinkers in Birmingham in the UK. I met him at the launch of a tiny-housing project years ago and have been following his work ever since, captivated by his capacity to zoom out and see the system design that underlies the symptoms we're usually trying to address. He calls that stuff institutional infrastructure, or 'deep code'. His company, Dark Matter Labs, do research and run projects that experiment with the deeply held, unquestioned assumptions we base our society and economy on, such as the fundamentals of ownership, our culture of individualism and our perceived dominance over nature. That's the stuff that's written into the source code of our competitive, consumer, linear system, and the system failure going on all around us now should be a signal to us that it needs an overhaul.

One of Dark Matter's latest projects is for the UK's innovation foundation Nesta (which used to be called the National Endowment for Science, Technology and the Arts), which has given them an opportunity to look at the relationship between place and innovation. If you want to stimulate more activity, productivity and connection, the very things that entice us to live in cities, can you use land value – the thing that usually prices that creativity out – to fund the space, support and infrastructure that generates a fair and productive society?

Usually, when governments fund innovation they have a narrow focus on grants and workspace for a certain kind of tech start-up. But those things have little impact on the talent pipeline that's required for enterprises to succeed. Training talent is vital, sure, but there have to be affordable places for those people to live in the city, and the kind of cultural and social life that attracts talent like flowers do bees. Dark Matter Labs say innovation policy barely touches the tip of the iceberg. While it supports entrepreneurs directly, until now policy has neglected the institutional, cultural and social conditions that make places and businesses bloom.

Dark Matter Labs have proposed a solution in the form of a national network of city endowments – imagine venture capital funds for cities – drawn from a range of revenue sources, including capturing some of the gains made through value uplift. That means when a developer might stand to make a 'windfall gain', a large profit thanks to being able to add ten more storeys to a building, then a slice of this – say the value of three floors – might be contributed back to a fund for the community around them. Indy says:

Actually, there's a correlation happening between how innovative a city is or can be, and land value. We said, 'Well, why don't we link these two things?' [What] if we could take, say, 1 per cent of transaction costs or uplifted transaction costs to fund an endowment which would actually then fund the city in a structural innovation capacity? You start to create a sustainable mechanism to build this institutional civic infrastructure for innovation. And that can operate at a cultural level, as well as what I'd call economic communities of purpose, as well as the institutional infrastructures levels of building the conditions for that stuff.

It's appealing for many reasons, not least of which is how tied to place this plan is. It's harder to dodge a development-tied contribution than it is for many cashed-up companies to minimise their tax contributions. From a city-making perspective, I also love the idea that you could see a tangible benefit from a development – which typically generates disruption in the vicinity – actually being delivered in the same area.

Dark Matter Labs have proposed that ten major cities in the UK could each start with a £100 million endowment, sourced in part from the money generated from value uplift, and they could use the interest to fund the kinds of commons and civil society infrastructure that we need to make our cities creative and fair. A rolling, growing fund could pay for affordable workspace to incubate new businesses of all kinds, as well as affordable housing for those workers to live in. It could fund training programs and support staff, people doing the essential work of connecting the dots and helping businesses and organisations find customers and sources of income.

Dark Matter write:

Their mission would be to unlock and embed long-term innovation capacity across our city-regions, enabling firms, communities, individuals and the public sector to grow new ideas that drive inclusive growth, tackle the challenges our society faces and change the world for the better.

To achieve this, the endowments need to be financially independent and highly localised – down to precincts, like Business Improvement Districts have been applied in other parts of the world – as well as being transparent and accountable to local communities. Ideally, forms of participatory governance and budgeting like the ones we've seen at work elsewhere would also be applied so that the people closest to the place and the 'productive communities of purpose' (that is, contributors to the project or the urban milieu) can make decisions about how investment could have the most impact.[8]

While they have deep local roots and empowered communities driving them, the endowments should also be nationally networked so innovators and cities everywhere can share knowledge and learn from each other.

Most importantly of all, these funds should be used to ensure that the broader community benefits from development. They should be designed to propel sustainable and inclusive growth – the kind of democratic and regenerative local economies that we know are needed all over the world.

Wouldn't it be transformative to see high property values – a factor that drives gentrification and pushes creativity and diversity out of our cities – employed as a tool for generating opportunity and building fairness into the places we live?

10

Restart a civic conversation

We're reaching the end of our story, taking you through the movements and ideas and introducing you to the people that give me hope, those glimpses of the world that's within reach. As I write, the politics and the moment have become more and more toxic, quite literally.

I began writing this chapter in January 2020 working in 30-minute bursts with a sleeping 12-week-old baby strapped to my chest. That was hard enough, but the greater challenge – then and now – has been fighting to hold on to the optimism of these visions of utopia I write about when the daily news has kept delivering reasons for pessimism. The Coronavirus pandemic is taking that challenge to stratospheric levels. The world post-COVID-19 will need to reinvent itself. It's very early days on that score. I hope positive, transformative visions like the ones I explore in this book will be woven into that reinvention: I'm fearful we'll see policy responses like those brought in after the GFC. Approaches like austerity – which had even more damaging consequences than the original crisis – diverted money and focus from the climate action we urgently need, and which exacerbated and deepened inequality.

Meanwhile, I'm wondering what kind of world I've brought my tiny daughter into.

In the first few months of Elinor's life, Australia was burning: more than 11 million hectares of bush were destroyed in climate-change-related fires on Australia's east coast in the summer of 2019–20.[1] I became morbidly fascinated with the scale of the disaster, regularly superimposing a *Guardian* interactive map of the fire area over different parts of the globe. I watched as it exceeded the size of Belgium or Slovenia, doubled Belize or tripled the size of Lebanon, and then neared the size of England. By the end of January, the fires had doubled Australia's annual greenhouse gas emissions.[2]

The sky turned into an enemy, a foe to assess every morning. In her first three months of life Elinor was outside only a handful of times because air pollution soared to 11 times hazardous levels. When I went out, I came home with a headache and sore throat. It worried me that Elinor was snoring – surely something unnatural for such a tiny baby. Have I damaged her lungs by opening a window or daring to take her out on the wrong day? Friends loaned us an air purifier (they sold out almost everywhere) and my husband monitored the indoor air quality readings on an app with the same intensity with which some people watch the stock market.

We risked poor air quality to take our daughter with us to a rally called Sydney Is Choking. At only a few days' notice, 20,000 people were gathering at the Sydney Town Hall, angry at governments wilfully blind to the connection between the poisoned air, the burning country and our outsized environmental footprint. As ash rained from the sky and smoke permeated everything, the business district rang with the sound of fire trucks: the smoke in the air was so thick that it was setting off smoke alarms in buildings. The Town Hall was evacuated and city workers had to sit outside in the thick haze for two hours until it was confirmed that the air, not the building, was on fire. As the biggest city in the country choked, politicians on teams blue and red alike decided this was the day to pose with the CEO of the World Coal Association and declare bipartisanship on Australia's toxic role as an exporter of fossil fuels.

Four weeks earlier, I'd been at another rally, outside the state parliament building, on a day labelled catastrophic for fire danger. In fact, authorities had to create a whole new fire rating category for it. Six hundred schools were closed for the day, and residents of huge areas like the Blue Mountains, to the west of Sydney, were advised to evacuate. Among them were my parents and my sister's family, and so by that afternoon, we all found ourselves holed up at my small inner-city home. Yet the conservative Liberal–National state government made this the day to introduce legislation to prevent climate change from being considered as a limiting factor in new mine or gas-field proposals. They wanted to be able to override court rulings that – like in the Netherlands' nitrogen crisis, as we saw in chapter 6 – had tried to make the connection between what governments say they're committed to and what they permit in practice.

In other parts of the country, supposedly progressive leaders went out of their way to criminalise the actions of Extinction Rebellion protesters as tabloids and talkback radio hosts frothed at the idea that activists might stop traffic or inconvenience people going to work. If you think someone blocking a road is inconvenient, just wait till you hear about what climate change will do...

Through it all, our representatives refused to make the connections common sense demanded, to see the country on fire as a desperate trigger to action and for a change of policy direction. Predictably, all the while Australia's Murdoch-controlled media kept up their deadly game of savaging any leader who dared to deviate from the thoughts-and-prayers script. That's why tens of thousands of us were on the street demanding action; by 12 December 2019, the business sector was haemorrhaging $50 million a day in lost worker productivity and sales in Sydney alone,[3] yet none of it was enough to prompt reflection or action.

If our leaders don't seem to value human health, the environment, democratic engagement or economic productivity, what do they value? How do we have a conversation about values in society today?

It seems like we have more and more places to talk – festivals of ideas and comments sections and Facebook pages to name but a few – but are we only talking in our tribes? What seems to be lacking is a healthy, civil, compassionate public sphere, a place where we can have the overarching conversations about what we should prioritise as a society and how we should get there.

If our public sphere – whether the public square of protest or the discussions in media – is an echo chamber or an ideological cul de sac, where do we have the conversations about what matters, what we want to elevate to the top of the list, and what we are prepared to sacrifice or fight for?

I left this chapter till last as I thought that it might be the easiest problem to solve. When I started, I thought, *Surely the toughest nut to crack will be redesigning work to be more useful for people or the planet? Isn't reforming the voracious beast that is banking and finance a harder ask than simply having a place where a conversation can take place?* With a bit of techno-optimism still coursing through my veins, leftover from my 20s, I kept thinking: *I'll find it when I get there. There'll be that one project, the 'killer app' of democracy that will reveal itself, the plan to rebuild media and the public sphere.*

How hard could it be to work out how to talk with people about this stuff?

As I went on, writing, interviewing and researching for all the other chapters, I chipped away at this one. Yet, somehow, it felt like the one I made the least progress on. Every conversation I've had while writing this book sparked another conversation, a lead to follow, an organisation to look up or a new visionary to admire. But every time I asked the interviewees about where they see this civic conversation happening and how we spark it, instantly, even the most optimistic people in the world sank into despair.

Then I realised that we can have all the good ideas in the world – and this book has proven to me that we in fact do have a world bursting with great ideas – but if we don't have a better way of talking to each other, we can't make them a reality.

Exit the echo chamber

If your social media feed looks anything like mine, you're surrounded by people in furious agreement with you. We tend to live our lives online in self-selecting media channels, listening and talking to people who share our perspectives on the issues that divide the planet, which is why we can be so surprised by outcomes – like election results – that don't match our worldview.

If you pop out of the bubble and post political opinions online, you can sometimes end up a little bruised, particularly if you're a woman or a person of colour. I've had more than one troll – a random stranger who's irritated by me or my politics, savaging me on anything from my stance on issues to my weight, or under the mistaken impression that I'm somehow living large on their dime – and many people I know have had it much, much worse. It's not hard to see that there's something antisocial that arises when you hold most of your political conversations online, when you don't have to look the people you're arguing with in the eyes or deal with the impact your harsh words have on a living breathing human being.

The less we hear from people with different views and the more we have these conversations in disembodied ways, the less real or reasonable people with different views can seem to us. In turn, this can create a more toxic political discourse, accelerating the fragmentation of society into tribes and making it harder for shared positions to be reached. It's a horrible state for us as individuals, and as we've seen, when it comes to conversations on the issues that really matter, like saving our planet and building a fair world, we're not doing well.

It's a counterintuitive idea, but instead of only talking to people we agree with, it's possible that charging deliberately at disagreement is a strategy for rebuilding our fractured, bruised public life.

It has been championed by Maria Exner, Deputy Editor-in-Chief of Germany's *Die Zeit* Online, and some of her colleagues. 'With filter goggles, we interact with "the Other" – in societal terms – less and less: with people who think differently, have a different background and have a different social reality. So, we thought, "We want to bring people into these conversations,'" Maria tells me. 'People who think differently about politics should talk to each other.'

As a newspaper, the *Die Zeit* team recognised that if they were caught up in an echo chamber and came to believe wholly in one perspective on the events of the day, their legitimacy would collapse. They'd already seen it happen to their peers around the world.

In early 2017, the Brexit referendum was just behind us; the American election where Donald Trump won; the French election was on a margin, going to Macron and not to the far right. In this environment, we were thinking about our own election coming up in the autumn of 2017, the general election in Germany. We thought, 'How can we do our political reporting differently around our election? How can we enhance this by something that makes sure that we don't fall prey to the same illusion that some of our colleagues in other countries had experienced?' Their reporting was 100% sure that Hillary Clinton was going to win, that the Brexit referendum is going to be voted with a 'No'...

We felt that some of our quality-journalism colleagues in these countries had kind of lost connection with some parts of the country and didn't grasp what was really going on, and so they didn't see that coming. We thought, 'Okay, how can we be in a better position? How can we bring more of what people really think into our awareness?'

So, we thought, 'What would help, what would be a good intervention in this?' And we thought, 'Maybe people should just talk, you know, to each other more about political things that they care about, and where they are really of a very different opinion [and probably not likely to get into a conversation] about these political topics.'

Maria and her team designed a system to identify people with strongly opposing points of view on some hot-button topics in Germany: it wasn't flashy or complicated, and they didn't expect too much from it. They called it Germany Talks and started by putting out the spikiest questions of the day in as neutral a tone as they could.

The first version of Germany Talks was really more or less a Google spreadsheet, with a nice front end on our website, with five questions asking, for example, if Germany had accepted too many refugees in 2015 – that was the most contentious topic – and is to this day. We asked if Germany should return to the Deutschmark, as opposed to the Euro, if quitting nuclear energy was the wrong decision ... We thought maybe 1000 people will sign up ... People started answering the questions and, I think, within a week, we had 5000 people signing up for this. That was the moment where we thought, 'Oh, this is going to be bigger than we thought.' And in the end, for the first edition, we had 12,000 people.

Using that spreadsheet of answers, and information like postcodes to find opposing matches near each other, participants were paired up with dialogue partners: people whose views were as different as possible. About 50 per cent of those participants went ahead and met in person, sparking 3000 discussion pairs of 6000 people who might usually be arguing with each other on the internet. Or, worse still, be oblivious to or mystified by each other.

Amazingly, pairing up people who disagreed on major issues resulted in very few conflicts: rather than creating tensions, this process dissolved them. Maria tells me about the astonishing feedback she received:

People were really just so excited to have met somebody they wouldn't have usually met in their life and to have this kind of conversation that many of them said, 'Even with my friends, or even with my family, I don't have this kind of deep political conversation about why I really think certain things about certain topics.'

Many of them reported back that, even though they had really different opinions about a question like the refugee question, they often found a kind of common ground. They would reply something like, 'You know, we disagree, but I can understand why she or he thinks the way she thinks.' And probably the most interesting result of these conversations is that people stopped thinking that somebody who thinks differently on that question is a bad person, or 'I cannot at all understand why would anyone would think positively or negatively about refugees', and they really find something in these conversations that makes them relate to the other opinion in a different way.

Germany Talks disrupted the usual path of arguments by putting a real face to a range of political positions: the experience helped people realise that the people they disagree with are just like them, and have their own reasons for reaching their points of view.

'We have until today had 100,000 sign-ups on the platform, and we have not had a single really negative feedback,' Maria says.

Rather than being an engine for aggravation, a recipe for shouting matches and grandstanding, pairing up people who disagree has generated understanding and nuance. The magic of this approach seems to be the personal connection that arises in a conversation one-to-one rather than the tension of a group dynamic. It seems that we are more open to relating to each other, more generous or gentle with each other, when it's two people making eye contact.

The only thing that really makes me change my mind is if I have a one-on-one conversation with another person, because this is a surrounding where I can feel comfortable enough to maybe open my mind a little bit. As soon as I'm in a public setting – even in a conference setting, with somebody on the stage, and maybe I'm part of the group of people in the audience – these are all kinds of settings where people will not be able to change their mind, because they have other humans watching them. And this one-on-one conversation is a setting where I can actually say to another person, 'Oh, yeah, actually, you're right about this. You know, maybe I'm wrong?' Or maybe, 'I'm thinking about what you're saying.' This is about the only setting where that is possible.

The success of Germany Talks resonated in media circles; Maria says they received messages of interest from as far afield as Argentina. Then it was scaled up ahead of the 2019 European Parliamentary elections to become Europe Talks. Powered by 16 media partners across the continent, on 11 May 2019 more than 16,000 participants from Norway to Greece and Bulgaria to Belgium travelled to meet each other to debate major questions about the fate, values and foundations of the EU.

As they met on that Saturday afternoon in parks and cafes and plazas across Europe, the participants broke through their echo chambers, ditched the small talk and dived right into the biggest issues dividing the continent: does the EU improve the lives of its citizens? Are there too many immigrants in Europe? Should richer European countries support poorer ones? Should European countries increase taxes on gas to save the climate?

What I find surprising is that people actually *want* to meet others who are different to them. The wisdom – which meshes with my own experience – is that we're all essentially tribal: we tend to gather with and befriend people who share our perspectives or our beliefs. But this project reveals that there's a yearning to be challenged, one that isn't being met by the comfortable filter bubbles we're in.

'I think it's really a need and something that people would like to do who care about society,' Maria says. 'People who think that we are driven more and more apart economically, that gentrification is really not a good development, and want to stay in contact and want to contribute something that stops this development. They fear there's something missing that they even don't talk to friends about political things that they feel uncomfortable with.'

Of course, there's an element of self-selection: Europe Talks participants are all readers of 'quality' journalism and are more likely to be politically informed and middle-class. While you can break out of the filter bubble, class bubbles are harder to pop, and this project hasn't evolved to that level yet.

'What we haven't yet tested – and I'm not sure if [we'd ever] be able to find out – is [whether people] from a more socially deprived background ... have any kind of interest in this kind of conversation. I think that they have so many things in mind how to go on with their lives that this may not be a priority,' Maria says.

***

Following the European edition, My Country Talks evolved and it has rolled out in single-country editions in Sweden, Denmark and Britain. Maria hopes to see foundations get on board to back the project as a way of supporting more inclusive, thoughtful civil society conversations. I'd love to see it grow too. The lesson I take away from My Country Talks is that we shouldn't underestimate each other, even when we disagree passionately about core issues. I've been as guilty as anyone of painting someone as irretrievably flawed, impossible to talk with, because we disagree on things I regard as core values – on whether we welcome refugees, or take action on climate change, for example. Now I recognise that this is easy to do when people are just shadow puppets, icons on Twitter, and so much harder when they're sitting across from you.

I always talk about how we need to build an inclusive future, to find constructive ways of working through disagreements with respect and patience, appreciating that people can have valid reasons for their positions, even when we disagree on what we value. It's not easy to do, but Maria is onto something with these platforms.

Her advice is to begin by asking questions, not making statements, to try to remove emotion and aggravation from the conversation. Lead with interest in the other person's position and, above all, ask why.

Why it works is that we try really hard to put the questions in a way that is very non-judgemental. We try to frame the questions in a way that people feel comfortable either answering yes or no, because we asked a neutral way. And that's also the first thing that we do – you come across My Country Talks when you read something online in the newspaper, there will be a kind of a small box, just asking you, 'Do you think Germany has taken into many refugees? Yes/No.' So, we don't advertise: 'Hey, this is a project where you should meet somebody who thinks differently than you.' The first thing that people interact with are these questions that ask for their opinion. We believe that's how you create the openness and the interest in the project, because people feel comfortable answering your question. And then we ask, 'Oh, do you maybe want to meet somebody who has answered the exact same questions in a completely different way?'

We don't advertise it as, you know, some kind of 'positive civil society, engage against the filter bubble' kind of thing. But it's really coming across as, 'Hey, we asked you to give your opinion on something that is important to our society at the moment.' And I think that's the way that we 'trick' – quote, unquote – people into participating.

It's a 'trick' that works. The big lesson I'm talking away from my conversation with Maria is this: if we truly believe that every person has a role to play in building the world we want, we need every person to feel valued and heard. We do that by asking them the *why* behind their positions and respecting the beliefs and experiences that got them there.

It seems basic, but it shows how far we've strayed from a civil civic conversation that we so rarely have a space to engage with people who have different perspectives, in a meaningful way. It could help us all feel more connected to each other, and that's a powerful way to counter the polarisation that is tearing us apart.

'One thing that we asked was if people would like to stay in contact with the person they met, and 80 per cent of people said yes,' Maria says. 'We asked: "Was it a positive experience?" Well, 83 per cent of people who answered said yes, and also 80 per cent would like to do it again.'

The My Country Talks model is the first step in rebuilding the public sphere – opening the lines of dialogue about our differences. The next step is talking about what we can agree matters to all of us.

We have to find a shared basis, something like the love we have for our kids or our nephews and nieces, our love of the natural world or of the ideas and creativity that people have used to explain and expand our world. Then we have to find a way to equate that love with the action we need to take now, the changes we have to make, the questions we need to ask, and think of our obligations beyond our own lifetimes.

Define the social space for action

All this stuff is great in theory: don't judge people who disagree with you, ask questions rather than make statements, have discussions rather than give lectures: you know the deal. But it's considerably harder in practice.

Just as I finished writing about My Country Talks, a family member sent me one of those climate-change-didn't-cause-the-bushfires videos that were doing the rounds in early 2020 and all my good intentions turned to dust. Instantly, I was outraged, indignant and self-righteous (even more so than usual). I didn't reply asking why she felt the way she did or asking why she wasn't convinced that extreme weather was getting worse. I forcefully told her that it was. She told me that people deserved to make up their own minds, and I retorted that climate change is too big, too existential a threat to be a matter of debate. She hit back by asking, 'Well, if it's so important, what are you doing about it?' We were moments away from an argument about who takes too many flights and who recycles. This wasn't going well.

I'd retreated into my corner of the ring, and she hers. This was someone I've known all my life, someone in my own family who I love: I should know better. I sent her media articles discrediting the particular theory she was spreading, articles published precisely because a version of this conflict was happening in every family and every workplace. Things had gone a bit far by then and I don't think they made one scrap of difference.

More information isn't going to dig us out of the trenches we're in. The usual method we employ at times like this is turning to knowledge: stacking up piles of research on either side of some kind of invisible scale, putting our hands on our hips and yelling *Q.E.D.* at the opposing party – shorthand for 'See: this proves it' – until they capitulate or walk away. Or we suddenly turn into the high school debating team, forgetting for a minute that they're often the most annoying people in school, and thinking our reasoned, bullet-pointed argument is going to be scored by some moderator. It's like watching politicians from teams blue and red on television in shows like ABC TV's panel discussion program *Q&A:* do we think they're somehow going to argue their way towards consensus?

'More knowledge is not going to solve this,' Professor Kees Dorst says, and then explains why. 'Because they don't want to take responsibility for innovation or for actions, people like to fall back on research, because "That analysis shows that we should do this." You're just not taking responsibility for something that is actually a creative step, which is also a moral step, that you should get behind and own. So, it's a giant cop-out.'

That's not the kind of talk you'd usually expect from an academic: for too long, academics have resolutely tried to stay out of proscribing action. Through the Sydney Policy Lab, for example, I've been in lots of conversations with researchers who are distraught that their system pushes them to do research, draw conclusions, but rarely to go the step beyond towards advocating for real-world application – in their world, that's often deemed too activist or political a stance. Kees doesn't stick to those rules. One of the most unconventional problem-solvers I've ever encountered, he uses design to solve wicked systemic problems in a range of different contexts.

I've been a fan of Kees's work since I first invited him to speak at one of my events – it was about a project he did trying to remedy violence in Sydney's night-time hotspots (this was before the lockout laws – but that's a whole other story). Since then, the challenges he's tackled have scaled exponentially in complexity. Today, he's the director of Transdisciplinary Studies at the University of Technology, Sydney, and he's working on the biggest problem set we have: achieving the United Nations' Sustainable Development Goals (SDGs).

Kees is telling me how we've got problem-solving all wrong. Unusually, for an academic, Kees thinks we need to cool it with the research.

Our talk turns to this issue that's plaguing me: how do we have a civic conversation about what we value and about building a future that includes us all? According to Kees, we need to stop thinking the civic conversation will be won in the battle of the footnotes. What's actually required is a moral, values-based discussion, but one with enough empathy to give people room to include change and action within their existing worldviews. It's more complicated and difficult than simply telling someone they have to care: it's finding common ground on the fundamentally human, then recontextualising these burning issues in a way that resonates on the deepest level.

'My father used to say, "You can put a lot of pressure on people, but you first have to design them a way out,"' Kees tells me. 'Because, if not, they're not going to accept it as a problem. Because something is only a problem if it could be solved in principle. If it can't be solved in principle, then that is something that you ignore.'

In other words, people need to see some light at the end of the tunnel. Kees believes that's one of the reasons we have to find and promote examples of solutions to our biggest social and environmental challenges. Currently, much of our discourse tells people that the planet is on a doomsday countdown, spells out the staggering inequality and the climatic disruption before us, and then demands that people take seemingly disconnected positive action in the face of it. When there's a hefty disconnect between the scale of the problem being presented and the nature of the individual contributions people are being asked to make, the action seems nonsensical. The future of humanity is at stake and so ... all we have to do is sort our rubbish and recycle? The gulf between haves and have nots is growing into a vast chasm, and so ... we should make this small monthly payment to an NGO?

When the solution to a substantial issue is conveyed in language like *should, duty and sacrifice, debt and obligation* for people who are unconvinced, there's nothing very appealing or particularly compelling about it.

What would compel someone who's sceptical or reluctant to take action? How do you work out what people are willing to contribute on behalf of the rest of society or for the benefit of future generations? To find that out, Kees says you've got to determine what someone's 'social space' is, and it's the first thing he does when he goes into a project.

To explain, Kees tells me about a project he's collaborating on with the City of Amsterdam. Although the city is renowned for its canals, over the years Amsterdam's officials have been less than diligent in the upkeep of these waterways, and now there are bridges sinking and quaysides crumbling. It's a massively expensive and disruptive project: 110 kilometres of quayside need to be completely rebuilt over the next 20 years. Imagining what those community information sessions sound like makes me go cold. What Kees explains is fascinating:

Of course, local city government is expecting revolts from all of the people, because you're going to dig up their environment completely, and it's a very long process – the sand has to settle before you can build. So, we did a little workshop with them in June. We asked, 'What is the social space of people?' They love living on a canal. They also live in an old, old house. Now, Amsterdam has its old city archives intact; my brother lives on the canal there in a house from about 1450. So, you know about all the previous owners of your house, who [perhaps] were wig-makers and hat-makers and so on. So, you're actually more a steward of that house for a limited period of time, rather than that you own it.

And that idea of stewardship works: that idea of 'Okay, we're in this generation now; this has to happen now, and we'll do a bloody good job.' It's like what happened in Paris when Notre Dame's roof burned, that people said, 'This is happening on our watch, and it shouldn't collapse on our watch.' So, there is this sense of taking care of the commons, but it's not on a city-wide scale. It's on your stretch of it. So, they're now splitting up the project, as it always was going to be split up, of course, but they're no longer saying, 'It's nine billion over 20 years', they're talking about just your stretch.

It's less about appealing to people's big-picture sense of altruism and obligation to the city as a whole than, in this case, expanding their picture of how each person as an individual fits into the bigger picture of a place in time. The project is now reminding people about the scale of time during which these houses, canals and quays have existed. When your house and street is six hundred years old, the reframing goes, what's a six-month closure in the scheme of things? While it's not immediately transferable for every social justice and climate conversation, Kees's example asks us to connect with people where they are by identifying and understanding what motivates them, what touches their sense of pride in the places they live or the groups they belong to.

You're not trying to reset someone else's values; rather, it's about having empathy that, even though we aren't all motivated by the same things, that doesn't mean we don't have common ground. We all have different triggers or paths to connecting with what matters to us.

'What you're doing is you're going for people's positive drivers, people's real intrinsic motivation that they already have. Taking care of their environment or being a good steward is one of those intrinsic motivators. You can't impose that on people but you can actually touch it. In this case, it was much stronger than I thought it was,' Kees says. 'They're all very proud Amsterdam people that are also very over-assertive. But this idea of stewardship, which is a subtle one, they've got it: 'We're doing justice to our street or the city or to some something we already have a bond with. So, using those existing trust bonds, that's how you build society. It's not rocket science. If you go back to that value level, things can be so simple.'

To understand what people's 'social space' is, that sweet spot of what they're willing to contribute for the greater good, Kees always opens a project with any group by asking three questions, and reading between the lines of the responses:

The first question you ask somebody is, 'Okay, what do you want?' And then they say what they want, which means that they sound like egoistic idiots. The second question is, 'What's good for the neighbourhood or for the street or whatever?' And from the difference between the answers to the first and the second question, you can see what their social space is: how far they're actually willing to let go of their own self-interest for the others that they know. And then the third question is 'What's good for the country or for the city?' People haven't thought about that. So, they go back to: 'What's good for me is good for the country.'

I'm surprised by that, but it's a reminder that we need to engage with each other as we are in reality – as our own complex, busy, conflicted selves – not as we say we are in surveys or polls. Understanding the social space you're working in is a more realistic way of devising a campaign to engage people with the big ideas that need to be tackled or motivate people to action. Kees says that, whether progressive or conservative, there are some core intrinsic motivations that are common across groups, such as the hard-wired value people everywhere have that the next generation should do better than the last.

That's one of my key motivations for writing this book. I hope that there's enough time left on the clock to make it so. Occasionally, I'm filled with sadness and unease that there might not be if we don't change course urgently, and it feels like I'm coming full circle to be talking about this in the context of the burning world and smoky cafe Kees and I are sitting in.

I'm particularly glad Kees is now applying his designer's mind to the biggest goals we've set ourselves as a society – the United Nations' SDGs, which I've touched on a couple of times in our story. They consist of 17 overarching goals broken down into 169 targets – a framework for each signatory country to use in tackling the environmental, social and economic challenges we're facing. The SDGs have been a great force for good, focusing the work of many countries and NGOs, and it's incredibly helpful to have some definition of what we want the world to look like in 2030. But by their very nature as a set of global aspirations, the targets are quite general. They also don't go as far as we need to in challenging the fundamentals of the system that got us into this mess in the first place.

'One of the problems is that they're UN Sustainable Development Goals and, from goals, everybody starts to negotiate with one another within the existing systems,' Kees points out.

What you need to do is step back and have a value discussion. Because from a value discussion, you can start thinking about new systems that achieve that value. But if you set goals, people start thinking from there. And if you really want to achieve the Sustainable Development Goals, you need systems change. You can't get there with negotiating within the existing systems.

There's plenty of best-practices-like things around, so that people can do better stuff than they did before. But that's becoming *less bad;* it's not changing the system. It's actually not getting to the Sustainable Development Goals at all. But because there's so many low-hanging fruits, everybody thinks that they're tracking really well. Yeah, but this isn't even becoming hard yet, because you haven't done anything before. So, the system-change stuff is really important: to get that in the different sectors, to get that going now.

With an eight-person committee that has 'gone completely rogue', Kees is working under the cover of the United Nations' Development Programme on 'mainstreaming' action towards the SDGs, focusing on how they're being adapted in the contexts of different countries. Reading the report on their work, it's interesting seeing how innovation springs forth everywhere, and how the interplay works between the big-picture aspiration that an organisation like the United Nations can co-ordinate, and the thousands of small-scale, locally relevant and more closely felt projects that would actually make those aspirations achievable. The global and the local have to happen at the same time, pointing in the same direction, and there has to be a way to feed back discovery and learning between the two levels and across the whole network. That's the values platform Kees is working on, which he explains:

> In the platforms that I'm setting up for the UN now, the value discussion on that general level is very important. It's actually modelled on the arts, because I used to be on these arts committees, and you realise that there is a general discussion going on about 'What is good art?' and that's not a discussion that's ever going to end. It's not meant to end

but it does give you the terms and the thinking, and it feeds off the artworks and it also influences the artworks that are happening.

So, you need a kind of local discussion and you need a very general discussion – feeding off one another. The general discussion is, 'What is a good city?' – those kind of discussions. It needs to be ongoing and needs to be fed. And then you need local things where you're actually applying it, trying things out. Interesting things happen that feed that bigger discussion. But you can't confuse those two discussions. They are different things.

Working from within this set of big goals for our planet and society, Kees is building a way for people making change to learn from each other. He's also bringing to this project his understanding of what motivates people to shift their perspectives. I'm inspired by the fact that he's embedding into that process this deeper conversation about values and also questioning the system itself.

***

If we want to have these conversations about the new systems we need to deliver on our real, core human values, we'll have to reimagine more than the media or our ways of talking to each other. We need entirely new institutions, adapted for the world we live in today, that embrace the diversity that many have fought hard to daylight, and which don't aim to shore up the status quo, the way our civil society institutions have in the past.

An activist friend, Michael Bones, observes that people who seek change have a fairly limited palette of options when it comes to having our voices heard. We mobilise online and spread petitions like memes. If we're deeply outraged, we protest: we make signs and adopt our own counter-slogans to the government slogans we deride as being too simplistic; we stand outside a building to listen to people we already agree with making short speeches; and then we walk to another building, waving those signs and shouting those slogans.

Of course, protest is important: it's a way of making our dissatisfaction visible and it helps us all feel less alone. I love the feeling of standing in a crowd at a rally, complimenting people on their signs and sharing in the mutters and chants, for an hour or two at least feeling a sense of solidarity and society, knowing that I'm not alone when it feels like the world isn't pointing toward a positive future. But, then what? Protest is a tool to campaign *against* something, not a way to design the alternative: to imagine the world we want then put forward a case for something better.

But Michael spotted an existing mechanism and wrote an opinion piece about it. He wonders if we can learn from churchgoers – people who come together every week to contemplate, learn, tell stories, raise funds and make connections. For an atheist like me, it can be confronting to think about the power of religion, but in essence this is about members of a community of belief – with institutions and rituals – coming together in a regular, committed way to live out their strongly held beliefs here in the real world.

Is there a way we could do that in the secular world? Even if we take heaven out of the equation, there's something divine about the power we could derive from each other if we made space and time to talk, work together and bring the world that could be into being.

I think back to those Bellamy Clubs of the 18th century, where we began our story, places where people could come together to dream about the future and then organise the steps needed to get there. Imagine Bloch Parties where we could share glimpses of the potential futures we see emerging all around us. Where would you go today for that kind of hope? Where could we turn optimism into solidarity and action? If this space doesn't exist yet, could we create it?

CONCLUSION

What now?

To get that world we can see glimpses of in these pages, there's much that needs to change and so much work to be done. It's understandable to feel a bit intimidated by the depth and breadth and width of the mountain range of changes that need to be scaled. Uncertainty can be debilitating. When you don't know where to begin your ascent, it's natural to just think: maybe I'll start tomorrow.

First of all, you don't have to do this on your own. In fact, changing the world is never a solo sport. This isn't to say one person can't make a huge impact and wield enormous influence – it's been so exciting to watch a young woman, Greta Thunberg, become a global icon over the year I've been writing this book, and I hope the path she's forged has been eye-opening for those young girls I first set out to write this book for, among many many others.

But all massive steps forward in human history have been taken by people working together: led by a courageous few pushing through the thicket of the status quo with will and their bare hands. The first difficult branches are cut back by many more, often at much personal cost, and then, as the course of history turns, thousands of others have pushed through to trample the undergrowth and carve a way ahead where before there was only wilderness.

You may have to be brave but you will not go alone. Maybe somebody else is in on it.

Importantly, you don't have to start from scratch, either. So many of the transformative ideas I've covered in this book are creative reimaginings of ideas from other times and other contexts: we'll scale mountains faster standing on the shoulders of giants. Many great ideas or movements have already begun and all they need is those first few followers, amplifiers and advocates who can add their energy to the task or bring their network into the fold. Join and contribute, or take ideas that have inspired you and spread them wider.

Another thing to keep in mind is that talking helps. We always hear about the storms approaching but rarely about the slow, constant, positive work that many are doing. As Kees told me, we need to show more people there are other ways our world could be organised, and so talking about the good as well as the bad is part of spreading hope that there can be a solution.

If you've got this far, it's likely that you're already interested in politics. Why not find out how you could take that interest further? Lend your voice to the push for deep-seated structural change either by joining a party you could influence to take meaningful action on these issues or by supporting independents and social movements that actively intervene in politics or lobby on behalf of a livable future. (If by chance you're as mad as I am and could see yourself running for office, well, please drop me a line. We need you.)

And maybe you could think of people in your family, or in your social circle, who are less engaged with politics, and find gentle ways to draw out their own interest. Every vote matters, even when we live in 'safe' seats and may not feel heard. There's opportunity to make change at every level of government.

The goal is shifting the system – the work we do and the work we reward, the way our money works on our behalf, the way we make decisions, how we live and where, and how we talk to each other. We need to question it all, rethink, reform, restore, redesign and refocus to get the world we want and the future the next generation deserves.

In the meantime, if you still want a quick takeaway on what you can do today and what we need to ask for, here are a few ideas from the visionaries I had the privilege to meet through this book.

Move your money. As ethical banker Kat Taylor said, if your money isn't doing good, it's working against you. Your superannuation fund and your mortgage, if you have either, are the two biggest pools of wealth most people have access to. It's faster and easier than you'd think to move your money to funds and banks that act ethically and refuse to sink money into fossil fuels.

Water deep roots. A democratic economy is one with public good at its core, and that's more likely to happen when companies are tied to place. Think about where you spend money: are there ways you can support businesses that are locally owned and connected to other places in your community, help to tilt the balance in their favour? Follow the Preston example and keep your money circulating here in the real world.

Share your experience. If you've felt the precariousness of the economy in your own life and career, try to share this experience where you can, particularly with people outside your industry or generational cohort who might not understand how widespread and unsettling it is. It's important for people to put a human face to these global trends. I'd also say join a union, because so much of what we expect as our workplace rights today was hard won by unions. Having said that, I've struggled to find a union that has kept pace with the reality of work in the 21st century, but I'd love to be proven wrong on this.

Demand more from data. In your day-to-day life, including your digital interactions, ask for the principles of the data commons to be respected. James Mansell from Predator Free New Zealand points out the need for a social contract for the new millennium. We have the right to demand prosocial rules and standards to ensure that data is managed and used as a common pool resource.

Care for the carers. If you engage with carers in your own life, think about how you can support care businesses that empower their workers. Or you might make common cause with the care sector politically, to help improve the way we reward this life-giving work.

First Nations, first. So many of the solutions we need are embedded in the philosophies and spiritualities of First Nations people, but these aren't to be considered as a grab-bag of policy tactics. Listen to and support Indigenous-led holistic approaches to land management and community wealth-building, as a start. But as a foundation for a mature future, our country – like many others – must also address its original sin of dispossession and genocide.

Expose the subsidies. In Australia, we spend about $29 billion of our money a year to make fossil-fuel use cheaper; globally, it's more than $400 billion. Yet some dare to say we can't afford a just transition to a sustainable economy. Spread the word: we have the money. All we lack is the political pressure to demand that our money works in the interests of our planet.

Push to price the externalities. We need our tax system to work in support of the circular economy – so it's more expensive to pollute than it is to take responsibility for your production process. Support businesses that have achieved or are working towards circularity.

Build a model, not a building. Learning from a systems thinker like

Jeremy McLeod from Nightingale, champion innovation that disrupts business-as-usual mindsets rather than providing more of the same. Having said that, be critical of disruption; it has little value in and of itself. Support the kind of disruption that rebalances unequal power dynamics and reboots the trickle-up economy we have today.

Join a co-op. Whether you go with a food co-operative or a mutual banking society, you're putting your money to work in an organisation that's designed to benefit members and helps make the shift towards the democratic economy.

Enable bottom-up creativity. In so many places, and in almost all instances, the people closest to the problem have devised creative solutions that need to be amplified. Resist the temptation to import from the outside and empower the communities you engage with to lead themselves. I'll be thinking about Razia Sultana's green shoots in the slums of Dhaka and keeping my eye out for their counterparts in every project I do.

Participate in participatory politics. It can be a big commitment of time, but if your local government is running citizens' juries or participatory budgeting projects, consider signing up. It's a wonderful way to get a deeper understanding of the decisions that need to be made in your community, and you're likely to be expanding the diversity of representation just by adding your voice. You'll probably also meet motivated, engaged people with whom you can share ideas and take local action.

Daylight the invisible. There are a lot of people and places being left off the map, figuratively and literally, in informal settlements like Mukuru but also in workplaces that fly under the radar, or that are behind the closed doors of private homes. When you've got the opportunity to be at a decision-making table, say through one of the participatory processes we've heard about, think about who doesn't have a seat at the table, and seek to have their voices included.

Policy over technology. Innovations aren't always tech solutions: sometimes the transformations to celebrate and push for are technical, unglamorous policy changes, as Mat Santamouris's really smart smart-city work shows us.

Vote for change. It almost goes without saying that one of the most important things you can do is vote for progressive candidates and parties that prioritise climate action and social justice. You can go one step further and volunteer or support candidates who fight for change. Or work out where you'd have the opportunity to make an impact and run yourself.

Distribute, decentralise, devolve. So many of the most promising ideas I've encountered centre on decentralising – moving decision-making away from a top-down, centralised model, which is often distant and removed from the experiences and assets of citizens or users. From child care to renewable energy to political decision-making, support solutions that maximise local participation for tailored solutions. Invariably, the outcome is more resilient and relevant, empowering and efficient.

Question the assumptions. There's a lot of 'deep code' – stuff we simply assume has always been that way, such as ownership of land and how it's used, what we tax and subsidise, or which jobs attract high pay. None of these things arise from laws of nature; they're all constructions of culture, and they can all be changed. We have to start by figuring out who these assumptions serve and whether they continue to have social value in the context of the world today.

Build space for community. People are very good at designing solutions, building community and helping each other: but we need places to connect, build understanding and do this work. Many of the projects I got to learn about through writing this book were focused on building social spaces for people, whether that was in city-making in Portugal or China or in designing citizen participation as in Taiwan. Make like Ateliermob and start with the kitchen table.

Ask your neighbours. Do you think I've diagnosed the ills of our time correctly? Do you think there are other root causes to the situation we find ourselves in? What would you change first to make a fairer world? I loved the open-ended questions Mesa de Unidad Social proposed for people to run their own town hall meetings right up and down Chile. If you can spark deep reflection and bring people together to imagine solutions socially, you're on the path to positive change. As My Country Talks shows us, the most powerful question you can ask is why.

Show, don't tell. As Caren Tepp and Cuidad Futura do in Rosario, Argentina, model the future you want to give others a sense of what that glorious, generous future could be.

A lot of this is ambitious. Monumental problems require equally transformative solutions.

Some might say it's impossibly naive to think we can update all these fundamentals, rewrite all this deep code, all at once. I think that's the kind of ambition our age demands. Following the script, obeying the rules and playing it safe have got us to a dangerous place: it's time to try something different. The future we need is closer than we might think, but we need to have the courage, and each other's company, to make a leap of faith to it.

ACKNOWLEDGEMENTS

Thank you to everyone I interviewed for this story, who shared their experiences and ideas with me: this book only exists because of the hope you inspire through your dedicated efforts towards a more just world. I'm so grateful you took the time to talk me through the work you do and to help spread your optimism in action to more people.

My thanks also to the people I interviewed while feeling out the shape of this book, who also generously gave their time but whose stories didn't make it to the final edit. Many of your ideas helped lay the groundwork or pointed me in the right direction, and I'm sorry our conversations didn't land in this version of the story. Particular thanks to Lorena Zarate (Habitat International Coalition), Jack Self (REAL Foundation), Associate Professor Paul Jones (Sydney University), Maria Aiolova (Americas Arup University Leader and Terreform ONE), Ludovica Rodgers (Platform Cooperativism Consortium), Leonard Ng

Keok Poh (Ramboll), Justine Saunders and Daniel Richards (Natural Capital Singapore) and Rosalia Contreras (National Domestic Workers Alliance). There are so many more glimpses of the world we need, and people like you who are doing the work, and I hope one day to be able to share your stories too.

It's hard to thank all the people whose leads, introductions, recommendations and book loans contributed to this process, but I'd like to single out Marc Stears from the Sydney Policy Lab, Selena Griffiths from the University of New South Wales, Jason Twill from Urban Apostles, Stella Gwee and Adib Jalal from Shophouse and Co. Thank you to my first reader and critical friend Amy Denmeade for your insightful reflections and gentle redirection, and to the incredible people who made time to read the (almost) finished version of this book, despite the fact that they're so busy making impact in so many fields: Christiana Figueres, Jan Fran, Jess Hill, Benjamin Law, Bill McKibben, Blair Palese, David Ritter and Edwina Throsby. I'm so grateful you carved out time to dive into unknown territory from a first-timer and your support gave me a boost in the home stretch.

Thank you to the brilliant Eva Cox for lending your expertise to the child-care section and challenging me on my ideas: I am so lucky to be able to argue with you over UBI versus UBS, or anything else really. I've admired your advocacy and fervent belief in a good society for as long as I've known of your work and I'm honoured that you would take the time to help me sharpen and clarify my thoughts.

I'm fortunate to be able to work with one of my heroes, and to see up close the persistence and passion, focus and courage that is required to deliver a better world. In my lifetime Clover Moore has reshaped Sydney and proved it isn't naive to believe that politics can be a tool for positive change, and that even though it takes immeasurable personal fortitude to stand at the forefront, history is on the side of the hopeful. Thank you Clover for your leadership and for proving that cities are the place to push progress forward.

I'm honoured to be able to work with you, over the last four wonderful years I've learned so much from you and our CMIT colleagues on council: Jess Miller for your radical (in every sense) energy and green vision, Philip Thalis for your deep knowledge of place and sense of justice, and Robert Kok for your humour, global perspective and big picture thinking.

Public libraries are one of the most crucial pieces of social infrastructure we have and I owe a great deal to them in my life. This book was written in libraries across Sydney and Melbourne, providing books and journals and space and a sense of community through the silent and often solitary process of pushing ideas around a page. Particular thanks to the State Libraries of New South Wales and Victoria for giving me a place to think over many many months.

Editor Anne Reilly has read this book more times than anyone else, dedicated vast amounts of time to helping clarify my message, and held my hand (metaphorically – no iso rules were broken) through a process that shook out all my doubts and insecurities. Thank you Anne for your thoughtful comments and questioning, you've contributed so much towards helping me tell this complex story in what I hope is an accessible way. Thank you to publisher Lex Hirst for your confidence that I had a story to tell and a vision for a better world I needed to get out of my head and into a tangible form: when I lay awake at night drowning in doubt for having the temerity to attempt such an ambitious book, your sustained belief in me was a rock I could cling to, or at least a very buoyant flotation device. Thanks for your patience too, for sticking through more than one false start. The whole Pantera Press team carried me through the valleys of the process and gave me faith in this story and its worth. I could not have landed in a better place than with a publisher who wears their heart on their sleeve and dedicates themselves to social purpose: and that aims to change the world as their reason for being in business.

The writing of this book spanned my pregnancy and the first eight months of my daughter Elinor's life, so in my memory the haze of the newborn days flows into a daze of deadlines and rereads and edits. The book and Elinor and I really all benefited from a wonderful village: thank you to all my friends who cooked and cared and bounced and wrapped us all in love, especially Clare Buttner, Emily Collins, Allie Rosen, Emma Scott-Child, Joanna Townsend and Aletha Wilkinson. Thanks Linda Mateljan for that holiday during which I wrote an earlier unsuccessful version of this book and was a colossally annoying travel companion as a result. Thank you Mandy Edkins for keeping me relatively sane for so many years, helping me do the work and delivering on the things I said I'd do.

My family – on both the Scully and Armstrong sides – have made so much of this book possible by helping look after Elinor. My parents Trish and Bryan made me an optimist through their unfailingly positive outlook on life. No matter what the world has thrown at them, no matter what happened yesterday – even when it makes no sense at all and it drives me completely bonkers – they wake up smiling every morning. Their enthusiasm and resilience are limitless. Mum and Dad, you energise everyone you meet and whatever I have of that, I owe to you. I already had a funny, creative sister Cass and then through marriage I scored three more – thank you Claire, Helen and Kate for all your encouragement – special thanks to Aunty Kate for helping us so often with Eli. My in-laws Angela and Peter have been so warm and supportive from day one; thank you for welcoming me into your family and for raising the most caring man I've ever met.

I don't even know where to begin in thanking my husband Pat. Even at my most optimistic I never dreamed there was a man in the world as curious, considered and considerate as you. Thank you for all the links and long conversations that fed into this book: for your wide-ranging sweep of interests and your ability to dive in and get into detail when my patience fails me. I can't believe I get to talk to you every day, about the kinds of things that would bore the socks off most of the planet, and that somehow we're both delighted and intrigued by. Thank you for taking care of me through this process and for taking a year off to be a full-time dad to Elinor. I love you.

Thank you, Elinor, for showing me that the future is even more glorious than I could ever imagine, because you're in it.

ENDNOTES

Introduction: Rays through the storm clouds

[1]   Introduction: Rays through the storm clouds

[2]   Robin McKie, 'Why is life expectancy faltering?', *The Guardian,* Sunday 23 Jun 2019

[3]   Raj Chetty, David Grusky, Maximilian Hell, Nathaniel Hendren, Robert Manduca & Jimmy Narang, 'The Fading American Dream: Trends In Absolute Income Mobility Since 1940', *Science* 356(6336): 398–406, 2017, December 2016

[4]   Richard Samans, Margareta Drzeniek-Hanouz, Gemma Corrigan & Marcus Burke, 'The Inclusive Development Index 2018', World Economic Forum, 22 January 2018

[5]   Riccardo Mastini, 'Degrowth: the case for a new economic paradigm', opendemocracy.net, 8 June 2017

[6]   Kate   Raworth,   *Doughnut
        Economics: Seven Ways to Think
        Like a 21-stcentury Economist,*
        Random House, London (UK),
        2017

1: Rethink utopia

[1]   Nigel Gladstone & Craig Butt,
        'Living long and prospering:
        Some Sydney babies to outlive
        peers by a decade', *Sydney
        Morning Herald,* 30 October 2019
[2]   Natassia Chrysanthos & Ann
        Ding, 'Food fault lines: mapping
        class through food chains', *Honi
        Soit,* 22 September 2017

2: Recentre the citizen

[1]   Brendan Coates, Matt Cowgill,
        Tony Chen & Will Mackey,
        'Shutdown: Estimating the
        COVID-19 employment shock',
        *Grattan Institute Working Paper
        No.2020–03,* April 2020
[2]   Maggie Astor, 'How the Politically
        Unthinkable Can Become
        Mainstream', *New York Times,*
        26 February 2019

[3]   Simon Kuznets, 'National Income, 1929–1932', *Senate document no.124,* 73rd Congress, 2nd session, 1934

[4]   'Understanding the unpaid economy', PwC discussion paper, March 2017

[5]   City of Sydney Community Wellbeing Indicators Report (2019); City of Sydney Strategy and Urban Analytics Unit, 2019

[6]   http://www.andi.org.au/

[7]   Mike Salvaris, 'Submission to The Senate Inquiry on Sustainable Development Goals by Australian National Development Index (ANDI) Limited and The University of Melbourne', 29 March 2018

[8]   Amartya Sen, *Development As Freedom,* Oxford University Press, Oxford (UK), 1999

[9]   Simon Hunter, 'Spain's guaranteed minimum income scheme will come with €5.5bn price tag', *El Pais,* 19 April 2020

[10]   Anna Coote & Andrew Percy, *The Case for Universal Basic*

Services, Polity Press, Cambridge (UK), 2020

[11]   Jonathan Portes, Howard Reed & Andrew Percy, 'Social prosperity for the future: A proposal for Universal Basic Services', Institute for Global Prosperity, University College London, 2017

[12]   Ibid.

[13]   Dan Wellings, 'What does the public think about the NHS?', The King's Fund UK, 16 September 2017

3: Refocus politics

[1]   Yascha Mounk & Roberto Stefan Foa, 'This is how democracy dies', *The Atlantic,* 29 January 2020

[2]   Naaman Zhou, 'Australian millennials' faith in politics and big business collapsing, poll finds', *The Guardian,* 16 May 2018

[3]   Edmund Burke, *Reflections on the Revolution in France,* J.G.A. Pocock (ed.), Hackett Classics,

Indianapolis, 1987 (1st published 1790); see also https://thegreat thinkers.org/burke/introduction

[4] Alice Workman, 'The typical Australian politician is a 51-year-old white man who owns two homes', BuzzFeed News, 12 April 2017

[5] Tony Yoo, 'Revealed: Exactly how much each party spends on their election campaign', Yahoo!Finance, 15 May 2019

[6] SA Government, 'South Australia's Citizens' Jury on Nuclear Waste: Final Report', November 2016, available at htt ps://yoursay.sa.gov.au

[7] newDemocracy Foundation and United Nations Democracy Fund, 'Enabling National Initiatives to Take Democracy Beyond Elections', newDemocracy Foundation, Sydney 2019

[8] Jon Henley, 'Finland enlists social influencers in fight against Covid-19', *The Guardian,* 2 April 2020

[9] Teija Sutinen HS, 'The majority considers government coronavirus

measures to be well timed and appropriately rigorous', *Helsingin Sanomat,* 5 April 2020 (translated from Finnish)

[10]   https://citiesfordigitalrights.org/

[11]   Protest slogan quoted in BBC News World, 'The 6 big social debts for which many Chileans say they feel "abused"', *Tele13,* 22 October 2019

[12]   Chile's extraordinarily deregulated financial system played a role in the country's extreme inequality. There's a whole book to be written about Chile's insane retail credit cards, with supermarket and department store credit cards charging colossal interest rates – four times as many of them as every bank credit card in the country – and the way that people are kept in constant, mounting, rolling debt.

[13]   *El Tiempo* editorial with EFE and AFP, 'The most controversial points of the Constitution that Chile hopes to modify', *El Tiempo,* 15

November 2019 (trans. from Spanish)

[14] Abdullah Öcalan, *Democratic Federalism,* Transmedia Publishing Ltd, 2011

[15] Rojava Information Center, 'Beyond the frontlines: the building of the democratic system in North and East Syria', December 2019

[16] Ibid.

[17] Naomi Klein, *On Fire: The Burning Case for a Green New Deal,* Allen Lane, London, 2019

[18] Robert Hockett, 'Our Money's Not Green Enough', forbes.com, 12 November 2019

4: Redesign work

[1] Joseph Schumpeter, *Capitalism, Socialism, and Democracy,* Harper & Brothers, New York, 1942

[2] Fidan Ana Kurtulus & Douglas L. Kruse, 'How Did Employee Ownership Firms Weather the Last Two Recessions? Employee Ownership, Employment Stability,

and Firm Survival: 1999–2011', W.E. Upjohn Institute for Employment Research, Kalamazoo, MI, 2017

[3]   ABC News Breakfast, 'Insecure work the "new norm" as full-time job rate hits record low: report', ABC.net.au/news, 7 June 2018

[4]   https://www.shine.com.au/service/class-actions/isg-management-classaction

[5]   David Marin-Guzman, 'Workforce contractor Tandem hit with class action over "shame contracts"', *Australian Financial Review*, 21 November 2018

[6]   Ellen Huet, 'Google Contractors Want to Be Included in New Policies on Sexual Misconduct', Bloomberg, 28 November 2018

[7]   Jessica Irvine & Adam Gartrell, 'Seven charts revealing the truth about wages and the Australian economy', *Sydney Morning Herald,* 30 March 2018

[8]   William Lazonick, 'Profits Without Prosperity', *Harvard Business Review,* September 2014

[9]   Sascha Lobo, 'Auf dem Weg in die Dumpinghölle', *Spiegel Netzwelt,* 3 August 2019

[10]   Jill Sheppard & Nicholas Biddle, 'Class, capital and identity in Australian society', *Australian Journal of Political Science,* Vol 52, Issue 4, 14 August 2017

[11]   Jessica Bruder, *Nomadland,* W.W. Norton & Company, New York, 2018

[12]   Guy Standing, *The Precariat: The New Dangerous Class,* Bloomsbury Academic, London, 1999

[13]   Ibid., pp.19–20

[14]   Neil Irwin, 'To Understand Rising Inequality, Consider the Janitors at Two Top Companies, Then and Now', *New York Times,* 3 September 2017

[15]   Lauren Kaori Gurley, 'Gig Workers Are Forming the World's First Food Delivery App Unions', *Motherboard VICE,* 10 October 2019

[16]   Takashi Yoshida & Naoko Murai, 'Uber Eats staff forms union, wants security delivered hot',

The Asahi Shimbun, 4 October 2019

[17] Alison Braley-Rattai & Larry Savage, 'Despite Foodora ruling, app-based workers face uphill union battle', *The Conversation* (Canada), 15 March 2020

[18] Bethan Staton, 'The upstart unions taking on the gig economy and outsourcing', *Financial Times,* 19 January 2020

[19] According to the Living Wage Commission in the UK, at the time of writing the London Living Wage rate is £10.75 per hour and the rate for the rest of the UK is £9.30 per hour, calculated based on the real cost of living in the UK capital. There's a global push to set more realistic living wages and base them on the real costs of living in different parts of countries. See www.livingwage.org.uk/calculation

[20] https://www.uvwunion.org.uk/strippers

[21]   https://www.uvwunion.org.uk/design-culture-workers

[22]   '47% of PAYE freelancers fear they won't qualify for government support', BECTU.org.uk, 30 March 2020

[23]   Hannah Reich, 'Coronavirus has shut down the Australian screen industry but most workers aren't eligible for JobKeeper', ABC Arts, 18 April 2020

[24]   Marjorie Kelly & Ted Howard, *The Making of a Democratic Economy: Building Prosperity For the Many, Not Just the Few,* Berrett-Koehler, Oakland, 2019

[25]   Ed Mayo, *A short history of co-operation and mutuality,* Co-operatives UK, Manchester, 2017

[26]   Giles Tremlett, 'Mondragon: Spain's giant co-operative where times are hard but few go bust', *The Guardian,* 8 March 2013

5: Reward the human

[1] Larry Elliott, 'World's 26 richest people own as much as poorest 50%, says Oxfam', *The Guardian,* 21 January 2019

[2] Michael Savage, 'Richest 1% on target to own two-thirds of all wealth by 2030', *The Observer,* 7 April 2018

[3] Thomas Piketty, *Capital in the Twenty-First Century,* The Belknap Press of Harvard University Press, Cambridge (USA), 2014

[4] Eva Feder Kittay with Bruce Jennings & Angela A. Wasunna, 'Dependency, Difference and the Global Ethic of Longterm Care', *The Journal of Political Philosoph*y, Vol 13, No.4 (2005), p.443

[5] Ai-jen Poo, 'The work that makes all other work possible', TEDWomen 2018 video on TED.com

[6] David Graeber, *Bullshit Jobs: A Theory,* Simon & Schuster, 2018

[7] https://joboutlook.gov.au/

[8]   Gloria Steinem, *Moving Beyond Words: Essays on Age, Rage, Sex, Power, Money, Muscles: Breaking the Boundaries of Gender,* Open Road Media, New York, 2012

[9]   Hannah Arendt, *The Human Condition,* 2nd edn, with foreword by Danielle S. Allen (2018), introduction by Margaret Canovan (1988), University of Chicago Press, Chicago, 2018

[10]   Ibid.

[11]   John Kenneth Galbraith, *Economics and the public purpose,* Andre Deutsch Ltd, London, 1973, p.33

[12]   Silvia Federici & Power of Women Collective, *Wages against housework,* Power of Women Collective, London, 1975

[13]   Laura Addati, Umberto Cattaneo, Valeria Esquivel & Isabel Valarino, 'Care work and care jobs for the future of decent work', International Labour Organization, 28 June 2018

[14] National Health Expenditure Accounts 2018, accessed at ht tps://www.cms.gov/

[15] Dan Harrison, 'Audit slams Rudd's primary school building program', *Sydney Morning Herald,* 5 May 2010

[16] Jerome De Henau, Susan Himmelweit, Zofia Łapniewska & Diane Perrons, 'Investing in the Care Economy: A gender analysis of employment stimulus in seven OECD countries', a report by the UK Women's Budget Group commissioned by the International Trade Union Confederation, March 2016

[17] Alexia Fernández Campbell, 'Kamala Harris just introduced a bill to give housekeepers overtime pay and meal breaks', Vox.com, 15 July 2019

[18] Barbara Ehrenreich & Arlie Hochschild (eds.), 'Love and gold', *Global Woman,* Owl, New York City (USA), 2002, pp.15–31

[19]   Michael Birnbaum & William
         Booth, 'Nursing homes linked
         to up to half of coronavirus
         deaths in Europe, WHO says',
         Washington Post, 24 April 2020

[20]   Summer Woolley, 'Coronavirus
         Australia: NSW   aged   care
         homes linked to more than a
         third of state deaths', 7News.c
         om.au, 29 April 2020

[21]   Pat   Armstrong,   Hugh
         Armstrong, Jacqueline Choinière,
         Ruth   Lowndes   &   James
         Struthers,   'Re-imagining
         Long-term Residential Care in
         the COVID-19 Crisis', Canadian
         Centre for Policy Alternatives,
         April 2020

[22]   Dr Hans Henri P. Kluge, WHO
         Regional   Director   for   Europe,
         press statement, 23 April 2020,
         Copenhagen, Denmark

[23]   https://en.wikipedia.org/wiki/20
         20_coronavirus_pandemic_in_W
         ashington_(state)

[24]   Moira Wyton, 'BC Boosts Pay
         for Long-Term Care Workers
         amidst COVID-19', *The Tyee,* 1
         April 2020

[25]   Charles Breton & Mohy-Dean Tabbara, 'How the provinces compare in their COVID-19 responses', Policy Options Politiques, 22 April 2020

[26]   Mike Hager & Andrea Woo, 'B.C. health officer takes over nursing-home staffing as coronavirus spreads', *The Globe and Mail,* 31 March 2020

[27]   Pat Armstrong et al., op. cit., p.14

[28]   Leah Ruppanner, 'HILDA findings on Australian families' experience of childcare should be a call-to-arms for government', The Conversation, 30 July 2019

[29]   Jessica Longbottom, 'Emergency workers lose child care in "unintended consequence" of coronavirus rescue package', A BC.net.au, 21 April 2020

[30]   Jen Jackson, 'Quality childcare has become a necessity for Australian families, and for society. It's time the government paid up', The Conversation, 16 February 2020

[31]   OECD, Net childcare costs (indicator).   doi: 10.1787/e328a9ee-en (Accessed 29 April 2020)

[32]   Laing & Buisson, cited by Miranda Hall & Lucie Stephens, in 'Quality Childcare For All: Making England's Childcare A Universal Basic Service', in *Childcare UK Market Report,* 15th edn, D. Barrett-Evans & D. Birlean (eds), New Economics Foundation, London, 2020

[33]   The Senate Education, Employment and Workplace Relations References Committee, 'Provision of childcare', Commonwealth of Australia, Canberra, November 2009

[34]   Emma Rush & Christian Downie, 'ABC Learning Centres: A case study of Australia's largest child care corporation', Discussion Paper Number 87, June 2006

[35]   Peter Hurley, Jen Jackson & Kate Noble, 'Australian Investment in Education: Early

Learning', Mitchell Institute, 16 February 2020

[36] Juliet Rix, 'Is this Hackney nursery the future for London's childcare industry?', *The Guardian,* 18 January 2017

[37] Laing & Buisson, op. cit.

[38] Ibid.

[39] Martin Woodhead, 'Early childhood development in the SDGs', Young Lives Policy Brief 28, January 2016

[40] Jen Jackson, 'Every $1 spent on preschool will return $2', Mitchell Institute, 15 July 2019

[41] Peter Hurley, Jen Jackson & Kate Noble, op. cit.

[42] Monica Nilsson, Beth Ferholt & Karin Alnervik, 'Why Swedish early learning is so much better than Australia's', The Conversation online, 6 March 2015

[43] Stephanie Gutierrez, *An Indigenous Approach to Community Wealth Building: A Lakota Translation,* The Democracy Collaborative, Washington, 2018

[44]   Bruce Pascoe, *Dark Emu*, Magabala Books, Broome, 2014

[45]   Sarina Locke, 'Explainer: What is carbon farming and the Emissions Reduction Fund?', ABC Rural, 9 April 2017

6: Recoup the investment

[1]   Dennis M. Kelleher, Stephen W. Hall & Frank Medina, 'The Cost of the Crisis: $20 Trillion and Counting', Better Markets, July 2015

[2]   Jonathan Ponciano, 'The Largest Technology Companies in 2019: Apple Reigns As Smartphones Slip And Cloud Services Thrive', forbes.com, 15 May 2019

[3]   Silvia Amaro & Arjun Kharpal, 'EU reveals a digital tax plan that could penalize Google, Amazon and Facebook', CNBC, 21 March 2018

[4]   Mariana Mazzucato, *The Value of Everything: Making and Taking in the Global Economy*, Penguin Random House, London, 2019

[5]   Mariana Mazzucato, *The Entrepreneurial State: Debunking Private vs Public Sector Myths*, Anthem Press, London, 2013

[6]   Tesla valuation as at May 2020

[7]   This sounds like a terrible deal, right? In a report to the United States Securities and Exchange Commission on 29 March 2010, Tesla revealed this would likely be the terms of a venture capital cash injection.

[8]   Scott Wooley, 'Tesla Is Worse Than Solyndra', Slate.com, 29 May 2013

[9]   2017 Annual Report and Financial Statements, Sitra, The Finnish Future Fund

[10]   There is no suggestion Malcolm Turnbull acted improperly, however he was named in the Panama Papers as a 'former director of a British Virgin Islands company set up and administered by law firm Mossack Fonseca to exploit a Siberian gold prospect' in Neil Chenoweth, 'Malcolm Turnbull named in Panama Papers',

Australian Financial Review, 12 May 2016

[11] 'Paradise Papers: Queen's private estate invested £10m in offshore funds', BBC, 6 November 2017

[12] Thomas Piketty, 'A global progressive tax on individual net worth would offer the best solution to the world's spiralling levels of inequality', London School of Economics Blog, 17 April 2014

[13] Elizabeth Byrne, 'Mining giant Glencore loses High Court Paradise Papers fight to force ATO to return documents', ABC News, 14 August 2019

[14] 'Paradise Papers: Apple's secret tax bolthole revealed', BBC, 6 November 2017

[15] Neil Chenoweth, 'Is News Corp still paying zero tax?', *Australian Financial Review,* 10 May 2019

[16] Martin Farrer, 'Rupert Murdoch's empire receives $882m tax rebate from Australia', *The Guardian,* 17 February 2014

[17] Simon Bowers, 'Leaked Documents Expose Secret Tale Of Apple's Offshore Island Hop', International Consortium of Investigative Journalists, 6 November 2017

[18] Patrick Hatch, 'Apple's Aussie profits grew but its tax bill went down', *Sydney Morning Herald,* 26 January 2019

[19] www.taxjusticenet/topics/corporate-tax/taxing-corporations

[20] Amy Wilson-Chapman, Antonio Cucho & Will Fitzgibbon, 'What happened after the Panama Papers?', International Consortium of Investigative Journalists, 3 April 2019

[21] https://www.icrict.com/icrict-documentsthe-declaration

[22] Richard Murphy, 'The Big 4 accountancy firms have finally endorsed public country-by-country reporting', Tax Research UK, 24 January 2020

[23] Sol Picciotto (ed), *Taxing Multinational Enterprises as Unitary Firms,* Institute of

Development Studies, Brighton (UK), 2017

[24]   https://www.taxjusticenet/topics/corporate-tax/taxing-corporations

[25]   ICRICT response to the OECD Consultation on the Review of Country-by-Country Reporting (BEPS Action 13), 6 March 2020

[26]   Edward Helmore, 'Google says it will no longer use "Double Irish, Dutch sandwich" tax loophole', *The Guardian,* 2 January 2020

[27]   Conrad Bower, 'Silicon Six "aggressively avoid" $100bn in tax, Manchester's Fair Tax Mark reports', *The Meteor,* 10 December 2019

[28]   https://www.iea.org/topics/energy-subsidies

[29]   David Coady, Ian Parry, Nghia-Piotr Le & Baoping Shang, 'Global Fossil Fuel Subsidies Remain Large: An Update Based on Country-Level Estimates', 2 May 2019

[30]   Kalpana Kochhar, Catherine A. Pattillo, Yan M. Sun, Nujin Suphaphiphat, Andrew J. Swiston, Robert Tchaidze, Benedict J. Clements, Stefania Fabrizio, Valentina Flamini, Laure Redifer & Harald Finger, 'Is the Glass Half Empty Or Half Full? Issues in Managing Water Challenges and Policy Instruments', International Monetary Fund, 2 June 2015

[31]   http://www.internal-displacement.org/countries/bangladesh

[32]   Marinella Padula, 'Undermining the Resource Super Profits Tax', Australia and New Zealand School of Government, 2013

[33]   Michael West, 'Australia's Top 40 Tax Dodgers 2019: Chevron Australia Holdings Pty Ltd', Michael West Media, 5 August 2019

[34]   Michael West, 'Australia's Top 40 Tax Dodgers 2019: Exxon Mobil Australia Pty Ltd', Michael West Media, 5 August 2019

[35]   Labour   Market   Information
         Portal: Mining,   Australian
         Government, lmip.gov.au
[36]   Naomi   Klein,   *On   Fire: The
         Burning Case for a Green New
         Deal,* Allen Lane, London, 2019

7: Reform finance

[1]   'Australia's   banks   the   most
         profitable   in   the   world',   The
         Australia   Institute,   5   August
         2016
[2]   Nassim   Khadem,   'Banks
         increasing exposure to fossil fuels
         despite promises to fight climate
         change: report', ABC News, 16
         January 2019
[3]   Servaas Storm, 'Financial Markets
         Have Taken Over the Economy.
         To Prevent Another Crisis, They
         Must   Be   Brought   to   Heel',
         Institute   for   New   Economic
         Thinking, 13 February 2018
[4]   Christine Berry, Duncan Lindo &
         Joshua Ryan-Collins, 'Our friends
         in the City: why banking's return
         to business as usual threatens
         our economy', New Economics

Foundation, London, UK, February 2016

[5]   Jonathan Shapiro, 'The greatest rotation: How Baby Boomers will totally reshape financial markets', *Australian Financial Review*, 12 April 2017

[6]   Toby Shapshank, 'Global Remittances Reach $613 Billion Says World Bank', *Forbes*, 21 May 2018

[7]   https://globalfindex.worldbank.org

[8]   Gaea Katreena Cabico, 'Philippines is 3rd top remittance receiving country in the world', Philstar.com, 23 April 2018

[9]   'More Philippine rural banks, microfinance firms embrace digital technology for expansion', Asian Development Bank, 18 September 2018

[10]   Emma Doherty, Ben Jackman & Emily Perry, 'Money in the Australian Economy', *Reserve Bank of Australia Bulletin*, 20 September 2018

[11]   http://www.gabv.org/about-us/our-principles

[12] Adriana Kocornik-Mina, 'Real Economy – Real Returns: The Business Case for Values-based Banking', Global Alliance for Banking on Values, January 2020

[13] Ibid.

[14] Sakis Kotsantonis & Vittoria Bufalari (KKS Advisors), 'Do sustainable banks outperform? Driving value creation through ESG practices', European Investment Bank, Global Alliance for Banking on Values and Deloitte, 2019

[15] Umar Moghul, *A Socially Responsible Islamic Finance*, Palgrave Macmillan, New York (USA), 2017

[16] Umar Moghul, 'A Landmark Impact Investment: Could This Innovative Experiment with Islamic Finance Provide a Model for Both Sectors?', NextBillion, 17 June 2019

[17] Islamic Finance Development Report 2019, Refinitiv Islamic Finance

[18]   Abayomi Alawode, Ahmad Hafiz Abdul Aziz & Ana Maria Aviles, 'Sustainable Development Goals and the role of Islamic finance', World Bank Blogs, 15 February 2018

[19]   Aamir A. Rehman, 'Islamic finance for social good', United Nations Development Program (blog), 23 January 2019

[20]   Francine Pickup, Ifran Syauqi Beik & Greget Kalla Buana, 'Unlocking the Potential of Zakat and Other Forms of Islamic Finance to Achieve the SDGs in Indonesia', UNDP and Baznas, 2018

[21]   Ibid., p.6

[22]   'First In Indonesia: Zakat Financing Gives "Rays Of Hope" To Four Villages In Jambi', United Nations Development Program (press release), 6 April 2018

[23]   'Connecting Malaysia's Islamic and Sustainable Finance to the World', The World Bank, 18 April 2019

8: Restore the commons

[1]   Ben Martin, 'Communal ownership drives Denmark's wind revolution', Green Economy Coalition, 20 September 2017

[2]   Virginia Eubanks, *Automating Inequality: How High-Tech Tools Profile, Police and Punish the Poor,* St Martin's Press, New York, 2018

[3]   Rachel Siewert, 'What I learned about poverty and mental health chairing the robo-debt inquiry', Crikey, 31 May 2019

[4]   'The objective of this new set of rules is to ensure that personal data enjoys a high standard of protection everywhere in the EU, increasing legal certainty for both individuals and organisations processing data, and offering a higher degree of protection for individuals', https://edpb.europa.eu/legal-framework_en

[5]   Elinor Ostrom, 'Beyond Markets and States: Polycentric Governance of Complex Economic

Systems', The Nobel Foundation, Stockholm, 8 December 2009

[6]   Ibid.

[7]   Data Commons Manifesto, https ://datacommons.barcelona/our-v ision/

9: Rebuild for equity

[1]   Edward Glaeser, *The Triumph of the City: How Our Greatest Invention Makes Us Richer, Smarter, Greener, Healthier, and Happier,* The Penguin Press, Brooklyn, 2011

[2]   Josephine Kaviti Musango, Paul Currie & Blake Robinson, 'Urban Metabolism for Resource-efficient Cities: From Theory To Implementation', UN Environment, 2017

[3]   https://www.youtube.com/user/W anavijiji

[4]   Lorena Zárate, 'They are not "informal settlements", they are habitats made by people', *The Nature of Cities,* 26 April 2016

[5]   'Kolorob: lighting up the city', Urban Sustainability Exchange

[6]   http://www.kolorob.info/

[7]   UN-Habitat, 'Case Study 6: Dhaka's extreme vulnerability to climate change' in 'State of the world's cities', 2008/2009, United Nations, unhabitat.org, 2008

[8]   Damian Carrington & Sarah Marsh, 'Deaths rose 650 above average during UK heatwave – with older people most at risk', *The Guardian,* 3 August 2018

[9]   Federación Uruguaya de Cooperativas de Vivienda por Ayuda Mutua, 'Producción Social del Hábitat', https://produccions ocialhabitat.wordpress.com/

[10]   Joost Beunderman, Indy Johar & Chloe Treger, 'Network of City Endowments: Investing in creativity, innovation and invention', Nesta and Dark Matter Laboratories, December 2019

10: Restart a civic conversation

[1]   Joel Werner & Suzannah Lyons, 'The size of Australia's bushfire

crisis captured in five big numbers', abc.net.au, 5 March 2020

[2] NEW ENDNOTE (MAYBE): I also reference a Guardian interactive map here. Should I endnote it? Nick Evershed, Andy Ball & Naaman Zhou, 'How big are the fires burning in Australia? Interactive map', *The Guardian,* 24 January 2020

[3] Andrew Freedman, 'Australia's greenhouse gas emissions effectively double as a result of unprecedented bush fires', *Washington Post,* 24 January 2020

[4] Jessica Irvine, 'The economic cost of bushfires on Sydney revealed: up to $50 million a day and rising', *Sydney Morning Herald,* 12 December 2019

ABOUT THE AUTHOR

Jess Scully is a politician, public art curator, festival director and media producer who uses creativity and the arts to engage communities. Since 2019 she has been Deputy Lord Mayor for the City of Sydney.

An advocate for the knowledge economy, creative and cultural sector, Jess was the founding director of Vivid Ideas, Australia's largest creative industries event, and has curated creative sector events including Junket, TEDxSydney and Curating Participation. She was a founding contributor to the Sydney Culture Network, launched in late 2017. Jess has directed the Qantas Spirit of Youth Awards and the Creative Cities East Asia project.

She began her career as an editor, working on publications such as *Yen, Empty* and *Hotpress.*

Glimpses of Utopia is her first book.

www.ingramcontent.com/pod-product-compliance
Lightning Source LLC
Chambersburg PA
CBHW071658280326

41926CB00099B/1675